THE NATION STATE AND
NATIONAL SELF-DETERMINATION

ALFRED COBBAN

THE NATION STATE
AND
NATIONAL
SELF-DETERMINATION

THOMAS Y. CROWELL COMPANY
NEW YORK
Established 1834

The bulk of this book first appeared as *National Self-Determination* (Oxford University Press for the Royal Institute of International Affairs, 1945). Shortly before his death, the author revised it and brought it up to date, incorporating at the same time his article on the Nation State which was first published in *History* (new series VOL. XXIX, No. 109, March 1944). The present work is published in exactly the form that the author left it, with no further editorial alterations.

First published in the United States of America in 1970

Printed in the United States of America

L.C. Card 73-112487

Contents

PART II. THE THEORY

PART III. THE CONTEMPORARY WORLD

PART IV CONCLUSIONS

Preface

THIS BOOK was originally written for the Institute of
International Affairs and was published in 1944 under
the title *National Self-Determination*. It has been out of print
and virtually unobtainable for many years. I have been
pressed to have it reprinted but was reluctant to do this
until I was able to make the desirable revisions. So much has
happened in the past quarter of a century that the text
could not be left without extensive additions and alterations. The subject, however, as a whole has not become
less relevant to contemporary conditions. Indeed, I would
say that it has become more relevant. At the end of the
Second World War it seemed evident that three or four
great empires would bestride the world. Nearly twenty-five
years later, the same empires have vanished, or are struggling to maintain their imperial power and prestige against
satellites asserting their independence or small nations
obstinately refusing to recognise overwhelming military
superiority. But while the current of international politics
may have changed, I believe that the fundamental issues,
which can be seen at work through a long historical evolution, remain the same, and that the theory of the nation
state is still equally necessary to an understanding of its
practice.

The book was written in the belief that theory and practice in politics are never safely divorced, and that the
practical difficulties, which were encountered when
nationalism in the form of the theory of self-determination
was proclaimed as the basis of a new international order,
largely arose because there was such a divorce. My starting-
point, therefore, is not the statement of a right, but an
attempt to discover how national self-determination has
operated as an actual historical process. The demonstration
of its practical inadequacy naturally leads to a recognition

of the need for a fundamental re-examination of the theory. In the third place, having discussed its historical foundations and theoretical implications, I turn to the analysis of the contemporary world, with the object of discovering the positive conditions which will determine the mode of application of as much of the ideal of national self-determination as still retains its validity. So-called realists, who believe that international relations are a pure struggle for power, unaffected by ideals or ideas, and sentimentalists, who close their eyes to the factor of power or believe that it can be argued away, will find little to their taste here. Others, it is hoped, will find in the facts given here a collection of relevant material on one of the greatest issues of the day, and in the opinions at least a reasonable basis for discussion.

I must express my indebtedness to the Royal Institute of International Affairs for permission to use the book I wrote for it as the basis of the present one. I am also indebted to the Editor of *History* for permission to incorporate an article on 'The Nation State' in the present edition. The preparation of the original study was facilitated and made pleasant by the kindness of Miss Margaret Cleeve, then Deputy Secretary of the Royal Institute of International Affairs. Professor R. A. Humphreys gave me advice on the material for Chapter X. The whole original manuscript was read and re-read by Dr. E. H. Carr, to whom I am deeply grateful for a thorough and constructive criticism which helped me to eliminate many faults. For those that remain, and for all statements and opinions in the book, I, of course, am entirely responsible.

A. COBBAN

University College, London

PART I

The History

———————

I. The Problem of Nationalism

THIS BOOK was first composed while international relations were still in the turmoil of war, nor can it be pretended that with the restoration of peace a stable situation developed. It was not intended to be a study of the transient phases of a rapidly changing balance of power, but an analysis of a basic element in the modern international system, and one which underlies many of the surface phenomena of peace as well as of war. Geopoliticians and neo-Machiavellians, who would have liked to eliminate the unmeasurable quantities from the international equation, must have been disappointed at the persistence of such a principle as national self-determination, which constitutes a disturbing and incalculable element in the neat *schema* of power politics. It seemed to them like a survival of a dead age, the ghosts of Garibaldi, Mazzini, Byron, Bolívar, come back with a faded scent of nineteenth-century liberalism to haunt an age in which all that they stood for no longer has any right to exist. But the idea of national self-determination is far from dead, and the aspirations it embodies have still to be taken into account in any serious attempt to deal with the problems of the international order.

A simple statement of some of the concrete issues of the day will be sufficient to prove this. It must, of course, be conceded that in one area the principle of self-determination appears at first sight to have been conspicuously ignored, in a way that should rejoice the hearts of political realists. The Soviet Union, on the conclusion of the war with Germany, took strategic safeguards and territorial compensation by annexations from Germany, Finland, Poland, Czechoslovakia, and Roumania, and by reuniting the Baltic states to Russia. There are easily comprehensible reasons for these annexations, which consisted largely of former possessions of the Tsarist empire, but it is very difficult to justify them on the principle of self-determination. Yet the more significant fact is perhaps not these territorial changes, which in any previous age would have been taken for granted as the natural consequence of the collapse of German and the revival of Russian power, but the fact that no attempt was made to reabsorb Finland or Poland, although the whole of the one and a large part of the other were incorporated in the Russian empire as recently as thirty years earlier. This is nothing if not a testimony to the strength of the sentiment for national independence. Despite overwhelming local power, military occupation, and a strong sense of the requirements of strategic security, the Russian government obviously felt itself under the necessity of exercising its influence in the states on its European borders through national governments and in as veiled a manner as circumstances permitted. Perhaps it has not been quite veiled enough, for in respect of the states controlled by the U.S.S.R., the Western powers, and particularly America, have found occasion to present themselves as defenders of their right to independent statehood. This virtuous role is not a monopoly, however. Where Western influence was the stronger, as in Greece, the Russians appeared as the defenders of the rights of national independence, including freedom from interference, or at least acknowledged interference, by foreign powers in internal political struggles. In Germany the situation was not dissimilar, because there Britain, the United States, and Russia appealed to, or rejected, the rights of self-determination, according as their recognition appeared to promote or to injure their respective interests.

The situation became more complicated where, as in Iran, as well as a state with national rights of its own, a party appeared, putting forward a new claim to national self-determination on behalf of a minority. Russian support of the Azerbaijan national movement against the dominance of Teheran was opposed by American and British defence of Iranian national independence against foreign interference, and in this case both sides could plausibly claim to be upholding the principle of national self-determination. An even more desperate situation appeared in Palestine, because here it was not a mere minority that demanded rights of self-government, but two nations, each claiming possession of the same state, and simultaneously demanding national independence for themselves and rejecting it for their opponents. Even more than in the Iranian situation here was a potential cause of world war, if, for any reason of domestic or foreign policies, two Great Powers were to take opposing sides in the conflict.

Such a development, as Korea and Vietnam have shown, remains by no means a remote possibility. Circumstances may, of course, keep national struggles dormant, but it would still be a little optimistic to believe, for example, that the states of Eastern Europe will know no more of the internal conflicts which weakened them so greatly before 1939. Even a state with as long a history as Spain has still a Catalonian and a Basque question; and Italy has not yet solved the problems of Sicilian or Tyrolese government.

In Europe, however, nationalism is temporarily held in check. It finds a freer field of action in the Arab countries, in Africa and in Asia. Here also national independence raises more problems than it solves. Where the nationalist movement remained in the stage of revolutionary agitation, the difficulties arising from the absence of a homogeneous nationality did not appear. With practically no minority problems to complicate the issue, the Egyptians successfully shook off the British Protectorate and military garrisons, though they did not succeed in winning acceptance of the thesis that the Sudanese are really Egyptians. Even Egypt, however, serves to remind us that national self-determination solves no economic problems. Egypt is now a completely independent state, poor, overpopulated, free to take advantage of the world market and to negotiate with America, Britain or Russia on equal terms, her chief advantage the possibility of playing off one against the other.

When we turn our eyes to Asia, India and Pakistan present us with a classic case of self-determination, and a series of problems as fascinating to the social pathologist as their incidence and outcome may be distressing to the humanitarian. The Burmese set their feet in the path of national independence and civil war. Malaya and Singapore have decided that they are different nationalities.

Not only British but also the French and Dutch possessions changed their character rapidly. There is one factor in the Far Eastern situation, however, to which too much attention can hardly be paid. The Japanese conquest proved a flash in the pan, but while European control had been weakening, Chinese immigration in all these regions had been growing steadily. In one country which remained free from Western conquest, Thailand, national sentiment turned against what it regarded as Chinese imperialism. It required no gift for prophecy to see the same development coming in Indonesia. The principle of self-determination was here directed not against the control of foreign officials and armies, but against peaceful penetration by the hardworking, law-abiding Chinese merchant, peasant and labourer, with behind him the might of a huge if distracted empire, conscious of the ties of race and the rightful claims of the 'outland' Chinese. In the maintenance of their national claims against Chinese pressure, Thais, Malay, Javanese, and the rest, are faced with new and interesting problems.

It is evident that no power, great or small, can escape the incidence of the problem of nationalism. Even the United States of America, offered the choice of either filling some of the more important areas of power vacuum left by the war or else seeing a rival power fill them instead, has become increasingly conscious of the difficulty of reconciling power with principle. Oil companies are not armies of occupation, dollars are not bayonets, influence is not empire, yet the problems that economic connexion between a small and poor state and a great and wealthy one involve belong fundamentally in the same class as those we have already mentioned. Where, as in the Philippines, the United States had agreed to withdraw her power, she discovered that she still needed strategic bases; while the Philippines for their part are not unaware that economically they cannot afford to cut their connexions with America. In Puerto Rico the national question is primarily an economic one. In Korea the German situation is repeated on a small scale.

The demands of nationalism, therefore, still stand on the agenda of world politics. We may hail the nation-state as the supreme political achievement of Western civilisation, or we may regard nationalism as a disease which if not taken in time will destroy civilised life—and it is not uncommon for both views to be held at once—but neither approval nor disapproval is very relevant to something that may be regarded, at least for our time, as a natural force, a mighty torrent which is equally capable of serving the purposes of man or destroying him. Our duty is not to shut our eyes to it, and not to pretend that it does not have the consequences which it does have. These consequences fall primarily into two groups, according as we look at the demand for national self-determination from the point of view of individual states or of international relations. Internally, nationalism has passed from the stage of state-making to that of state-breaking. The newer nation-states of Asia and Africa have hardly even had the time to be born before reproducing the situation, which it used to be thought was peculiar to imperial régimes, of two or more nations warring in the bosom of a single state.

Secondly, zones of small, internally divided states constitute the belts of greatest weakness in the thin crust of international peace. This is not, of course, the result of the deliberate policy of the smaller states themselves, nor is it the necessary consequence of the disproportion between them and the Great Powers. Where, as in Central America, a belt of small states lies entirely in the shadow of a single great state, even though they are weak and internally unstable, their existence normally constitutes no threat to general peace. But other zones of small and internally divided nation-states lie in the penumbra where the shadows of two great powers intersect. Such zones are faults in the political structure of the world, and like geological faults they are the areas in which disturbance is most likely to arise. The danger of war undoubtedly comes primarily from Great Power rivalries, but small states, where they are divided and unstable and subject to the influence of more than one Great Power, may act as the priming which will set off an explosive situation.

The solution is not the abolition of small states. The forces which have enabled small states to survive to the present day, and even, during the last years, to increase considerably in number, have not ceased to operate. To say that we do not believe in small states, to denounce nationalism, or to repudiate the principle of national self-determination, may be emotionally satisfactory but is no constructive solution. Denunciation will not change the facts. An important antithesis in the modern political mind is that between the liberal idealists and the advocates of power politics. The new Machiavellians made great play with the failure of the liberal hopes for world order, perhaps without realising that the very force of national sentiment, which had been most influential in bringing about this failure, was also playing a large part in preventing the concentration of effective power in the hands of the two or three world powers, whose existence alone as powers the realists were prepared to recognise. The dilemma of national self-determination is not the whole problem of world peace, but it is a very important part of it. Unless we are prepared to say that the problem is insoluble and to sit back in philosophic expectation of the worst, the only constructive line of thought is to attempt to restate the issue in different and less irreconcilable terms. It is the aim of this book to do that, taking, in the words of Rousseau, men as they are and institutions as they might be.

During the first World War it was generally believed by public opinion in the Western democracies that there was a right of national independence which the Central Powers had overthrown, and that the primary object of the Allies was the reinstatement of this right. The democratic conception of government being added to it, the combined ideal obtained widespread recognition as the principle of self-determination. The second World War was again a struggle against a German bid for hegemony in Europe and as such could be regarded as partly fought in defence of the independence of the smaller nations, but on the future of these the most diverse opinions were expressed, ranging from an assertion of unlimited national sovereignty to proposals for the complete absorption of all nations in a world state.

While representatives of the smaller nations insisted on their absolute rights of sovereignty and independence, opinion in the greater powers tended to attribute the collapse of international peace to the 'balkanisation' of Europe, and looked with alarm on the possibility of a re-creation of the conditions that proved so unstable before 1939. 'The idea of nationality as a basis for independent statehood,' wrote G. D. H. Cole in 1941, 'is obsolete.'[1] 'In the case of great states surrounded by smaller neighbours,' he argued, 'it is inevitable, if state sovereignty is to remain the basis of political relationships, that the great states should seek to engulf their neighbours, and the small states be kept alive, if at all, only when they are in the position of buffers between the great.'[2] An American writer similarly proclaimed the necessity of eliminating 'great differences in military strength between states within the same power zone', and concluded that an unspecified number of small states would have to sacrifice their independence, as constituting 'a political hazard to the whole international community.'[3] 'It is unlikely,' said another, 'that the small sovereignties destroyed by the Nazis can be restored. It is

[1] G. D. H. Cole, *Europe, Russia, and the Future*, 1941, p. 13.
[2] *id.* p. 101.
[3] N. J. Spykman, *America's Strategy in World Politics: the United States and the Balance of Power*, 1942, p. 463.

doubtful that the small nations of Europe will rise from their servitude to Nazi tyranny as small nations.'[4]

A critical attitude toward small states had in the past found more frequent expression in German than in British political thinking. The German political mind, conditioned by a long struggle for national unity against the small states, because of whose rivalries Germany as a whole remained weak and exposed to the constant menace of foreign invasion, had a deep-rooted dislike of what it called *Kleinstaaterei*. The German worship of size, and contempt for small nations, reached its climax with the rise of the Nazi Party. 'What,' asked Hitler in a speech of March 1938 on the Austrian question, 'what can words like "independence" or "sovereignty" mean for a state of only six millions? . . . To-day it is only under quite peculiar presuppositions that such small state formations can have a possibility of life . . . Even the German Reich is too small: it needs a complement of colonies: how should a state which was but the size of a single province succeed?'[5]

Great Britain and America, on the other hand, explicitly denounced and repudiated this method of dealing with the lesser nationalities. The Atlantic Declaration of August, 1941 said: 'They respect the right of all peoples to choose the form of government under which they will live; and they wish to see sovereign rights and self-government restored to those who have been forcibly deprived of them.' The Anglo-Russian Treaty of Alliance of May, 1942 was less specific, but it contained an acceptance of the principle 'of not seeking territorial aggrandisement for themselves and of non-interference in the internal affairs of other states.'

A factor that was sometimes forgotten in the discussion of this problem was the opinion of the smaller nationalities themselves. These became increasingly restive in the face of signs of great power mentality on the part of their Allies.

[4] R. Strausz-Hupé, *Geopolitics: the Struggle for Space and Power*, 1942, p. 191.
[5] N. H. Baynes, *The Speeches of Adolf Hitler, April 1922–August 1939*, 1942, II. 1, 437–8.

To give but one example: 'When writers, diplomatists, men of action and men of imagination so loudly discuss an Anglo-American direction of world affairs,' wrote the President of the Norwegian Parliament, 'they will be met with these questions: what should entitle those two powers to act for all countries and particularly for the small nations? Is there anything in their near political past that gives them the full confidence of the rest of the nations? Have their politicians and their diplomats shown a wisdom, a foresight, a moral courage to which the world can look for guidance? Were they prepared? Could they read the script on the wall? Or is the present holocaust largely due to the sins of commission and the sins of omission of those responsible for great power policy since the last war?'[6]

The determination of the peoples of Europe to throw off the alien yoke was, moreover, almost as important a factor in 1944 as it had been in 1919. 'It was easy enough,' writes Harold Butler, of the Versailles Treaties, 'to condemn the peace settlement as the "balkanisation of Europe" from arm chairs in London. It was all very well for the economists to demonstrate by industrial and banking statistics that the new grouping of the states was unworkable, and to a large extent they were right. But national sentiment takes little account of statistics. To the traveller who witnessed the ecstasy with which all the liberated peoples were revelling in their newly won freedom, it was obvious that the peace settlement was in its broad lines not only right but inevitable.'[7] Whether we agree with this conclusion or not, the same forces of national feeling have certainly not ceased to operate, nor have they become weaker in the course of the last half century. We may approve them, or we may condemn them, but we cannot ignore them; and they will pay little heed to either our abstract approval or condemnation.

This brings me to the problem discussed in this book. Given the strength of the sentiment of national independence, and the existence in Europe and throughout the world

[6] C. J. Hambro, *How to Win the Peace*, 1943, pp. 99–100.
[7] H. Butler, *The Lost Peace*, 1941, p.124.

of an array of separate nations, conscious of their identity and requiring satisfaction in the form of political rights, the real task is to integrate them into the fabric of a stable, prosperous, and peaceful world. This problem has been much debated in the past, and will doubtless be discussed even more in the near future. My object is not to add another to the many *ex parte* statements, but to attempt a study of the fundamental issues involved in the demand for what was called in 1918 the right of self-determination. Such a study appears to fall into four main divisions: first, a historical account of the rise of the concept of national self-determination, its triumph in 1918, and its subsequent collapse; secondly, an analysis of self-determination as a theoretical and practical principle; thirdly, an examination of the methods adopted, with more or less success, by the three great allies, Britain, the United States, and the U.S.S.R., in dealing with the smaller nations within their spheres of influence; and, fourthly, a discussion of the economic and strategic implications of self-determination in the contemporary world.

II. The Nation State

ONE OF THE difficulties of the history of ideas is that names are more permanent than things. Institutions change, but the terms used to describe them remain the same. This is true of words as familiar as democracy, sovereignty, monarchy or nation. It is with the last of these that we are concerned here, and more particularly with what is called the nation state. The assumption is often made that the nation state is a peculiar development of modern history, dating from the sixteenth century and symbolising the breakdown of the medieval world. Whatever interpretation we give to the term nation state, this view is untenable. In one sense it attributes to the sixteenth century what was really the work of the Middle Ages; in another it pre-supposes developments that only came about in the nine-teenth century. The objection that must be faced at the out-set is that this is a matter of interpretation, and that before we can say anything about the nation state we must define what we mean by the term. This method of procedure is common, but dangerous. Historical phenomena are not abstractions to be neatly tied up in the academist's defini-tions. They are, as I have already said, changing things, and their real meaning is apparent only in their history. All we need assume, to begin with, is that the term nation state corresponds to some concrete political form, and that we are not using meaningless jargon when we describe France, Spain, Norway or the United States as nation states. What such states have in common might, of course, be decided by a purely contemporary analysis, but a more instructive approach is to attempt to trace the historical origins of the nation state, as fact and idea, and discover how in both respects it came to be what it is to-day.

As a political unit the nation state is normally larger than the tribe or the city-state, and smaller than the empire; but it must not be supposed that any necessary historical development is implied in this comparison, for if we examine the sequence—tribe, nation state, empire—we find that the middle term is often left out. Society, when it progresses beyond the tribal stage, may crystallise in the city-state form, and from this pass directly into empire. This was in the main the line of development followed by the classical world. Taking the whole course of history, it will be found that the nation state is by no means a common phenomenon. Pre-European Africa and America never really developed beyond the tribal stage, except in so far as conquering tribes such as the Aztecs and the Incas subjected neighbouring peoples to their rule. The Arab peoples passed directly from tribe to empire. In Asia, until very recent times, nation states may be considered to have developed only in a few areas where geographical isolation provided favourable conditions, as they did, for example, in Iran, Burma, Thailand and Japan. Only in Europe has the development of the nation state been the rule rather than the exception.

It has been maintained that many of the states of the pre-classical world—those of the Egyptians, Sumerians and Assyrians, for example—possessed the essential characteristics of the nation state.[1] By the continual wars in which they engaged, however, these states destroyed or weakened one another, and the political conceptions of the city-state civilisation of the Greeks and Romans triumphed throughout the Mediterranean and the Middle East. During the classical period there were no nation states: the Latin term *natio* was applied only to the barbarian tribes outside the Roman world. It is often assumed that there is an established historical connection between these tribal 'nations'

[1] M. T. Walek-Czernecki, Le rôle de la nationalité dans l'histoire de l'Antiquité, in the *Bulletin of the International Committee of Historical Sciences*, 1929.

of the barbarian world as the Romans knew them, and the nation states of modern times. Far older than the nation state, it has been said, 'reaching back into the misty dawn of pre-history, is the national community which, founded on the personal life of the nation, yet exercised most of the functions of the state.'[2]

In this interpretation there seems to be an assumption of permanence in the tribal 'nations,' which is hardly justifiable. Even a superficial study of the American Indian, as well as of other tribal societies, says an American ethnologist, 'will quickly dispel the idea that they are simple or permanent units.'[3] There are two other considerations which make the thesis of the tribal origin of the modern nation state unacceptable. In the first place, for the political scientist there are differences between the primitive tribe and the state which are not to be overcome by including them both in the category of nation. In primitive tribal conditions doubtless some of the raw materials of statehood already existed, but for the study of what Aristotle called politics, to include a congeries of related tribes, or a transient and partial military confederacy such as the Gauls under Vercingetorix, the Germans at the time of Arminius, or the Angles, Saxons and Jutes when they invaded Britain, under the same heading as modern France, Germany, the Netherlands or the United States, is to introduce an element of hopeless confusion. The existence of linguistic and cultural affiliations between a number of tribal communities is a fact of importance for the student of language and culture: until it has had some permanent institutional embodiment it cannot be regarded as a political fact, or as belonging to the same order of things as the nation state. The second implication which we cannot accept is that the modern nation state is the descendant of earlier tribal nations. Primitive tribalism has been described as a 'small-scale nationalism,'[4]

[2] C. A. Macartney, *National States and National Minorities*, 1934, p. 21.
[3] J. R. Swanton, *The Evolution of Nations*, 1942, p. 1.
[4] C. H. J. Hayes, *The Historical Evolution of Modern Nationalism*, 1937, pp. 1–2.

but for the creation of nation states the importance of a tribal inheritance of common language and culture can easily be exaggerated. In the development of the nation states of to-day a common language and culture have more often been a result than a cause. Even the names of the nation states rarely correspond to any former anthropological, linguistic or ethnographical unity.[5]

In the making of nation states non-tribal elements, such as the semi-Latinised population of Gaul, or the Norman conquerors in England, generally played a leading part. The process was sometimes a ruthless one, as is seen in the conquest of southern France by the feudal barons of the North. Groups of related or unrelated peoples were welded into political unity during the medieval period by the force of feudal overlords, supported by their baronage. Where no single military supremacy was established, nation states were late in developing, or never developed at all. Where such supremacies approached, or overlapped one another, lands of uncertain allegiance appeared. Thus during the eleventh and twelfth centuries strong dynasties laid the foundations of English, French and German nations, while lesser rulers, such as the Ramon Berenguer dynasty, were creating smaller nationalities like the Catalan. The constituents of practically all the medieval nations are diversified and without any common tribal or cultural background. J. B. Trend writes of the Catalan nation, which developed a clearly marked identity earlier than the larger nations of the West, that it 'is above all a historical product . . . On to the old Iberian stem have been grafted stocks that were Greek, Roman, Goth, Arab and Gaul . . . It is the Catalan tradition which counts, not the descent of the Catalan race.'[6]

It was long before the medieval nation states acquired names of their own; usually they were known by the title of their chief province. Thus France was so called from the Ile de France, Saxony or Franconia equalled Germany,

---

[5] A. van Gennep, *Traité comparatif des nationalités*, 1922, I. 211.

[6] J. B. Trend, *A Picture of Modern Spain*, 1921, pp. 90, 95.

Polonia gave its name to Poland. By the twelfth century in Western, and the thirteenth century in Eastern Europe, a considerable number of nation states existed. 'The formation of a state nationality,' says M. Handelsman, 'marks, properly speaking, the end of the Middle Ages.' For many nations the fourteenth century is the climax of this age of nation-making.[7]

It must be emphasised that throughout this period, when nations in the modern political sense of the word, or what we may call nation states, were in process of creation, the word nation continued to be understood in a non-political and mainly linguistic sense. It was thus that it was employed in the medieval universities. The advocacy by Dante of the Tuscan vernacular as a literary language for all Italy might be looked upon as a manifestation of national feeling, as perhaps in one sense it was. But the arguments with which he supports his case are almost exclusively linguistic and literary, and his political ideals, as exhibited in the *De Monarchia*, were far wider than anything that could be included under the concept of the nation.

The growth of the nation state during the Middle Ages was, of course, purely a practical development. Medieval states were political entities, and there was no belief in any necessary connection between cultural and political ties. The creation of the Swiss confederation is the most striking illustration of this fact. If the modern conception of the political importance of a common culture had been accepted, the Swiss state could never have been formed. At the same time, although the work of the great medieval monarchies was primarily one of political consolidation, the development of political unity naturally stimulated the growth of a common language and culture, and the assimilation of alien cultural elements. There are possibly indications that language was beginning to be thought of to a

---

[7] In this paragraph I have followed the interpretation of M. Handelsman, in 'Le rôle de la nationalité dans l'histoire du Moyen Age,' in the *Bulletin of the International Committee of Historical Sciences*, 1929, *cf.* pp. 237–240, 242, 247.

certain extent as a factor in politics by the fifteenth century, but in the present state of our knowledge we cannot say more.

During the Middle Ages the political divisions of Europe were constantly changing, some centres of power rising, while others were declining or even disappearing. Provincial sentiment remained a strong rival of national consciousness. The French distinguished themselves from Normans, Lorrainers or Burgundians, Aquitainians from French, Bretons from Normans. But the feeling of loyalty to broader political unities was increasing, and by the sixteenth century a number of recognisable nation states existed in Western Europe.[8] The trend towards the formation of nation states had in most cases been arrested at an earlier stage in Central and Eastern Europe. Many factors contributed to this differentiation. The absence of suitable geographical barriers,[9] an excessive intermingling of alien elements, the existence of wide divergencies in cultural level, the failure to produce a succession of strong rulers such as medieval England enjoyed, or a long unchallenged and unbroken hereditary succession such as that of the French crown, the complications resulting from the ambitions and rivalries of the Papacy and the Holy Roman Empire, the undue extent of Germanic territory, which, along with the persistence of tribalism well into the Middle Ages and the strength of centrifugal feudal authorities, made it an impossible task, under medieval conditions, to establish an effective government for Germany as a whole, the crystallisation of the city-state form in Italy early in the Middle Ages—these were some of the causes of the weakness of the nation state in Central Europe. In some countries the process of building up the nation state was checked,

[8] On the development of national sentiment in France, see D. Kirkland, 'The Growth of National Sentiment in France before the Fifteenth Century,' *History*, June 1938, vol. xxiii, pp. 12–24.

[9] It is to be noted that the two countries in Central Europe which were the most like geographical regions, Bohemia and Hungary, were also those in which medieval monarchies came the nearest to success in the building up of nation states.

before it had reached completion, as a result of foreign attacks. Such was the fate of Hungary and Bohemia. The Balkans, which had not been behind Western Europe in their political development during the earlier Middle Ages, suffered severely, for the Ottoman conquest destroyed the material bases of their civilisation, wiped out their old aristocracies and middle classes, and even in some cases obliterated their traditional frontiers.[10] On the other hand, Poland fell into a condition of arrested development for internal reasons, because of the power retained by her nobles, which prevented the monarchy from completing the task of political unification.

From what has been said it may reasonably be concluded that the nations of Europe developed in, and were essentially adapted to a medieval political environment. This environment was rapidly changing during the fifteenth and sixteenth centuries, when the basic conditions of political life were profoundly modified both in practice and in theory. The states of the Middle Ages had not been sovereign states in the modern sense of the word; indeed sovereignty in its classical conception had almost completely vanished, except in so far as it survived in the Papal claim to *plenitudo potestatis*. It has been said, with some justice if the term is used in its modern connotation, that the only state in the Middle Ages was the Church. The idea of secular sovereignty only re-appeared when the Middle Ages were drawing to their close. As was to be expected, the influence of the new political ideas was first felt in Italy. There, in a society of small independent states—mostly city-states—the least medieval of medieval countries, was a situation to which they were eminently applicable. From Italy they spread over the rest of Europe, and though their influence varied from country to country, it was sufficiently widespread to constitute a real political renaissance. And since the principle of sovereignty was revived in a society in which the nation state had become the strongest form of political organisation, out of this combination the new

10 *Cf.* C. A. Macartney, *Problems of the Danube Basin*, 1942, p. 32.

political ideal of the sovereign nation state ultimately emerged.

The rise of the idea of sovereignty was not altogether favourable to the continued growth of nation states, however. It emphasised the rights of government, and so intensified the process of unification in nation states which were already set in that path; but it also militated against the development of the process where different political entities prevailed, as in the petty states of Germany and Italy, or the great dynastic empire of the Habsburgs. The process of formation of nation states therefore experienced a setback at the end of the Middle Ages, from which it did not recover until the nineteenth century. During the early modern period also the word nation changed its significance: it lost its linguistic and acquired an almost exclusively political meaning. The possession of a separate government came to be the criterion of nationhood, though the smaller independent states were not commonly termed nations. Vattel, in the very first sentence of his treatise on international law, assumes that state and nation are synonymous. By the eighteenth century, in fact, most of the cultural and linguistic significance had been emptied out of the word nation. It merely meant the state considered from the point of view of the ruled rather than the ruler. The Dictionary of the *Academie Française* as late as 1878 was still giving as its primary definition of the nation, 'the totality of persons born or naturalised in a country and living under a single government.'

Already, however, by the end of the Middle Ages, a number of nation states existed, in which political unity was combined with a greater or less degree of cultural unity. The history of Europe is unique in that nowhere else, and at no other time, has such a considerable group of nation states survived in geographical contiguity and close association with one another over a period of many centuries. Nowhere else, moreover, until we come to the contemporary extra-European development of nationalism under Western inspiration, do we find a civilisation passing out of medieval conditions and yet continuing to be organised largely on a national basis. It is therefore justifiable to regard the development of a widespread civilisation, in which nation states have not passed away before the attack of the imperial principle, as a peculiar characteristic of the Western world. During the modern period in Europe, it is true, there has been a tendency towards the amalgamation of the medieval nations into larger political units. The persistence, despite this tendency, of the political divisions of Europe is to be explained in the first place by the absence of any power capable of uniting the whole Continent under its military dominion. Lacking such a unifying force, the peoples of Europe, instead of being assimilated to one another, grew more distinct. The unifying forces of Latin Christendom became weaker after the Reformation and the shifting of the focus of European society from the Mediterranean to the Atlantic coastline; while a further source of political cleavage was to be found in the division into Latin, German and Slav, three large groups none of which was strong enough to conquer or absorb the others.

The consequence was that European politics were kept in a perpetually unstable equilibrium on the system of balance of power. Such a result is inevitable wherever a number of independent states, none of them strong enough to establish a permanent dominion over the rest, are in continuous contact with one another. The relations of the city-states of ancient Greece presented a similar situation and a similar consequence. If any state grew powerful enough to threaten the balance, sooner or later it drew on itself the enmity of a more powerful coalition. The island state of Great Britain played an essential part in the maintenance of this balance. Too small and too separate to aim at continental empire, it was at the same time protected from conquest by its naval power. In every century since the decline of the Middle Ages British power has intervened to prevent the establishment or consolidation of a European hegemony by a dominant military power. The advantages and disadvantages of this system of balance, and of the survival in Europe of so many independent states, are both obviously great, but it is not for us to discuss them here.

Out of this division of Europe into a large number of independent states there gradually evolved the idea of a right of independence on the part of these states. Grotius and his successors in the development of international law upheld this principle, which found its most striking expression, towards the end of the eighteenth century, in the reaction against the partitions of Poland. A new factor appeared in the protests against the extinction of the Polish state, as it had in those provoked, a little earlier, by the sale of Corsica by the Genoese to the French. 'Thus,' said Burke of the latter, 'was a nation disposed of without its consent, like the trees on an estate.'[11] 'It is making fools of people,' wrote Rousseau, 'to tell them seriously that one can at one's pleasure transfer peoples from master to master, like herds of cattle, without consulting their interests or their wishes.'[12] We can see in such quotations the beginning of a new association between the ideas of the political state and the national community, in consequence of which the idea of the nation state at last appears in its modern form. But to understand its new significance we must turn to what was a necessary preliminary to the new stage in its history, the assertion of the right of democratic self-government.

The long history of representative institutions, which, like the nations themselves, are a product of the Middle Ages, may seem to contradict the attribution of a recent origin to democracy. But medieval representative institutions were extinguished in many countries, and declined in importance in practically all, when the New Monarchy of the sixteenth century appeared, and with it the later medieval or renaissance conception of sovereignty. Although in one or

[11] *Annual Register*, 1768, Historical Section, i. p. 2.
[12] J. J. Rousseau, *Political Writings* (ed. C. E. Vaughan), 1915, i. 340–1.

two states, such as England, the history of representative institutions forms an unbroken chain from the Middle Ages to the present day, their revival and extension throughout Europe were not a direct consequence of these survivals, but of the attempt at the end of the eighteenth century to create a democratic government of a new type in France. The French Revolution must not be thought of as no more than a struggle to establish in France principles of government that already existed, although perhaps in an imperfect form, in those countries where medieval representative institutions survived. It was a revolution of a far wider compass than this would imply, a revolution not only in the institutions, but in the political ideas of the Western world. By proclaiming the principle of popular sovereignty, the French revolutionaries fundamentally altered the prevailing conception of the state, and opened a fresh chapter in the history of the nation state. It was through the combination of the revolutionary idea of democratic sovereignty with the new importance attached to national differences that the nation state ceased to be a simple historical fact and became the subject of a theory.[13]

The nation states of the Middle Ages, as I have said, had been the creation of the political power of the monarchies, though it was also held that the people were an active participant in the political power of the state. This attitude of mind, which was inherited by the Contractual school of thought, came to be generally accepted in the seventeenth and eighteenth centuries. It was maintained, in the words of Locke, that, 'Wherever any number of men so unite into one society as to quit every one his executive power of the Law of Nature, and to resign it to the public, there and there only is a political or civil society.' The belief that their agreement to establish a common legislature and government was the factor which made a collection of individuals into a state was still the prevailing view on the eve of the French Revolution, when Sieyes defined the nation as 'a

[13] I have discussed this development more fully in *Dictatorship, its History and Theory*, 1939, pp. 161–174.

body of associates living under one common law and represented by the same legislature.' There was one fundamental
change, however. The great achievement of revolutionary
political thought, for good or evil, was the conception of
government as a manifestation of the democratic will, and
the identification of the state as sovereign with the people.
This was the meaning of Sieyes when he said that the *tiers
état*, the people, was nothing and ought to be everything;
and it was what the revolutionaries meant when they declared, 'Sovereignty is one, indivisible, inalienable and im-
prescriptible: it belongs to the nation.'

During the last century and a half, beginning with the
revolt of the American colonies, there has been a renewed
wave of nation state making, but in place of a feudal
monarchy the unifying power has been the will of the
people, or at least of the politically conscious classes, though
a part has also been played in this movement by military
powers such as Piedmont and Prussia. It is to be noted that
both in the medieval and the modern periods of the formation of nation states, the process has been a political one,
initial differences of language, race or culture being of comparatively minor account. The Americas provide many
modern examples of this fact. Belgium and South Africa
belong to the same class of political nations, of which the
classic example is Switzerland.

The modern conception of the nation state did not remain purely political, however. A new meaning, as I have
said, had been acquired by the nation during the second
half of the eighteenth century, a development parallel with,
although distinct from, the rise of the democratic idea of the
state. It was an important element in the early romantic
movement, and is particularly associated with the medieval
revival. Among the manifestations of a new attitude towards the nation are: the writing of the first national hymn
of Norway and the first history of Norway inspired by the
idea of Norwegian independence, both in 1772; the development of national ideas in the Austrian Netherlands and the
revival of the term *Belges*; the writing of a Finnish national

poem; the demand for Parliamentary independence in Ireland; the appearance of the American nation.[14] Many other examples might be found of the increased significance of the idea of nationality in this period, which was also that in which Herder, the best-known and the most influential of the prophets of the new idea of the nation, was writing. There is no need to summarise here the well-known history of the nationalist movement, though it is to be noted that histories of nationalism which find its origin in the French Revolution and the Napoleonic Wars omit its initial phase. The point to be emphasised is that whereas before the French Revolution there had been no necessary connection between the state as a political unit and the nation as a cultural one, the combination of these two elements in a single conception was the significant fact in the phase that now opened in the history of the nation state.

Although nation states had existed for centuries, before the nineteenth century no specific relationship had been posited between culture or language and the political state. Some states were more or less culturally united, others were composed of culturally disparate elements. The matter was not one that was regarded as of fundamental importance. It did not occur to anyone to criticise the Habsburg Empire on the ground that its peoples spoke different languages, had different cultures, and apart from their allegiance to a common dynasty were even separate political communities. For the *ancien régime* one state was as good as another. In the definition of the state communal ties, and all aspects of social life that were not narrowly and directly governmental, played no part. The state was a juristic and territorial concept. It was the land, and its ruler the lord of the land. The new idea of the nation changed all this. In October, 1789 the *roi de France et de Navarre* became *roi des Français*, and during the next half-century the nation state entered on a new stage in its history. Hitherto it had been a historical fact: now it became a theory. It was embodied in

[14] Halvdan Koht, *L'esprit national et' idée de la souveraineté du peuple*, in the *Bulletin of the International Committee of Historical Sciences*, 1929.

the theory of nationalism, which posited as an ideal the identification of cultural and political communities in a universal system of nation states.

As an agency of destruction the theory of nationalism proved one of the most potent that even modern society has known. Empires or states that were not homogeneous in culture and language were undermined from within, or assaulted from without; nation after nation broke away from its traditional allegiances. But there was less success in the task of rebuilding a stable system of states on the ruins of older political structures.

An admirable example of the consequences of the attempt to fuse together the political and cultural ideas of the nation is provided by Hungary, which was at the end of the nineteenth century the solitary survivor in Central Europe of the medieval nation states of the type of England and France. Her tragedy was that, as a result of Turkish and Habsburg domination, she had never been able to push the process of nation-making to completion throughout her territories, and her unassimilated peoples were consequently caught up in the cultural nationalist movement of the nineteenth century. In place of the slow but successful assimilation that had gone on in previous centuries, a desperate policy of compulsory Magyarisation was now adopted, which only accelerated the onset of disaster. The fatal conflict of two different ideas of the nation comes to the surface in the Hungarian Law of Nationalities of 1868, which declares, 'All citizens of Hungary . . . form a single nation—the indivisible unitary Magyar nation—to which all citizens of the country, irrespective of nationality, belong.'[15] At a time when the other peoples of Central Europe were struggling to convert their cultural nationalities into politically independent states, Hungary was still attempting to force her way in the opposite direction, from political to cultural unity.

During the nineteenth century the belief in the ideal

[15] Macartney, *National States and National Minorities*, p. 119. This translation is perhaps not quite fair to the nuances in the original.

identification of cultural or linguistic nation and political state obtained widespread acceptance, though among the voices raised in protest against the new nationalist gospel were those of Proudhon, Le Play, Bakunin, Lecky and Acton. The conception of the nation state which was embodied in nineteenth-century nationalism attained its highest point in 1919 and the following years, but it was a mistake to suppose that this was the end of its history. Already there was ample justification for asking whether the idea of the nation state that prevailed would be a permanent factor in political ideology. We must at least observe that the assumption of a necessary coincidence between the political and cultural divisions of mankind, far from enshrining the wisdom of the ages, is a modern invention. If it looks back to anything it is to tribal barbarism; but in the Middle Ages, when actually the modern nations were being made, such a faith as nationalism would have been appropriate only to the heretic and the traitor.

At different times different institutions have embodied the political ideals of man. We need not here pass judgment on the historic process which has at one time fixed men's hearts on the city or the nation, at another on a civilisation or an empire. The truth is that while loyalty to the community in which for the time being are enshrined the highest aspirations of social organisation is a perennial quality in human nature, the object of that loyalty has varied widely from age to age. There is little to suggest that the combination of cultural and political unity in the idea of the nation state is the last, or that it is the highest, of those mortal gods to which men have sometimes paid undue adoration. This does not mean that we are free to choose one or another, as the fancy takes us. We are children of our age, and must obey its dictates, but we should be careful not to read the history of five thousand years in terms of the last one hundred and fifty. Nations and states grew up and flourished in the medieval world long before such a faith as nationalism was thought of. The state system of Europe has changed century by century, and there are no signs that its evolution has come to an end. The least we can say in conclusion to this brief outline of its history is that we should be prepared to examine with as open a mind as our day and generation permits the still dominant idea of the culturally and politically united nation state.

III. The Rise of National Self-Determination up to 1918

I. *National Self-determination as a Theory*

THE RIGHT of national independence, which came to be called, during the first World War, the principle of self-determination, is, in general terms, the belief that each nation has a right to constitute an independent state and determine its own government. This description, however inadequate by itself, is sufficient to enable us to answer one necessary preliminary question. Before venturing on a study of national self-determination, it is reasonable to ask what kind of thing it is. Our answer must be that it is a theory about the relationship that should prevail between the nation and the state, the latter being understood as any separately governed political community. Logically, therefore, we should begin with an attempt to define the nation. It is clearly not enough to avoid the issue by saying that we know a nation when we see it: there is only too much evidence that we do not. But on this subject an extensive literature has already accumulated to which the reader can be referred. To attempt a definition of the nation, or of the concept of national self-determination, at this point, would be to prejudge the whole issue. If it is objected that we cannot study something we have not defined, the only answer is that, rightly or wrongly, historians and scientists are doing this all the time. To begin with a theoretical analysis would be to endanger the whole historical basis of our study, and to produce an essentially non-historical account disguised as history.

In this chapter I propose to give a brief survey of the principle of nationalism, not from the theoretical point of view, but as a practical historical force. It must be made clear at the outset that I do not include under this description every kind of national revolt. The movement for national independence, or self-determination, falls into the same category as utilitarianism, communism, or Jeffersonian democracy. It is, as I have said, a theory, a principle, or an ideal, and no simple, unconscious national movement can be identified with it. Struggles such as the rising of the French under the inspiration of Joan the Maid, or the Hussite Wars, are fundamentally different from the national movements of the last hundred years because of the absence of a theory of national self-determination, which could only appear in the presence of a democratic ideology, and democracy, in the modern sense of the word, was born in the second half of the eighteenth century. Such democratic tendencies as are to be found before this time take the form of assertions of a right of representing the people in the government, of checking the government by the political action of the people, or of directing it in the interests of the people. But with the French Revolution democracy became something more than this. It was not merely the representation of individuals, much less of classes or corporations, in a parliament exercising a constitutional control over the government: the people itself became the supreme authority, the single active principle in the state. It passed from the role of subject to that of sovereign.

The post-medieval form of the theory of the Divine Right of Kings, which had been the chief political gospel of the early modern period, received a mortal blow from the French Revolution. It was replaced by the Divine Right of the People. Under the influence of the new national and democratic ideas, the people ceased to be an atomic dust of individuals: it took shape and form, became a *whole*, was called the *Nation*, endowed with sovereignty, and identified with the state. The revolutionary theory that a people had the right to form its own constitution and choose its own government for itself easily passed into the claim that it had a right to decide whether to attach itself to one state or another, or constitute an independent state by itself. The effect of revolutionary ideology was to transfer the initiative in state-making from the government to the people. Nation states had formerly been built up, in the course of centuries, from above, by the influence of government: henceforth they were to be made much more rapidly from below by the will of the people. The logical consequence of the democratisation of the idea of the state by the revolutionaries was that nationalism took the form of the theory of national self-determination.

II. *Democracy and Nationality during the Nineteenth Century*

As France itself had not to be liberated from the sway of foreign powers, the strictly democratic element in revolutionary ideology was naturally the one to be emphasised inside France. The principle of national self-determination, however, also received practical application during the early years of the Revolution. It appeared in the attitude which the French Assembly adopted towards the proposal for the union with France of Avignon and the Venaissin in 1791, and of Savoy and Nice in the following year. A series of speakers urged that only the clearly expressed will of the population concerned could justify a change in sovereignty, and the Assembly decreed that before annexation a formal expression of the will of the people should be obtained by the holding of plebiscites, which were conducted on the whole with remarkable impartiality.

This idealistic frame of mind did not survive for long un-adulterated. The change in revolutionary policy was in-augurated by Cambon's Report of 15th December, 1792, in which revolutionary zeal carried the day over demo-cratic idealism. The Report in effect authorised the destruction of the existing authorities in the conquered countries, and the establishment of revolutionary governments by force. From this point onwards the Revolution rapidly diverged into paths of aggression, as a result of which its own principles were turned against it. The consequent rise of national feeling in the conquered countries proved the rock on which the Napoleonic Empire was to be shattered. The downfall of Napoleon brought the re-establishment of the anti-democratic and un-national governments of the *ancien régime*. But, defeated in the realm of practical politics for the time being, the new principle of democratic nationalism triumphed in the realm of ideas, and this was the vital fact for subsequent history. 'The self-consciousness of nations,' writes Sir Ernest Barker, 'is a product of the nineteenth century . . . In the world of action apprehended ideas are alone electrical; and a nation must be an idea as well as a fact before it can become a dynamic force.'[1]

This is not the place to re-tell the general history of nationalism since 1815. It was far from being a merely theoretical development. Great social and economic forces were at work: the rise of national consciousness cannot be separated from the growth of a new middle-class society. The principle of nationality reached its height between 1848 and 1870 and found expression in a series of plebiscites. It was recognised by an international Congress, when at Paris in 1856 it was decided that a plebiscite should be conducted under international supervision in Moldavia and Wallachia to determine their future. Mazzini was the greatest prophet of the new idea, and its greatest apparent triumph the union of Italy. But the theory of national self-determination, now fully launched on the tide of history, was disintegrating as well as unifying in its influence. Its logical consequence was that any state which could not persuade its people to regard themselves as a single national community, and so become a nation state, must lose its cohesion and its diverse elements fly apart. This is what happened to the Austrian and Turkish Empires. The history of self-determination is a

[1] E. Barker, *National Character*, 3rd ed., 1939, p. 123.

history of the making of nations and the breaking of states. In consequence of the appearance of the principle of self-determination out of the first and more democratic phase of the French Revolution, and its subsequent development in a series of prolonged struggles against the autocratic empires of Napoleon, the Sublime Porte, the Habsburgs, and the Romanovs, the connexion between the nationalist and the democratic movements became strongly established. The war of 1914 to 1918, which was fought, after the collapse of Russia, by a group of parliamentary states against three great autocratic empires, ranging on the one side the aggressive imperialist ambitions of Germany, and on the other all the nations in Europe threatened by them, seemed to confirm this association and carry it to its highest point. By 1918 nationalism and democracy were generally taken as synonymous in the thought of the Western nations. The nation state was regarded as the political expression of the democratic will of the people.

A more careful examination of the process of national liberation might have suggested doubts, arising from two different considerations. The success of national revolts in the nineteenth century, when they did succeed, is not to be interpreted as the triumph of democratic virtue unaided by force. On the contrary, nations only achieved their independence when they had the effective backing of a strong military power. Where this was lacking, as it was to the Poles, national independence was not achieved. Moreover, the democratic elements in the movement were very restricted. The wishes of the people were represented generally, not through a direct vote, but by the election of an assembly, often on a very narrow franchise. The Ionian Isles, when they voted for union with Greece in 1862, had a population of nearly 250,000, but in the plebiscite only 13,419 voted.[2] The Italian plebiscites of 1860 embodied a very rudimentary democratic procedure. *The Times* described the plebiscite in Savoy and Nice in these terms: 'The vote was the bitterest irony ever made on popular

[2] S. Wambaugh, *A Monograph on Plebiscites*, 1920, p. 129.

suffrage—the ballot box in the hands of the very authorities who issued the proclamation; no control possible; all opposition put down by intimidation.'[3] Doubtless in most cases the true wishes of the populace were represented by the plebiscites, but it has to be admitted that it was democracy with a difference. Bearing all these considerations in mind, we are bound to conclude that the association between nationalism and democracy, and therefore the theory of self-determination itself, may have been the result, not of their innate interdependence, but of historical accident. Recent experience has certainly thrown doubt on the belief that there is such an inevitable and inherent connexion between the two principles as the theory of self-determination has generally been taken to imply.

III. Development of the Expansionist Idea of the State in Germany

The identification of the nationalist movements of the nineteenth century with the ideal of democratic self-determination appears even more difficult when we examine the development of political thinking in Germany. Whereas national unity in France and England was the creation of the great medieval monarchies, Germany remained politically divided until the second half of the nineteenth century, and then the peculiar conditions of German political life and thought dictated a very different course for the national idea from that which it had followed in Western Europe. The absolute sovereignty of the state authorities had been accepted without qualification in Germany. Not that the petty German princes were in theory more absolute than the Bourbons in France, but, whereas in France absolutism had been constantly challenged both by practical and theoretical opposition, in Germany it is difficult to find a single voice raised against it from the sixteenth until the end of the eighteenth century,

[3] *The Times*, 30 April 1860, quoted in G. Schwarzenberger, *Power Politics*, 1941, pp. 292–3.

except in a few isolated centres of rather feeble constitutionalism. Moreover, at the time when the authority of the ruler seemed to have reached its crowning-point in Germany, with the career of Frederick the Great, France was on the eve of a revolution which was to strike a fatal blow at the roots of Bourbon absolutism.

Germany, of course, did not remain uninfluenced by the democratic current of opinion. The alliance between liberal Europe and the force of nationality reached its zenith in the Revolution of 1848, when the national and democratic principle of self-determination was accepted in the form of a policy of voluntary and democratic unification for all Germany; nor was there anything exclusive in the claim, for the same right was recognised as an attribute of other nations, just as it was by the founder of Italian nationalism, Mazzini. Thus the Austrian envoy, who was President of the Frankfurt Assembly, declared with reference to the problem of Schleswig: 'I believe that it would be no breach of faith to the cause of Schleswig, no treason against the cause of Germany, if, supposing that a part of Schleswig should express the desire not to remain as a part of Germany, this desire should be complied with.'[4] Even in 1864, when the Schleswig question again became critical, the Prussian government pressed for the holding of a plebiscite. After the war with Denmark, Prussia was no longer willing to accept this solution, and soon liberal Germany was a thing of the past.

It is to be noted, however, that even in the German Declaration of Rights of 1848 the emphasis was more on the sovereignty of the nation than on the rights of individuals. The democratic and liberal elements in the nationalism of the 1848 Revolution were very limited, and collapsed without great resistance when the task of achieving political unity was taken over by the Prussian monarchy. The decisive fact in the evolution of a nation state in Germany was the existence in that vast area of one powerful, closely integrated, absolutist state, with a great past en-

[4] Wambaugh, p. 879.

shrined in historic tradition, and the promise of an even
greater future. Prussia was the single hard crystal suspended
in the solution of German society. Only by solidifying round
Prussia could the formless, non-political, national feelings
of the Germans acquire political substance. In doing so they
took to themselves the peculiar character of the Prussian
state. This would not have been possible, of course, unless
similar tendencies had existed in German politics as a
whole. But while there had been diverse possibilities in the
Germany of the eighteenth century, the influence of the
Hohenzollern state system ensured that governmental
absolutism should be the dominant political trend of the
new German national state of the nineteenth century.

Thus during the nineteenth century two very divergent
political ideals, embodying two different conceptions of the
state, appeared in Western Europe and in Germany. But
the theorists and statesmen who advocated self-determination of nations as a principle of universal application did
not realise that it might mean different things in different
political contexts, and that the difference between the
democratic English and French idea of the state and the
autocratic German idea would vitally affect the development of the process of self-determination.

IV. Decline of Self-determination in the Latter Part of the Nineteenth Century

The weakening of the forces of liberal nationalism was not a
phenomenon peculiar to Germany in the second half of the
nineteenth century. A leading characteristic of this period
was the development in many states of a policy of positive
and energetic denationalisation towards minorities. The
Germans attempted ruthlessly to germanise their Polish
subjects. In 1870 Polish regiments in the Prussian Army
marched to battle behind bands playing their national airs.
A few years later such a thing would have been impossible.
Similarly Russia began a policy of russification in her border
provinces. The Young Turks rather later fired the train

that was to destroy their empire by attempting a policy of wholesale turkification.

During a period in which aggressive nationalism, in the form of imperialism, was advancing rapidly, the principle of self-determination naturally receded. A few years before the end of the century, Lecky could write that, 'On the whole, the doctrine of the absolute and indefeasible right of nationalities to determine their own form of government seems to me now less prominent among the political ideas of the world than it was in 1848, and at the period of the emancipation of Italy.'[5] The attack, moreover, did not come only from one flank. While the more reactionary forces in Western society were moving in the direction of a militant imperialism, at the same time the left wing, under the influence of socialist ideology, had come to regard the national movement as a bourgeois trick to divert the workers from their true destiny. Some schools of socialism, besides denouncing nationalism, also condemned democracy, at least as it operated in a capitalist society. Socialism thus looked with suspicion on both elements in the theory of self-determination. There were, of course, socialist parties in Austria and Russia which were prepared to support national movements as a means of weakening capitalist imperialism, but the influence of the socialist movement as a whole, with its cosmopolitan ideals, could hardly be regarded as favourable to the general development of national self-determination.

However, since socialism as yet exercised no decisive influence over the policy of any state, the effective opposition to nationalism came from the forces of imperialism and the expansionist tendencies with which they were associated. It can hardly be disputed that the greatest barrier to the further progress of national self-determination in Europe at the beginning of the twentieth century was to be found in the power and policy of the great empires of Central and Eastern Europe—Germany, Austria-Hungary, Russia, and Turkey. So overwhelming were these imperial powers that

Lecky, *Democracy and Liberty*, 1896, I. 418.

the lesser nations were driven back on the defensive, except in the Balkans, where the weakness of the Turks and the rivalries of the other empires gave them their chance.

The contemporary observer might very reasonably have felt doubt in 1914 about the future of the movement for national self-determination. Indeed, one of the soundest of French historians, Charles Seignobos, writing a year before the outbreak of a war which was to release the pent-up forces of a host of nations, could argue that the national movement was in its decline. Apart from Norway and the Balkans, no fresh nation had achieved independence for over half a century, while the annexation of undoubtedly non-German populations in Schleswig and Lorraine by the new German Empire marked a definite regression for the principle of nationality. Government, Seignobos believed, had become too strong to allow much hope of success to national risings in the future. 'The hope of winning their independence by force of arms,' he concluded, 'is closed henceforth to little nations oppressed by foreigners.'[6]

There seemed much evidence to support such a view. Great imperial powers dominated every continent, either by actual possession or through spheres of influence. So long as Germany, Austria-Hungary, and Russia ruled Eastern Europe, national self-determination was not practical politics for its many subject peoples. Russia and Great Britain between them controlled most of the continent of Asia, except where the rising sun of Japan's imperial power was dawning in the Far East. Africa was partitioned between the great powers of Europe and their satellites, except for Abyssinia, where the meeting of British and French spheres of influence had created a no-man's-land into which Italy had failed to penetrate. Finally, the Monroe Doctrine provided a rather threadbare disguise for dollar diplomacy and the overlordship in the two Americas of the United States.

The revival of the forces of national and democratic self-determination, and their rapid advance to a position of ap-

[6] Ch. Seignobos, etc., *Les Aspirations autonomistes en Europe*, 1913, p. x.

parently universal acceptance, only came as a result of developments that appeared after the outbreak of war in 1914. It was hardly to be expected, however, that in the early stages of the first World War the idea of national self-determination should play much part. The Belgian and Serbian issues could be generalised, but into no more than a defence of the independent sovereignty of small states. The French based their claim to Alsace-Lorraine on historic grounds, not on any right of self-determination. How far the Allies were from accepting any general principle of national self-determination is shown by the terms of the secret treaties signed with Italy, Roumania, Japan, and Russia.

V. *The Great Powers and the Subject Nationalities 1914-1918*

The national principle only slowly came to assume the dominant position it held in 1918, and it emerged rather through force of circumstances than as a result of deliberate policy on the part of any of the great powers. National liberation was to be, as it had been in the time of Napoleon, a by-product of war.

The outbreak of a general European war naturally encouraged discontented minorities everywhere, and the presence of such minorities on either side presented the enemy with an opportunity which they could not afford to neglect. In the earlier part of the war the Germans employed the national weapon much more extensively than their opponents. The Allies professed to be fighting for the rights of small states, and the invasion and occupation of Belgium and Serbia gave them at least a *prima facie* case, but the Central Powers had a not ineffective riposte, which was embodied in the simultaneous German and Austrian notes of 11th January, 1917. The Austrian note may be quoted here, as the German note used identical arguments. 'If the adversaries demand above all the restoration of invaded rights and liberties, the recognition of the principle of nationalities and of the free existence of small states, it will suffice to call to mind the tragic fate of the Irish and Finnish peoples, the obliteration of the freedom and independence of the Boer Republics, the subjection of North Africa by Great Britain, France, and Italy, and, lastly, the violence brought to bear on Greece for which there is no precedent in history.'[7] It is interesting to see reflected in this protest the difference between the Central European and the Western conception of nationality. For the latter the political fact of statehood, as in Belgium or Serbia, constituted the crucial issue; for the former the existence of a cultural or racial unity was just as important. That this distinction had a definite effect on war policy is shown by the readiness of the Germans and Austrians to dismember the Russian Empire, careless of the precedent they were establishing, and the reluctance of the Allies to appeal to the minorities in the Austro-Hungarian Empire.

The decisive factor affecting Allied policy on the national question was the bond with Tsarist Russia. So long as the Allies were tied to Tsarist imperialism, no general recognition of the principle of self-determination, even confined to Europe, could be expected from them. Not only had Russia her own minorities, which she had no intention of freeing, but also her foreign policy was dictated by imperialist and not by national, or even by pan-Slav ideals. Masaryk acknowledged later that not until the downfall of Tsardom did he feel easy in proclaiming that the objects of Allied policy were 'the liberation of small peoples and the strengthening of democracy.[8] The event which transformed the whole relation of the belligerents to the national question was the Russian Revolution. One of the first steps of the Russian Provisional Government was to announce, in March, 1917, that its aim was the establishment of peace on the basis of 'the right of the nations to decide their own destinies.' With this declaration the ice broke, and the dammed-up waters of nationality began a wild rush which

[7] *Official Statements of War Aims and Peace Proposals, December* 1916 *to November* 1918, prepared under the supervision of J. B. Scott, 1921, p. 44.
[8] T. G. Masaryk, *The Making of a State*, 1927, p. 132.

was to sweep onward until the end of the war and beyond, in an increasingly powerful and ultimately uncontrollable torrent.

During the months that followed the fall of the Tsarist régime the collapse of the Russian armies was completed, and power was seized by a Bolshevik government determined, in reply to a general demand, to make peace at any price. The Central Powers now had their opportunity to end the war on the eastern front, and at the same time to demonstrate in public their plans for the post-war world. At Brest-Litovsk, for the first time in the war, self-determination becomes a dominant interest. The Soviets in their peace declaration of 8th November, 1917 brought it into the centre of the stage, and there ever since it has obstinately clung.

By the terms of the Treaty of Brest-Litovsk huge areas were torn from the Russian Empire, and, whatever lip-service was paid to the principle of nationality, the despatch of German expeditionary forces and armies of occupation to all the liberated provinces, and the absence of genuine representative assemblies or effective national governments, except in Finland, and possibly the Caucasus, demonstrated clearly the true nature of the situation. Brest-Litovsk, indeed, with its system of satellite states, its frantic search for supplies from Eastern Europe, and widespread German military occupation, was a fore-shadowing of Hitler's New Order. As Mr. Wheeler-Bennett comments, 'The High Command by their treatment of Russia had disclosed to the world what defeat at the hands of Germany would entail, and, furthermore, that the supreme power in the country was exercised by them alone. In so doing they had contributed to the Allied cause that final and essential degree of co-operation and oneness of purpose which was necessary for victory.'[9]

By this demonstration of German aims, and through its influence on the Allied attitude to the problem of subject

[9] J. W. Wheeler-Bennett, *Brest-Litovsk: the Forgotten Peace, March* 1918, 1938, p. 366.

nationalities, the Russian Revolution proved to be the decisive event in the history of self-determination during the war. From an early date there had been currents of opinion in the Allied countries running in the direction of a clearer and more generous definition of war aims in relation to the national question; but an important difference between the Allied and the Central Powers in this respect was that whereas the Germans made use of the national appeal, when it suited them, as a part of their official policy, the general idea of self-determination developed on the Allied side out of unofficial thought. It had reached the British Foreign Office in the form of a Memorandum on Territorial Settlement by autumn 1916. This declared that 'His Majesty's Government have announced that one of their chief objects in the present war is to ensure that all the states of Europe, great and small, shall in the future be in a position to achieve their national development in freedom and security. It is clear, moreover, that no peace can be satisfactory to this country unless it promises to be durable, and an essential condition of such a peace is that it should give full scope to national aspirations as far as practicable. The principle of nationality should therefore be one of the governing factors in the consideration of territorial arrangements after the war.'[10] At the same time the Memorandum recognised that the British Government was limited by its pledges to its Allies, especially Italy, and in a spirit of realism concluded: 'Lastly, we should not push the principle of nationality so far as unduly to strengthen any state which is likely to be a cause of danger to European peace in the future.'[11]

The leading party in the development of the general ideal of national liberation into an officially recognised Allied policy of self-determination was played by President Wilson, whose ideas on this subject were part of a long-considered political philosophy. From general principles

[10] Quoted in D. Lloyd George, *The Truth about the Peace Treaties*, 1938, pp. 31–2.
[11] *id.*

the discussion of Allied peace aims gradually worked down
to specific proposals. Self-determination was already, early
in 1917, turning from a mere phrase into what Wilson later
called 'an imperative principle of action.'[12] In the Allies'
reply of January, 1917 to President Wilson's Peace Note,
they included, along with other aims, a demand for 'the
liberation of Italians, of Slavs, of Roumanians, and of
Czecho-Slovaks from foreign domination,' and 'the en-
franchisement of populations subject to the bloody tyranny
of the Turks.' At the same time they drew attention to the
Tsar's Manifesto declaring his intentions with regard to the
Poles.[13] It has been pointed out that their declaration did
not quite mean all it seems to on the surface. The original
reference was to 'Italians, Southern Slavs, and Roumanians,' by which the Allies were clearly thinking of the
territories promised to Italy and Roumania by the secret
treaties, and the Serbian hope of gaining Bosnia, Herze-
govina, and Dalmatia. The Italians, who did not wish to
encourage the Serbs, secured the deletion of the adjective
'Southern,' and Masaryk's influence in Paris resulted in
the addition of the Czecho-Slovaks, but it is unlikely that
the significance of all this was understood by the Allies.[14]

Early in 1918 Wilson crystallised his proposals in the
Fourteen Points and the Four Principles, but even now the
scope of the self-determination envisaged was strictly
limited. Both Wilson and Colonel House believed that
Austria-Hungary was a political necessity.[15] Hence the
President, while he promised 'the freest opportunity of
autonomous development' to the peoples of Austria-Hungary, did not as yet envisage its destruction.

The development of the principle of self-determination
was for a considerable period hampered by the unwillingness of the Allies to contemplate the disappearance of the
Austro-Hungarian Empire. There was never the bitterness
of feeling against Austria-Hungary that existed against

[12] 11 February 1918, Scott, p. 268.   [13] *id.* p. 37.
[14] C. A. Macartney, *National States and National Minorities*, 1934, pp. 184–5.
[15] C. Seymour, *The Intimate Papers of Colonel House*, 1926–8, III. 346.

Germany. Masaryk reports that he found everywhere that the idea of destroying Austria-Hungary had not entered the mind of the Allies. 'Austria,' he says, 'was generally looked upon as a counterpoise to Germany, as a necessary organisation of small peoples and odds and ends of peoples, and as a safeguard against "balkanisation".'[16] The British and French governing classes had been brought up in the belief that Austria-Hungary was a European necessity. They favoured it as a conservative influence, and—perhaps mistakenly—believed that the Dual Monarchy was naturally a pacific influence in European politics because of its internal difficulties.[17] The Quai d'Orsay, which feared that in the event of a disintegration of Austria-Hungary the German areas of Austria would unite with thé Reich, regarded the prospect with natural alarm. Indeed, up to the last months of the war French foreign policy desired the maintenance of the Dual Monarchy.[18] Circumstances, however, were to push the Allies farther along the road to complete independence for the dissatisfied nationalities of the Dual Monarchy than they had contemplated, or perhaps desired.

The year 1918 was spent in the extension of the principle of self-determination on point after point. The first important practical step was the holding of a Congress of Oppressed Nationalities at Rome in April, 1918, under Italian patronage. It included, as well as Italians, Roumanians, Poles, Czecho-Slovaks, and South Slavs. One of its most important consequences was the removal of an outstanding obstacle in the way of the recognition of the claims of the subject nationalities of the Dual Monarchy, by the signing of an agreement between the head of the Italian Parliamentary Commission and the leaders of the Yugo-Slav National Council, which engaged both peoples 'to decide

---

[16] Masaryk, p. 244; *cf.* pp. 136, 247.
[17] H. W. V. Temperley (ed.), *A History of the Peace Conference*, 1920–1924, IV. 176.
[18] T. Ruyssen, *Les Minorités nationales d'Europe et la Guerre Mondiale*, 1923, p. 56.

amicably . . . pending territorial questions on the basis of the principle of nationalities and of the right of peoples to dispose of their own destinies, and that so as not to prejudice the vital interests of the two nations, which will be defined at the moment of peace.' [19] The final clause, of course, reduced the rest of the Pact to nonsense, and even so the Italian Government carefully avoided any official commitment, but it served its purpose at the time.

Allied declarations gradually became stronger as the situation in the Dual Monarchy unfolded itself, until finally, on 18th October, 1918, in reply to an Austrian Note, Wilson refused to accept autonomy as a satisfactory answer to the aspirations of the subject nationalities of the Dual Monarchy, saying that it was for these people to decide for themselves 'what action on the part of the Austro-Hungarian Government will satisfy their aspirations and their conception of their rights and destiny as members of the family of nations.'[20] A more thorough discussion of the development of the national situation in the Habsburg dominions than we have space for here would, I believe, lead to the conclusion that, while the Allies played a certain part in stimulating the revolt of the nationalities, it was primarily a consequence, not of Allied propaganda but of the spontaneous action of the nationalities themselves and of the progress of the war. A similar process of disintegration was taking place in the Russian and Turkish empires, and everywhere national forces were moving in advance of Allied policy. During the closing stages of the war, wherever there was a minority or a subject nationality, national armies were gathering and national governments being set up. For the stronger and better organised of the subject nationalities, self-determination, which had gradually emerged as an Allied policy owing to the events of the war, was a *fait accompli* in Europe long before the Allied statesmen sat down to discuss the new order at Versailles. The Peace Conference was not faced with the task of creating new states. They had

[19] Quoted in H. F. Armstrong, *The New Balkans*, 1926, p. 65.
[20] Scott, pp. 428–9.

already created themselves out of the disorder into which the defeated powers fell. All that the Conference could do was to register accomplished facts and delimit the frontiers of the new states, and even in this task its hands were far from free.

The Western powers had not called the force of nationality into being: they had rather reluctantly recognised it when it appeared and used it, not to win the war, but to hasten its last stages. In so doing, and in the propaganda they had poured forth, they had committed themselves to the principle of self-determination. Under pressure from President Wilson they had, perhaps, gone farther than they intended. The practical difficulties that would be presented by the attempt to reconcile the principles of self-determination with the realistic national and imperial ambitions of the victors were not hidden from all the Allied statesmen. But opinion in all nations expected a settlement based on self-determination, at least in so far as it was in their own interests, and the Allies were, as a result of their official declarations during 1918, committed up to the hilt in its favour. To produce a coherent and stable international order founded on this principle was therefore the fundamental task that confronted the Peace Conference.

IV. The Application of Self-determination in the Peace Treaties of 1919

I. Allied Policy and the Principle of Self-determination

WHEN THE Peace Conference opened in 1919, its leading principle, or so the world thought, was to be self-determination for all nations. We have seen how rapidly the star of national self-determination had emerged in the course of a few war years from what now seemed to have been merely a temporary eclipse. To the tribes of man, sickened by four years of carnage, the product of a generation of imperialism and centuries of power politics, it appeared as the light of salvation, beaconing humanity onwards to a happier future. A sceptical observer might have reflected that circumstances rather than design had placed it in the forefront of Allied policy. The Fourteen Points and the Four Principles had proclaimed it to the world, but it is to be remembered that Wilson had in a sense forced these on his Allies. He issued the Fourteen Points when he did because of the failure of the American Mission to secure from an Inter-Allied Conference the manifesto on war aims he desired. By his announcement he hoped to counteract the effect of the revelation of the secret treaties by the Bolsheviks, keep Russia in the war, and launch an effective propaganda offensive against Germany.[1] Once the President's principles had been given publicity, his allies could not stand out against them. An Inter-Allied Parliamentary Commission of French, Belgian, Italian, and British representatives had, at

[1] Seymour, III. 324–6.

the end of October, 1918, proclaimed their acceptance of
the principle of nationality and of 'the right of people to
dispose of their own destiny.' In their reply to the German
proposals for an armistice, the Allied Governments declared their willingness to make peace on the terms laid
down in President Wilson's address of 8th January, 1918
and his subsequent speeches, subject to qualifications regarding the freedom of the seas and reparations. Into the
debate concerning the extent to which the Allies were
actually committed to Wilson's principles by the pre-
Armistice negotiations, and in particular to self-determination, we need not enter, but an observation in the note sent
by Balfour and Clemenceau to Tittoni in the course of the
dispute over the Italian frontier, deserves quotation. 'All
four,' they said of the Western powers, 'are pledged to the
principle of self-determination.'[2] It is true that there were
demands in the Fourteen Points which were hardly reconcilable in practice with self-determination, and that the
Americans and British—apart from a loose sentence by
Lloyd George—did not contemplate its application to
colonial populations. It is also true that the difficulties involved in a consistent working-out of the principle were not
entirely ignored in all quarters before the Peace Conference.
But the important fact is that world opinion certainly
thought that the victorious Allies were committed to the
principle of self-determination in its most absolute form,
and expected it to be clearly and unequivocally put into
practice.

1. THE ITALIAN VIEW

The statesmen who assembled in Paris had fewer illusions.
They had used the appeal to self-determination as an instrument of war, not necessarily hypocritically; but not many
were anxious to apply it where it conflicted with the interests of their own states in drawing up the terms of peace.
Their true sentiments can be gathered from their private

[2] 25 July 1919; D. Hunter Miller, *My Diary at the Peace Conference of Paris,*
1924–6, XX. 362.

rather than their public utterances. In the pre-Armistice negotiations, for example, the Italian statesman Sonnino had been anxious to introduce a reservation to Point IX, making it clear that Italy expected to receive the frontier which she regarded as necessary for her security, regardless of ethnic considerations or the wishes of the populations concerned. Under pressure from the Allies, who used the argument that the frontiers of Italy were not involved in the negotiations with Germany, which were the immediate issue, Orlando dropped the protest, and the reservation was never communicated to the Central Powers.[3] It is only fair to note, however, that strictly speaking the Austrian negotiations stand on a different footing from the German, in that the Armistice terms had already been despatched directly to the Austrian Government, without the intervention of President Wilson. This makes the formal position different, but at the same time the failure to explain publicly the Italian point of view was unfortunate, for it led to much misunderstanding and recrimination subsequently. The Italians, although they withdrew, certainly did not intend to abandon their claim; and they declared later that they did not regard Point IX as applicable to the frontiers of Italy.[4] President Wilson seems to have acknowledged this, for he said that he realised that Italy was not bound by the Fourteen Points in making peace with Austria.[5] He implied that on the other hand *he* was, and therefore he could not consent to some of the Italian proposals. The Italian delegation would have been well advised to have clung to the Treaty of London. Throughout the war Italian policy had been controlled by a single-minded devotion to what were supposed to be the interests of the state, conceived in the narrowest and most exclusive fashion. At the Peace Conference the Italian representatives continued the same policy; but with a kind of naïve Machiavellianism, which aimed at deceiving every one and succeeded in deceiving nobody, they made a self-stultifying effort

[3] R. Albrecht-Carrié, *Italy at the Paris Peace Conference*, 1938, pp. 61–6.
[4] Temperley, IV. 430. [5] Hunter Miller, *Diary*, XIX. 513.

to clothe *il sacro egoismo* in the language of Wilsonian idealism, which had only the effect of weakening their position.

2. THE FRENCH VIEW

The French attitude was much more complicated. The project the French Government had prepared for the Conference proposed, indeed, to remove one serious obstacle to the policy of self-determination by cancelling all inter-Allied treaties; and advocated the 'right of peoples to decide their own destinies by free and secret vote.' But of greater significance was the fact that the basis the French suggested for the Conference was not the Fourteen Points, but the reply of the Allies to President Wilson of 10th January, 1917. They insisted on the principle of 'a certain homogeneousness of states,' but as this was with specific reference to Bohemia, the Southern Tyrol, Dalmatia, and Luxemburg, it is difficult to see what it meant. On the whole, the French project[6] left the principles of the Fourteen Points conspicuously on one side, as might have been expected, seeing that the dominating figure in the French delegation was Clemenceau, who had little tolerance for Wilsonian ideals. In the course of the discussions he frankly declared, according to Lloyd George, 'that he did not believe in the principle of self-determination, which allowed a man to clutch at your throat the first time it was convenient to him, and he would not consent to any limitation of time being placed upon the enforced separation of the Rhenish Republic from the rest of Germany.'[7]

3. THE BRITISH VIEW

The British delegation was less reserved in its attitude towards self-determination, but it had its doubts also. Balfour, on the principle that strong frontiers made for peace, had earlier expressed to Wilson the view that strategic necessity should in some cases be allowed to override the principle of

[6] Hunter Miller, *Diary*, II. Document 4.
[7] D. Lloyd George, *The Truth about the Peace Treaties*, p. 286.

nationality.[8] In general, however, the British delegation was
prepared, at least until it discovered some of the ethnological difficulties, to support a consistent and thorough-
going application of the principle of self-determination. As
Lloyd George ingenuously put it, 'There were many
questions regarding which the great powers were perfectly
impartial. For instance, they were quite impartial regarding
the Roumanian claims on Hungary.' In such a case he
proposed a reference to the experts.[9] The real difficulty
from the British point of view arose from the existence of a
large subject empire. Harold Nicolson explains that, 'The
most ardent British advocate of the principle of self-
determination found himself, sooner or later, in a false
position. However fervid might be our indignation regarding Italian claims to Dalmatia and the Dodecanese it could
be cooled by a reference, not to Cyprus only, but to Ireland, Egypt and India. We had accepted a system for others
which, when it came to practice, we should refuse to apply
to ourselves.'[10] During the war Lloyd George had declared
that the principle of national self-determination was as
applicable in the case of the colonies as in those of occupied
European territories;[11] but the British Government did not
seriously contemplate putting the principle into practice in
its own colonies, or in the German colonies either, for that
matter. 'The German colonies in the Pacific and Africa,'
General Smuts wrote, 'are inhabited by barbarians, who
not only cannot possibly govern themselves, but to whom it
would be impracticable to apply any idea of political self-
determination in the European sense.'[12] A similar attitude
is reflected, over a broader field, in a Memorandum of the
British Foreign Office of November, 1918, which said: 'It
would clearly be inadvisable to go even the smallest distance
in the direction of admitting the claim of the American

[8] Seymour, III. 53.   [9] Hunter Miller, *Diary*, XIV. 177.
[10] H. Nicolson, *Peacemaking*, 1919, 1933, p. 193.
[11] In a speech of 5 January 1918; Temperley, II. 227.
[12] J. C. Smuts, *The League of Nations: A Practical Suggestion*, December
1918, quoted in Hunter Miller, *The Drafting of the Covenant*, 1928, II. 28.

negroes, or the Southern Irish, or the Flemings, or Catalans, to appeal to an Inter-State Conference over the head of their own government. Yet if a right of appeal is granted to the Macedonians or the German Bohemians it will be difficult to refuse it in the case of other nationalist movements.'[13]

4. THE AMERICAN VIEW:
THE PRINCIPLES OF PRESIDENT WILSON

Even the American delegation was not united on the question of self-determination. Wilson's Secretary of State, Robert Lansing, at a later date revealed his violent hostility to the chief plank in his leader's programme. He described the phrase as 'loaded with dynamite,' and said, 'it will raise hopes which can never be realised. It will, I fear, cost thousands of lives. In the end it is bound to be discredited, to be called the dream of an idealist who failed to realise the danger until too late to check those who attempt to put the principle in force. What a calamity that the phrase was ever uttered! What misery it will cause!'[14] Both Canada and the United States, Lansing points out, only continued to exist because of their denial of the principle. If self-determination had been accepted, the Southern States would have been allowed to secede and French Canada would have formed an independent state.[15] What effect, he asks, will it have on the subject peoples of the world—the Irish, Indians, Egyptians, Boers, Mohammedans of Syria and Palestine, and even of French North Africa? Considerations of national safety, historic rights, and economic interests, which would be overridden by it should, he held, all have preference over the principle of self-determination.[16]

Even the President himself possibly did not realise fully the significance of the truly explosive principle which he had done so much to set in action. His ideas demand fuller

[13] Quoted in A. Zimmern, *The League of Nations and the Rule of Law*, 1918–1935, 1936, pp. 199–200.
[14] R. Lansing, *The Peace Negotiations, a Personal Narrative*, 1921, pp. 97–8.
[15] *id.* pp. 100, 103.   [16] *id.* pp. 103–4.

treatment, for the idea of self-determination is so intimately associated with the thought and policy of Wilson that it cannot be adequately discussed without an attempt to discover what the term meant for him. The key to the understanding of Wilson's conception of self-determination is the fact that for him it was entirely a corollary of democratic theory. His political thinking derived, by way of the American democratic tradition, from the democratic and national ideals of the French and American Revolutions. Even if he belonged to the generation that had accepted the Union, as a Virginian and a Southern Democrat he had the right of secession in his bones. His whole political inheritance lay behind his address of 2nd April, 1917, recommending to Congress the declaration of a state of war, and associating together, as the two ideals to uphold which America was entering the struggle, democracy and the rights and liberties of small nations.

Self-determination was to Wilson almost another word for popular sovereignty. In this he followed the French and the American, rather than the British, political tradition. Hence his tendency to appeal to the peoples of the world over the heads of their governments, a tendency which had been a useful asset during the war, but which his fellow statesmen at Versailles found less desirable, and which provoked a violently hostile reaction when he attempted to influence the Italian people against their own government.[17] For Wilson *vox populi* was *vox dei*. Rousseau's General Will was for him no merely ideal will, but the actual will of the people, that only required to be freed from the ill will of autocratic governments for its innate goodness to be manifested. The idealisation of democracy was an essential part of Wilsonian ideology.

It was because he was firmly convinced of the goodness of the people's will that he believed in the possibility of building up a new and better international order on the basis of national sovereignty, in which he assumed the democratic will of the people to be embodied. The intimate association

[17] Manifesto of 23 April 1919. Albrecht-Carrié, pp. 144–5.

in Wilson's mind between self-determination and national sovereignty is shown by the comment, which he repeated many times, on Article X of the League Covenant. 'Then there was the question,' he said, to quote one passage, 'as to whether it interfered with self-determination; that is to say, whether there was anything in the guarantee of Article X about territorial integrity and political independence which would interfere with the assertion of the right of great populations anywhere to change their governments . . . There is absolutely no such restraint . . . We do not guarantee any government against anything that may happen within its own borders or within its own sovereignty.'[18] This combination of faith in the people with unwillingness to interfere with national sovereignty, as well as the practical difficulties, explains why Wilson rejected the idea of international government and relied as the ultimate sanction for international peace on world opinion, expressed through the independent nations of the world. To put it another way, his belief in the goodness and power of world opinion, which might be termed the General Will of humanity, and in its identity with the General Will of every democratic nation, enabled him to hold the view that the self-determination of nations, and national sovereignty, was a possible basis, indeed the only possible basis, of world peace.

In theory, Wilson's ideas form a closely integrated and logically consistent whole. I will not at this point ask wherein their theoretical defects lay, but it is undeniable that in practice they led him into a long series of inconsistencies and contradictions in which he finally became inextricably entangled. The vastness of the practical issues he was raising was perhaps hardly realised by him at first. He confessed later, in weariness of heart, to the Committee of Foreign Relations of the Senate, that 'When I gave utterance to those words ("that all nations had a right to self-determination") I said them without the knowledge that nationalities

[18] Speech of 24 September 1919. *Public Papers of Woodrow Wilson* (ed. Baker and Dodd), 1927; *War and Peace*, II. 375-6.

existed, which are coming to us day after day . . . You do not know and cannot appreciate the anxieties that I have experienced as a result of many millions of people having their hopes raised by what I have said.'[19] It must be admitted that the difficulties involved in the application of his principle of self-determination had largely been hidden from the President until he was harshly brought up against them at Paris.

The fundamental weakness of Wilson's ideas was his failure to realise how indeterminate a criterion nationality might be, and how little assistance it might sometimes give in deciding actual frontiers. Although he had spoken of self-determination as though it were an absolute principle of international right, from the very beginning he perforce allowed competing principles to influence his decisions and derogate from its claims. Even in the Fourteen Points he had introduced reservations in favour of historically established allegiances in the Balkans and in Poland, and had promised to both Poland and Serbia free access to the sea, as something justifiable in itself, without specific reference to the wishes of the populations affected. An even more serious breach of his own principles was involved in his approval, before he had left for Europe, of the Brenner frontier for Italy, although it was with the qualification that any German population thus given to Italy should have the right of cultural autonomy. This concession was doubtless an oversight, due to haste and failure to consult his experts[20] —he later said that his Brenner decision was 'based on insufficient study'[21]—but it greatly weakened his position at Paris.

The greatest limitation of all to the application of his ruling principle Wilson only admitted when he was driven to it in defending himself against his critics in America. At the beginning had acted and spoken as though it were the function of the Peace Conference to replan the world on the lines of self-determination. Was this correct? He

[19] Temperley, IV. 429. [20] Albrecht-Carrié, pp. 63, 65.
[21] Seymour, IV. 451.

was compelled to confess the contrary. 'It was not within the privilege of the conference of peace to act upon the right of self-determination of any peoples except those which had been included in the territories of the defeated empires.'[22] This was equivalent to an acknowledgement that a moral principle was being enforced on the defeated states which the victors refused to apply to themselves. Wilson's defence was that this limitation was forced upon him, but a certain personal bias is suggested by his attitude towards an Irish delegation, as recorded in the Hunter Miller *Diary*. Hunter Miller writes: 'He [Wilson] then spoke of the Irish question and said that he had been made very angry by a delegation of the Irish, who had visited him while in the United States, and had requested him to promise to ask the Peace Conference to make Ireland independent. Of course he had refused to promise anything about it . . . His first impulse had been, from his fighting blood getting up, that he had wanted to tell them [the Irish] to go to hell.'[23] Wilson consistently refused to take any notice of the many petitions from subject nationalities of the Allies which he received.[24]

II. Practical Difficulties in the Application of Self-determination

It is not necessary to pursue our analysis farther. Enough evidence has been adduced to suggest that the British and American delegations were anxious to confine self-determination to Europe, while the French and Italian delegations would have preferred to confine it to Utopia. So much for general principles. Turning from theory to practice, even if it had been desired to adopt a strict policy of self-determination all round in 1919, we may argue that it would not have been possible. We shall be looking at the question in the wrong perspective if we imagine the Allies sitting down with a blank map of Europe, a list of principles,

[22] Speech of 17 September 1919, Baker and Dodd, *War and Peace*, II. 244.
[23] Hunter Miller, *The Drafting of the Covenant*, I. 294.
[24] S. Wambaugh, *Plebiscites since the World War*, 1933, I. 4.

and a free hand in drawing up the new frontiers. In many cases the claims had already been staked out and occupied and only military action on a large scale could have ousted the new possessors.

Another difficulty was that the great powers in making their decisions, although in a few instances they sent commissions of inquiry to ascertain as far as possible the actual sentiments and composition of the populations concerned, inevitably took in most cases one or another group of national leaders as representative of the wishes of each nationality. The assumption that the point of view of the nationalist leaders was identical with that of the whole nationality was in some cases a grave injustice.[25] While peoples such as the Czechs, Serbs, and Poles were well organised and adequately represented, some of the lesser nations, or sub-nations, which were only just beginning to emerge into political consciousness, had views attributed to them which may possibly have represented the ideas of only a small section. It is questionable, for example, whether the union of the Slovaks and Ruthenes with the Czechs adequately represented the wishes, in so far as they had any, of these peoples. It has been authoritatively stated that the majority of the Slovaks were passive under what seems to the outsider the not very benevolent Magyar rule, and that only a handful favoured secession.[26] R. W. Seton-Watson estimates the number of conscious and active Slovak nationalists in 1918–19 at no more than 750 to 1,000.[27] Even among these it seems possible that a majority wanted independence and not union with the Czechs. Masaryk recounts the arguments by which he won the support of Slovaks in the United States for the union. He says, 'I was able to show the Slovaks how little they were known in the political world and how serious a failure we should have courted had they acted independently. The idea of an independent Slovakia could not be taken

[25] *Cf.* C. A. Macartney, *Hungary and her Successors*, 1937, p. 486.
[26] Macartney, *op. cit.*, p. 94.
[27] R. W. Seton-Watson, *Slovakia Then and Now*, 1931, p. 30.

seriously though there might be a theoretical possibility of Slovak autonomy under Hungary. But since this possibility was not practical in the circumstances, there remained nothing save union.'[28] To equate this argument with self-determination would require a very liberal use of the term. Again, on the question of the Bohemian Germans the Conference was informed that 'their own sentiment is reported to be chiefly in favour of the proposed union, provided they are guaranteed minority rights and economic equality.[29] To avoid doubt, however, their views were not ascertained.

Three other major obstacles emerged to the practical application of the principle of self-determination. In the first place, as has been said, the Allies had no intention of applying self-determination at the expense of their own empires. Secondly, it proved impossible, in altering frontiers or setting up new states, to avoid creating new minorities. These two weaknesses in the settlement were only fully appreciated in the years that followed the Peace Conference. Thirdly, and this was a point of immediate importance, there was the difficulty of discovering a generally valid definition of the conditions a nation should satisfy before it could legitimately claim a right of self-determination.

In this last difficulty was implicit the basic problem of the whole policy of self-determination: to what kind of community should it apply? The Germans at Brest-Litovsk had declared that 'the assertion that the right of self-determination is an attribute of nations, and not of parts of nations, is not our conception of the right of self-determination. Parts of nations can justly conclude independence and separation.'[30] The leaders of the nations that were to form the successor states of Austria-Hungary took the opposite point of view. The Serbs asserted that when President Wilson spoke of the self-determination of nations 'his thoughts never went as far as the small communities.'[31] Masaryk did

[28] Masaryk, p. 209.   [29] Hunter Miller, *Diary*, IV. 231.
[30] In the session of 14 January 1918; quoted in J. Mattern, *The Employment of the Plebiscite in the Determination of Sovereignty*, 1920, p. 155 and *n*. 9.
[31] The Yugo-Slav Memorandum of Claims, Temperley, IV. 209.

not attribute his own thoughts to the President, but he expressed the view that the principle, as Wilson had stated it, was too general. 'Does it apply only to a whole people,' he asked, 'or is it valid for sections of a people? A minority, even a big minority, is not a nation. Nor does "self-determination" carry with it an unconditional right to political independence.'[32] These were admirable sentiments, but one cannot help feeling that their main object was to prevent a principle which had been used to justify the secession of the Czechs and Slovaks from the Austro-Hungarian Empire from being used to justify also the further secession of the German population included within the historic frontiers of Bohemia-Moravia. In practice, it is true, the disintegrating process of self-determination had to be stopped at some point or other. But on what principle could that point be fixed? The advocates of the new states were hard put to it to discover an answer to this question.

III. Language as the Test of Nationality

Closely allied with this problem was that of discovering some means of deciding when a number of affiliated communities constituted a nation, and could therefore properly be grouped together in a single state. There was a general tendency to believe that language was an adequate test of nationality. 'In Central and Eastern Europe,' wrote Professor Toynbee, 'the growing consciousness of nationality had attached itself neither to traditional frontiers nor to new geographical associations but almost exclusively to mother tongues.'[33] As a general statement this was undoubtedly true. Unfortunately the exceptions were extensive enough to rob the language criterion of much of its practical value. Nor was it universally accepted by the nations claiming self-determination. Each nation clung to the language test where its effect was favourable, and rejected it where it worked against the national interest. Thus

[32] Masaryk, p. 386. *Cf.* p. 278.
[33] A. J. Toynbee, *The World after the Peace Conference*, 1926, p. 18.

the Poles claimed territory from Germany on the basis of the language spoken by its inhabitants, but refused to follow the same principle in the Russian provinces or East Galicia, where non-Polish tongues were spoken. The Germans claimed various border populations, and later Austria, at least partly on the basis of language. On the other hand, they severely criticised the language test in its application to the population of the southern parts of East Prussia. The German representatives observed that although they used a different language no one believed that Welsh or Bretons or Basques should be separated from the states of which they formed part.[34] Similarly, Venizelos, on behalf of the Greeks, claimed the Albanian-speaking areas of Northern Epirus, on the ground that they were Greek in national sentiment.[35] The results of some of the plebiscites did in fact suggest that language was not invariably a reliable guide to nationality.

IV. The Use of Plebiscites

If language was not a safe guide, there was certainly no other objective test of nationality on which the conference could fall back. Logically, therefore, if it wished to apply the principle of self-determination, it should have taken a popular vote wherever the issue was in doubt. The Germans, in their Reply to the Allies' Conditions of Peace, demanded plebiscites before any of their territory was ceded, though they protested against the holding of a plebiscite in East Prussia to determine what parts of this, if any, should go to Poland.[36] The British, having much less faith than the Americans in the objectivity of nationality, were generally ready to have recourse to popular votes in Europe.[37] The holding of plebiscites in some of the more debatable areas claimed by both Poland and Germany was largely a result of the insistence of Lloyd George. He wrote,

---

[34] A. G. de Lapradelle, *La Documentation Internationale: La Paix de Versailles*, 1929, XII. 148.
[35] Nicolson, p. 255. [36] Lapradelle, XII. 133, 140, 148.
[37] Wambaugh, *Plebiscites since the World War*, 1933, I. 14.

in a Memorandum to the Conference, 'I am . . . strongly averse to transferring more Germans from German rule to the rule of some other state than can possibly be helped.'[38] He was less successful in securing the holding of plebiscites in former Hungarian territory, but his belief in the ethnic principle is brought out clearly in the same Memorandum. 'There will never,' he wrote, 'be peace in South-Eastern Europe if every little state now coming into being is to have a large Magyar *irredenta* within its borders. I would therefore take as a guiding principle of the peace that as far as is humanly possible the different races should be allocated to their motherlands, and that this human criterion should have preference over considerations of strategy or economics or communications, which can usually be adjusted by other means.'[39]

The number of plebiscites that were in fact held was many fewer than might have been expected. They have been studied so thoroughly that nothing more need be said on them here.[40] But the connexion between the principle of self-determination and the plebiscitary device is so close that the causes of the failure to employ it more extensively should be examined. The American point of view was that their team of experts could provide better evidence of the lines of national divisions and affiliations than could be obtained from plebiscites of the populations concerned.[41] The Italians, who could have put their claims on a basis of treaty right or strategic necessity, unwisely chose to appeal to the right of self-determination, but, naturally, they could not contemplate the possibility of a plebiscite of the non-Italian populations they wished to incorporate in Italy. The anxiety of the Italian delegation to avoid any general acceptance of the plebiscitary principle came out plainly in the peace negotiations.[42]

While the Italians provided no very strong arguments in

---

[38] Memorandum of 25 March 1919. Temperley, VI. 239, *n.* 1.
[39] *id.* p. 548.   [40] Wambaugh, *Plebiscites since the World War.*
[41] *id.* I. 13; *cf.* Hunter Miller, *Diary*, XIX. 96, 99-100.
[42] e.g. Hunter Miller, *Diary*, XVII, 186-8.

support of their view, other delegations made greater efforts
to find a justification for the rejection of plebiscites in
territories they were annexing. The Roumanian delegation
protested forcibly against the suggestion that a plebiscite
should be held in Bessarabia. 'Has a plebiscite any meaning,' it asked, 'in a country where the uncontested autoch-
thonous nation still forms the absolute majority by at least
two-thirds of the total?' Somewhat inconsequently it
argued that the elections shortly to be held in Bessarabia
would be 'the best expression of the will of the Bessarabian
people and the most telling of plebiscites.' To strengthen
their case, the Roumanians added that while they were in
a state of war with the Bolsheviks a plebiscite was impossible, and that on the other hand its postponement
would cause agitation and unrest.[43] The French claimed
Alsace-Lorraine on historic grounds and some doubt was
felt 'whether "self-determination" in the shape of a plebiscite
would give a clear majority for re-union with France.'[44] A
French writer of the time put the difficulty bluntly: 'At
this moment in Alsace-Lorraine,' he said, 'any referendum
would be meaningless.'[45] It has been estimated that about
half a million French had left the conquered provinces
between 1871 and 1910, and some 300,000 Germans had
come in to take their place,[46] a sufficient proportion of the
whole population to produce at least an unpleasantly large
minority vote for Germany in a plebiscite. Significantly, the
Allies, in their reply to the German protest, stressed the
popular opposition to the annexation by Germany in 1871,
rather than the sentiments of the population in 1919. There
was a reasonable argument behind this position. Can a state,

[43] Memorandum presented to the Peace Conference by the Roumanian
Delegation on the Bessarabian Question, September 1919, in *Facts and
Comments concerning Bessarabia*, 1812–1940, compiled by a group of
Roumanian Press correspondents, 1941, pp. 23–4.
[44] Hunter Miller, *Diary*, XX. 342–3.
[45] R. Johannet, *Le Principe des nationalités*, 1918, p. 248.
[46] Vidal de la Blache, *La France de l'Est*, 1917, pp. 183–4. Temperley, II.
166, 168, gives the figure of 400,000 Germans entering the Reichsland
between 1871 and 1918.

it might well have been asked, annex territory inhabited by members of another nationality, remove large numbers of them by open or veiled pressure, or merely by the operation of their desire not to live under an alien government, introduce in their place its own nationals, and then claim the territory on the basis of self-determination? Such a consideration suggests the need of qualifying the use of the plebiscitary method.

On the whole, then, one is impressed with the reluctance to have recourse to plebiscites, though it would seem, at least in theory, that there can be no better means of securing genuine self-determination. In general the opposition to the plebiscitary mode of determining the future of communities came from the victorious Allies, especially from the lesser states, while the demand for plebiscites was a defensive weapon employed by the defeated powers. In the same way, at Brest-Litovsk the Bolsheviks had appealed for self-determination by means of plebiscites, while the Germans had declared them unnecessary.

The simplest explanation of these changes of policy would be that each side was prepared to appeal to the principle when it assisted in the defence of national interests, and to discard it when its influence was no longer favourable. But it is also true that, however carelessly leading politicians may have spoken, even those who most sincerely accepted the principle of self-determination at Versailles did not expect it to be applied with no regard to other considerations. Even where plebiscites were held they were not regarded as the only factor to be considered in the construction of frontier lines. In agreeing to the taking of a plebiscite in Schleswig, for example, the Allies, using a common formula, declared that the frontiers were to be drawn 'according to a line based on the result of the votes, and proposed by the International Commission, and taking into account the particular geographical and economic conditions of the localities in question.'[47]

[47] Hunter Miller, *Diary*, X. 133.

V. *Failure to Achieve General Self-determination*

The new states that were constituted by the Peace settlement, as might have been expected from all that has been said, were far from embodying the strict principle of self-determination. The union of Slovaks with Czechs represented an aspiration towards national identity, rather than an existent fact. In the same state the Ruthenes were treated practically as a colonial population, and there was only a pretence at consulting their wishes; while the Bohemian Germans were also included willy-nilly in the new state. Similarly in Poland a large Ukrainian and White Russian population was annexed, regardless of its wishes or natural affiliations, though it is true that the parts east of the Curzon line were taken by the Poles on their own responsibility and not by a decision of the Peace Conference. The new Roumania included millions of Magyars and a large body of Saxon Germans, as well as other non-Roumanian elements. The wishes of the partners in the Triune Kingdom were more adequately represented, but even here it is doubtful if the Croats would have accepted the union if it had not been for fear of Italian aggression.

Of the failure to achieve a replanning of the world on the lines of his guiding ideal, Wilson was partially aware, but he hoped through the League of Nations to provide machinery for the continuance of the process. 'If the desire for self-determination of any people in the world,' he said, 'is likely to affect the peace of the world or the good understanding between nations, it becomes the business of the League.'[48] In his original draft of the Covenant there was a clause specifically providing for the further progress of self-determination. His wording ran: 'The Contracting Powers unite in guaranteeing to each other political independence and territorial integrity; but it is understood between them that such territorial readjustments, if any, as may in the future become necessary by reason of changes in present racial conditions and aspirations or present social and

[48] 17 September 1919, Baker and Dodd, *War and Peace*, II. 244.

political relationships, pursuant to the principle of self-determination, and also such territorial readjustments as may in the judgement of three-fourths of the Delegates be demanded by the welfare and manifest interest of the peoples concerned, may be effected, if agreeable to those peoples.'[49] It would be difficult to reconcile this article with the principle of national sovereignty, which Wilson himself so strongly maintained. Sufficient pressure was brought to bear on him, however, as Lansing records with satisfaction, for the clause to be reduced to the non-committal form of Article X of the Covenant. Even as an ideal for the future, then, the forces antagonistic to the principle of self-determination were strong enough to hold it in check.

VI. The Substitute for Self-determination

It remains to ask how it has come about, if the settlement was not founded on self-determination, that it was believed to be so founded, perhaps even by many of those who drew it up, who were presumably not unaware of the wide divergences from the ideal. The answer to this question is to be found in the hardly noticed substitution in the peace negotiations of an allied but different set of ideals for that of self-determination. It would be superficial cynicism to maintain that the diplomats at Paris were moved by none but self-interested motives, and that no guiding principles inspired their work, apart from those represented in the establishment of the League of Nations, of which more than one interpretation is possible and which need not be discussed in this chapter. They had certain ideals which they perhaps unconsciously put in the place of self-determination; these were—a belief in small states as a justifiable part of the international order, a belief in the equality of states, great or small, and a belief in the right of absolute national sovereignty.

[49] Wilson's First Draft of the Covenant of the League of Nations, laid before the American Commission, 10 January 1919. Hunter Miller, *The Drafting of the Covenant*, II. 12. *Cf.* I. 42.

1. BELIEF IN SMALL STATES

It is not difficult to account for the dominance of this idea over the policy of the Allies. Great Britain had a long tradition of friendship with the smaller states and nations of Europe—Portugal, Greece, Belgium, Piedmont, Denmark could provide illustrations of positive aid, or at least sympathy. The recognition of the independence of the Spanish-American colonies had carried the same tendency into an extra-European field. In 1914 Britain had gone into the war, as we have said, ultimately perhaps for reasons of self-preservation, but immediately because of the attack by the Central Powers on two small states. Again, President Wilson, shortly before the United States also entered the war, had stated his view of the essential basis of world peace in terms of the rights of small nations. 'The equality of nations upon which peace must be founded if it is to last,' he said, 'must be an equality of rights; the guarantees exchanged must neither recognise nor imply a difference between big nations and small, between those that are powerful and those that are weak.'[50] France, for her part, had a tradition of reliance on the support of a group of client states against any strong rival on the other side of the Rhine. Thus when the war ended in the disintegration of three great empires, and the military collapse of a fourth, it was not unnatural that European peace arrangements should be envisaged in terms of free and independent small states.

2. EQUALITY OF STATES

In the second place we find the principle of the equality of all states. The influence of the idea of equal sovereignty was particularly strong in the American delegation. Lansing declared: 'Equality in the exercise of sovereign rights in times of peace, an equality which is imposed by the very nature of sovereignty, seemed to me fundamental to a world

[50] Address to the United States Senate on Essential Terms of Peace in Europe, 22 January 1917. Baker and Dodd, *The New Democracy*, II. 410–11.

organisation affecting in any way a nation's independence
of action or its exercise of supreme authority over its external or domestic affairs. In my judgment, any departure
from that principle would be a serious error fraught with
danger to the general peace of the world and to the recognised law of nations, since it could mean nothing less than
the primacy of the great powers and the acknowledgement
that because they possessed the physical might they had a
right to control the affairs of the world in times of peace as
well as in times of war.'[51] On the other hand, one of the
American legal experts, D. Hunter Miller, regarded Lansing's belief in the equality of states as mere verbiage, and
paraphrased it as meaning, 'The rights and obligations of
Albania as a member of the League are no more and no less
than those of the British Empire'—which seemed to him
nonsense.[52]

The crucial struggle came over the drafting of the League
Covenant. What was to be the position of the small states in
relation to the Council of the League? Colonel House, in
sending his suggestions for a League of Nations to Wilson
in July, 1918, proposed to confine it to the great powers. 'If
the smaller nations are taken in,' he wrote, 'the question of
equal voting power is an almost insurmountable obstacle.
Several of the smaller nations have indicated a willingness
to come into a League of Nations only upon condition that
the voting power of each country shall be the same—notably
Switzerland. If this were agreed upon, Mexico and the
Central American States could out-vote Germany, England,
France, Italy, Japan, and the United States, and yet in the
enforcement of peace or of any of the decrees of the League
of Nations they would not only be impotent but unwilling
to share the responsibility.[53] The British point of view, expressed by Lord Robert Cecil, was that 'the great powers
must run the League and that it was just as well to recognise it flatly as not.'[54] The British draft convention of 20th

[51] Lansing, p. 58.   [52] Hunter Miller, *Drafting of the Covenant*, I. 23.
[53] Seymour, IV. 24.
[54] Hunter Miller, *The Drafting of the Covenant*, 1928, I. 53.

January, 1919 therefore proposed a Council of Great Powers only,[55] and this was incorporated in the Cecil-Miller draft of 27th January, 1919.[56] The proposal was vigorously attacked by the representatives of the lesser states.[57] 'What you propose is nothing else than the Holy Alliance,' protested M. Hymans on behalf of Belgium.[58] The great powers for various reasons were not united in the determination to assert their authority in the League Council. On behalf of France, M. Bourgeois virtuously expressed the view that if too much power were given to the great powers they might seek for peace rather than for peace founded on justice.[59] French sympathy for the smaller states even went as far as a proposal to add Monaco to the list of states invited to accede to the League Covenant.[60] Italy added her support of the smaller states to that of France.[61] When the neutral states were brought into consultation by the drafting Committee, the cry for recognition of the equality of all states and the demand for increased representation of the small states was redoubled,[62] and in face of this opposition Great Britain and the United States had to accept the principle that the lesser states should be represented on the Council.

One comment on this development is provided in Lord d'Abernon's Diary: 'The tacit admission of the claim of minor powers to rank with great powers, the outburst of intrigue, of bargaining, and of recrimination which followed, have revealed the inherent defects of the League constitution. It was always unwise to attribute to small powers an equal vote and an equal influence with the great world powers. The inexpediency of this theoretical equality was to some extent veiled, or perhaps corrected, by the establishment of the Council. But the moment the right of Poland

[55] *id.* II. 107–8.   [56] *id.* II. 132.   [57] *id.* I. 137–8.
[58] Hunter Miller, *Diary*, V. 101.   [59] *id.* V. 53.   [60] *id.* XX. 93.
[61] Hunter Miller, *The Drafting of the Covenant*, I. 152–3.
[62] Hunter Miller, *Diary*, VII. 23, 27. For the Swiss insistence on the equality of states, *v.* Lapradelle, *La Conférence de la Paix et la Société des Nations*, 1929, pp. 255–6.

to a permanent seat was supported by France and by Chamberlain, the disproportion between real and attributed weight was bound to blaze forth.'[63] The principle of the equal sovereign status of all members of the League of Nations triumphed so completely that membership of the League came to be regarded as a sign of independent sovereignty. Thus Lord Robert Cecil in 1921 spoke of 'the sovereignty and independence of Albania' as being 'established by her admission to the League.'[64] When Iraq entered the League in 1932 the *rapporteur* of the League Committee declared that this was conclusive proof that it was 'now beginning life as a free and independent state.'[65]

The reasons for the successful establishment of their claims by the smaller states in 1919 are not very obscure. Two great powers, Germany and Russia, were temporarily excluded from effective intervention in world affairs. The remaining four great powers had divergent interests and views. France was hoping to create a system of client states in Europe, and the prospect of the support of some of these on the Council of the League was not unwelcome to her. Great Britain could not, out of deference to the susceptibilities of the Dominions, too strenuously resist the claims of the small states. President Wilson's personal sympathies were with them. Finally, progressive opinion was generally on the side of the small states.

3. NATIONAL SOVEREIGNTY

Along with the general belief in the virtue of small states, and in the juridical equality of all states, great or small, there went, in the third place, a firm conviction of the rights of national sovereignty. The French delegation was practically alone in its willingness to abandon the principle of complete, independent national sovereignty in the interests

[63] D'Abernon, *An Ambassador of Peace*, 1929–30, III. 235.
[64] M. W. Graham, *The League of Nations and the Recognition of States*, 1933, p. 32.
[65] Graham, p. 33.

of a new international order.[66] In our view, said Bourgeois, the sovereignty of each state is not an absolute idea.[67] National sovereignty, declared another French member of the Committee on the League, had for some time past been a fiction.[68] The French wished to convert the League into a great military alliance in which independent sovereignty should to an appreciable extent be sacrificed in the interests of military security. On the other hand, in his report to the Conference on behalf of the League of Nations Commission, Lord Robert Cecil asserted as one of the basic principles the view that the League should not in any respect interfere in the internal affairs of any nation.[69] President Wilson seems to have refused to acknowledge, even to himself, that there could be any conflict between the organisation of a peace system in the form of the League of Nations and the principle of national sovereignty. Certain nations, he said, have a sort of fetishism for the idea of sovereignty, and in the front rank of these is the United States.[70]

The small states found the British and American assertion of the rights of national sovereignty very much to their minds. In their anxiety that no sovereign rights should be lost to their states, Sir Robert Borden and W. M. Hughes, for Canada and Australia, both strongly insisted that the League Council was not an executive body, and should not be described as such.[71] Among the neutrals the Dutch were particularly emphatic that the sovereignty of individual states should not be in any way limited.[72] The new states, for their part, believed firmly in their capacity to add to their security by territorial acquisitions, and defend them by their own right hands.

This was quite a natural and not a new attitude on the

---

[66] The attitude of the Portuguese delegate deserves to be recalled as an exception to this statement, as the following passage shows. '*M. Jayme Batalha Reis (Portugal) estime que le fétiche exagéré de la souveraineté des états dont il a été parlé est un véritable obstacle à la construction solide de la Société des Nations. Il faut que celle-ci se résigne a déléguer une partie de leur souveraineté à créer une véritable fédération.*' Hunter Miller, *Diary*, VIII. 94–5.

[67] *id.* XX. 73.   [68] *id.* VII. 182.   [69] *id.* XX. 14—15.   [70] *id.* VIII. 92–3.

[71] *id* VII. 221, 241.   [72] Hunter Miller, *Diary*, VII. 23, 37.

part of small states. One cannot read a certain passage in a despatch of Castlereagh, written in 1815, without reflecting that it might, with only a change of names, have been written in 1919. 'It is curious,' wrote Castlereagh, 'to observe the insatiable spirit of getting something without a thought of how it is to be preserved. There is not a power, however feeble, that borders France from the Channel to the Mediterranean, that is not pushing some acquisition under the plea of security and ratification of frontier. They seem to have no dread of a kick from the lion, when his toils are removed, and are foolish enough to suppose that the great powers of Europe are to be in readiness always to protect them in the enjoyment of these petty spoils. In truth their whole conception is so unstatesmanlike, that they look not beyond their sop; compared with this the keeping together a European force has little importance in their eyes.'[73]

The great powers paid scant attention to the wishes of the smaller states in 1815. Castlereagh in particular devoted his efforts to the creation of a European balance which should not easily be overthrown, and the history of the nineteenth century bears witness to the success of his plans. The peacemakers of 1919 were far more generous in their attitude to the smaller states, but they hardly realised how impermanent would be the guarantees they had provided for the survival of these states in the event of a recurrence of the threat represented by the defeated power, or the difficulty of reconciling their belief in national sovereignty with the conception of a new international order embodied in the League of Nations.

When the draft Covenant was presented to the Conference, Orlando declared: 'We started from two absolute principles which *a priori* it might seem dialectically impossible to reconcile with one another. On the one hand the principle of the sovereignty of states, which is supreme and brooks no comparison or relation, and on the other the

[73] Castlereagh to Clancarty, 4 September 1815; *British Diplomacy*, 1813–1815, ed. by C. K. Webster, 1921, p. 375.

necessity of imposing from above a restraint on the conduct of states so that the sphere of their rights should harmonise with that of the rights of all the others . . . We were able to effect a reconciliation between these two principles on the basis of "self-constraint".' Léon Bourgeois added: 'This reconciliation has been effected, if I may say so, automatically and, to pursue the metaphor of our distinguished colleague, we have proved the existence of motion by moving.'[74] These eminent statesmen doubtless thought they were saying something in these observations, but it is a little difficult to discover what it was. The attempt to combine a faith in small states, equality of states, and absolute national sovereignty, with the construction of an international system of security, may indeed be considered the greatest theoretical weakness in the peace settlement.

It may well be asked how it came about that the potential danger involved in this contradiction was not more clearly apprehended, especially by the British and American delegations, which were the keenest on the new League organisation. The answer to this question brings us back to the principle with the discussion of which we are primarily concerned. Self-determination for various reasons did not have as decisive an influence over the territorial settlements as might have been expected, but public opinion was far from realising this fact. Many of the limitations on self-determination in the peace treaties were undoubtedly forced on the Conference by circumstances. Millions of Poles, Czechs, South Slavs and others had been freed from alien rule, and it was natural in 1919 that this should seem the dominating fact. However important the numerous cases in which self-determination had not been followed came to seem later, in 1919 it still retained its ideological predominance. The emancipation of the nations by self-determination was the point on which attention was concentrated. If the blunt opposition between sovereignty and the League system had been brought out into the open, the contradiction might have seemed too

[74] Hunter Miller, *Diary*, XX. 16, 18.

blatant. Consciously or unconsciously, by wrapping up national sovereignty in the idealistic language of self-determination the peacemakers concealed from themselves the flaw in the system they had created. When the many failures to apply self-determination consistently and impartially were discovered, and perhaps exaggerated, the idealism seemed to be torn away from the peace settlement, and the conflict between national sovereignty and the League assumed its true place as the fundamental issue presented to the world, the vital question that had not been settled in 1919, and was to be still unsettled in 1939.

In the last analysis we are bound to conclude that the force of self-determination had achieved its real triumphs before the Armistice, in a series of national revolts for which the conditions of the war had provided the opportunity. At the Peace Conference it had passed from the offensive to the defensive. The right of self-determination invariably made its appearance in the discussions before every territorial settlement, and wherever it was patently overridden the Conference was ill at ease. In many of these cases, force of circumstances, or the existence of conditions which rendered the application of the right impossible, could have been urged. Too often, however, instead of frankly admitting the difficulties, the Allied delegates glossed them over and presented a settlement determined on many other considerations as in conformity with the strict principle of self-determination. It might be said that in this procedure there was a fundamental intellectual dishonesty, which, both at the time and subsequently, did much to undermine general respect for the peace treaties. But if either the members of the Conference themselves, or subsequent commentators, thought that—to quote an American writer—'the Versailles settlement sacrificed economic and power considerations to the exclusive demands of the principle of self-determination,'[75] they were profoundly mistaken.

The more we study the work of the Peace Conference, the less it seems to have been under the control of the principle

[75] Spykman, p. 467.

of self-determination. This conclusion, of course, cuts both ways. If self-determination was applied with so many limitations, and was neglected in so many cases, this was doubtless because circumstances prohibited a more complete application. Politicians should have realised, as some of them undoubtedly did, and as the experts proved, that it was only one principle among many and could not claim an overriding authority. At the same time, if we accept this view of the peace treaties we shall have to drop the familiar but circular argument, which condemns the peace treaties because they were based on self-determination, and self-determination because of the ultimate failure of the peace treaties.

V. The Sequel to
the Peace Treaties, 1919-1939

I. The Minorities Problem after 1919

THE HISTORY of self-determination as a force in international politics does not end in 1919, but its incidence changes. Just as Brest-Litovsk had handed over the offensive on the front of self-determination from Germany to the Allies, so with Versailles and its subsidiary treaties the initiative passed back to the defeated powers. The minority population of Europe was smaller than in 1914, but it still existed, with the difference that the subject nationalities of 1914 were now the powers in possession, while Germans, Magyars, Russians, Bulgars were henceforth the nations with a grievance.

The survival of large and diverse minorities in many countries provided ample occasion for the continuance of the agitation for self-determination. Its intensity was not diminished by the fact that now two of the formerly dominant nations found themselves with a grievance on this count against their former subjects. There was, moreover, a feeling, which was not confined to German, Italian, and Magyar quarters, though, of course, it was most strongly felt by them, that, to quote an American commentator, 'Germans, Magyars, and Italians were being sacrificed to people whose cultural value was infinitely less . . . It is far preferable to have Poles under Germans and Yugo-Slavs under Italians than the contrary, if there is no other good alternative.'[1] It is not necessary to endorse this last view to

[1] Diary of G. L. Beer, 16 March 1919 (unpublished); quoted by Albrecht-Carrié, p. 119.

realise the dangerous elements in the situation. The members of the Little Entente, and Poland, which were likely to be the states most exposed to attack, were also the weakest internally by reason of their minorities. It was ironic that a settlement supposed to have been largely determined by the principle of nationality should have produced a state like Czechoslovakia, with minorities amounting to 34.7 per cent of its population, quite apart from the question of the doubtful identity of nationality between Czechs and Slovaks. Poland was not much better off, with minorities amounting to 30.4 per cent, or Roumania, with 25 per cent.[2] On the settlement in Eastern Galicia the verdict in the *History of the Peace Conference* was: 'As things stand, four and a half million people have by a tragic collocation of circumstances been deprived of their rights of self-determination, and a new Ireland has been set up in the heart of Europe—with what consequences no man may know.'[3]

At least, however, the lesson of the disintegration of the Austro-Hungarian Empire, of the Polish revival, and of the revolt of the border nationalities of Russia, it might have been thought, would have taught weaker states than the Habsburg, Hohenzollern, or Romanov empires had been, the wisdom of a generous policy, and of attempting to conciliate their minorities by the concession of extensive rights of local autonomy. The intense national sentiment of the new countries was fatal to such a hope. The nationalities which had emerged successfully from the war and the Peace Conference were determined to create united nation states. To them the issue seemed to be, in the words of Masaryk, the question of 'our state-creative capacity, our power of political construction, our activity in political leadership and ability to lead—a question whether we can be and, in the long run, remain, our own masters and the masters of our state.'[4] It must be remembered, too, that Masaryk was

[2] These figures are taken from Seton-Watson, *Britain and the Dictators*, 1938, pp. 322–3.
[3] Temperley, VI. 274.   [4] Masaryk, p. 366.

the most idealistic and the most liberal-minded of all the representatives of the new states.

Lloyd George made a bitter comment on the tendencies manifested by the newly liberated nations at Versailles. 'It fills me with despair,' he said, 'the way in which I have seen small nations, before they have hardly leapt into the light of freedom, beginning to oppress other races than their own. They are more imperialistic than either England or France, certainly than the United States.'[5] If Masaryk and Beneš won golden opinions—and increased territory—by their breadth of mind, and Paderewski by his sympathetic personality, the other nations were not so lucky in their chosen leaders. Pašić represented a devoted but narrow Serbian patriotism, and of Bratianu a favourable historian writes that his mind 'revolved within the limits of a rigid and unbending patriotism,' and that to him 'the whole ideology of Wilson was at once meaningless and highly suspect.'[6]

The danger of leaving large minorities at the mercy of small states with such an intense national feeling had not been unforeseen, and the Peace Conference endeavoured to guard against it by means of the minority treaties. In one way or another, every one of the lesser states in Central and Eastern Europe compulsorily or voluntarily undertook to guarantee certain rights to its minorities. Great hopes were placed on this widespread acceptance of what was generally, though mistakenly, believed to be the innovation of minority guarantees, but from the beginning it suffered from certain fatal defects.

On the one hand, few of the new states accepted the minority guarantees willingly. The experience of the minority treaties showed that it was unwise to expect small states to live up to rules which the great states refused to contemplate for themselves. Most of them regarded the compulsory signature of minority treaties as a mark of inferiority of status, which they bitterly resented. The general attitude is well summed up by a historian of

[5] Hunter Miller, *Diary*, XIX, 98.
[6] R. W. Seton-Watson, *History of the Roumanians*, 1934, p. 539.

Roumania, who writes: 'The minorities treaties are intended to promote the consolidation of Roumania and not primarily to perpetuate for all time alien communities within her borders.'[7] What the minorities were guaranteed were civil rights and liberties as citizens of a national state. This was far from all they wanted. Neither side was satisfied by the treaties and guarantees, and in place of a gradually improving minority situation, there was one which, in most cases, fairly steadily deteriorated.

There was one possible agency through which this deterioration might conceivably have been prevented. The minorities had been put, to a limited extent, under the wardship of the League of Nations. How would the League interpret its responsibilities? A hostile critic might suggest that its policy was directed more to protecting the states against their minorities than the minorities against oppression by the state. The right of self-determination sank into the background. A League Commission pointed out in 1920 that there was no mention of it in the League Covenant. The grant or refusal of the right, it declared, is, exclusively, an attribute of the sovereignty of every state which is definitely constituted.

This may be juridically a sound view, but one cannot but ask what had become of the principle of self-determination only one year after the Treaty of Versailles. The Committee of Jurists had no doubts on that point. 'Positive International Law,' it said, 'does not recognise the right of national groups, as such, to separate themselves from the state of which they form part by the simple expression of a wish, any more than it recognises the right of other states to claim such a separation.' It admitted that in an international crisis, when ordinary rules are not operating, self-determination may play its part, but in ordinary times it is only one factor among many.[8]

---

[7] J. S. Roucek, *Contemporary Roumania and Her Problems*, 1932, p. 200.
[8] 'Report of the International Committee of Jurists . . . upon the Legal Aspects of the Aaland Islands Question', *League of Nations Official Journal*, Special Supplement, No. 3, October 1920, pp. 5–6.

The minorities were therefore left to the protection of the minority treaties. The literature of the minorities question is extensive[9] and this is not the place to re-tell its history. Excessive delays and inadequacy of treatment were the rule, impartiality the exception. 'The acceptance of a settlement,' it has been said, 'has been more often proof that it offends no important interest than that it secures justice.'[10] The League took effective action only when it was pushed into it by the championship of a state powerful enough to have intervened in defence of the minority had there been no League or minority treaties at all.[11] In the annual League debate on minorities of 1930 the British delegates frankly adopted the view that where German minorities were concerned it was for the German Government to look after their interests.[12] It was natural, given this attitude, that most of the more important minority cases with which the League had to deal should have been in effect disputes between two states[13]—Germany and Poland, Poland and Lithuania, Bulgaria and Greece, Greece and Turkey, Albania and Greece, Hungary and Roumania. It cannot be claimed that the protection for minorities provided by the peace treaties was very effective in eliminating this cause of international disputes. The Upper Silesian experiment, it was declared, showed that the threat or actual employment of force was the only way of protecting members of a minority against the government or the majority of the country; and such a policy introduced all the dangers of intervention.[14]

While the minority treaties did not fulfil the hopes that had been attached to them, the illustrations given should not lead to the supposition that national problems were in any way peculiar to the successor states or confined to

[9] *Cf.* especially Macartney, *National States and National Minorities.*
[10] *Nationalism*, p. 292.
[11] Macartney, *National States*, p. 491; J. Stone, *International Guarantees of Minority Rights*, 1932, p. 265.
[12] Macartney, *op. cit.*, p. 376.   [13] Stone, p. 130.
[14] G. Kaeckenbeeck, *The International Experiment of Upper Silesia*, 1942, p. 528 and *n.* 1.

Europe. The British and French Empires were faced during this period with widespread secessionist movements. Violent nationalist movements threatened to make foreign rule impossible in Egypt and India. The Arab world from Morocco to Iraq was rising in a general demand for rights of self-government. The Philippines and the states of Central America were striving to throw off United States control. Insurrections broke out in Ireland, Palestine, Syria, and many other countries. The demand for national self-determination was appearing where it had never been expected, in the long-established national states of France and Great Britain, in Wales and Brittany, Flanders, Alsace, even Provence and Scotland. Belgium had to face a struggle between Walloons and Flemings. In Spain, Catalans and Basques were increasingly restive. It is impossible to claim, so far as concerns the problem of national minorities, that the condition of the world as a whole was any more stable after 1919 than before 1914. Indeed it was decidedly less so. We are bound to conclude that among the reasons for the long continuance of a state of crisis not the least was the constant tension resulting from minority unrest or other aspects of the continuing pressure towards self-determination.

But can it be said that herein lay the fundamental reason for the deterioration of the political situation to the point of war? There is no denying that the policy of Germany, Italy, and Japan was a major cause of the Second World War. The causes of this bellicose policy we need not examine, beyond asking whether the principle of self-determination played any part in producing it. For Italy and Japan, this question can without further inquiry be answered in the negative. There was after 1919 no *Italia irredenta*. Japan also had no members of her national community to redeem from foreign rule. Germany, however, was in a different position. There was a large German-speaking population outside the borders of the Reich, so that here the claim for national self-determination may possibly have operated.

II. Self-determination in German Policy after 1919

The study of German international policy between 1919
and 1939 must begin and end with the fact that Germany
never accepted the territorial settlement of Versailles as
either just or permanent. The frontier with Denmark was
an agreed one. There was for a time a tendency for Germany to reconcile herself to the loss of Alsace-Lorraine and
drop the demand for a plebiscite there.[15] Elsewhere the
settlement was bitterly resented by all parties in Germany.
The loss of territory to the despised Poles, and the putting
of Germans under the rule of what was regarded as an inferior race, was never accepted as other than a dictate of
force. The German hope of recovering her lost Silesian
territory, and confidence that it would be recovered, is
shown in the pressure exercised upon Upper Silesians of
German descent in the territory ceded to Poland not to opt
for German nationality, in order to maintain as strong a
German minority as possible in Polish Upper Silesia.
Poland, on the other hand, was trying to limit by all means
in her power the number of Germans who had to be accepted as Polish nationals.[16]

The revision of the Eastern frontier was repeatedly put
forward by Stresemann in his private letters and memor-
anda as the major aim of German policy. The Polish
frontiers, he declared, and obviously genuinely believed,
were a gross violation of the principle of self-determination.
In a letter to the former Crown Prince, he named as one of
the great tasks of German foreign policy in the immediate
future, along with the lifting of the Reparations burden,
'the readjustment of our Eastern frontiers; the recovery of
Danzig, the Polish corridor, and a correction of the frontier
in Upper Silesia.' It is interesting to note that he associated
with this as the third great object of German policy, 'the

[15] *Cf. G. Stresemann, his Diaries, Letters and Papers*, ed. and trans. by E.
Sutton, 1935–40, II. 112–3.
[16] Kaeckenbeeck, pp. 123, 130.

protection of Germans abroad, those 10 to 12 millions of our kindred who now live under a foreign yoke in foreign lands.'[17] There was no party division on this question in Germany. Some years later, in 1931, the Socialist Prime Minister of Prussia, Otto Braun, declared that the Eastern frontiers of Germany were unjust and unnatural and never to be recognised as equitable.[18]

The critical issue over which the cry of self-determination brought Germany into conflict with the Versailles settlement was the enforced separation of Germany and Austria. In November 1918 the Provisional Assembly of German-Austria had declared that 'German-Austria is a constituent part of the German Republic.' This declaration was repeated by the Constituent Assembly in March 1919, and in December the Tyrol Landtag, influenced particularly by the economic situation of Austria, proposed to secede to Germany.[19] 'Well,' commented General Hoffman on 29th October, 1918, 'Austria has capitulated unconditionally. I hope at least that we may thus get the German lands of Austria for Germany and so compensate ourselves for what we shall have to give up.'[20] The prohibition imposed on union between Germany and Austria came to be regarded as one of the major crimes of Versailles. Little in evidence in 1919, in 1925 Stresemann was referring to it as a violation of the right of self-determination and a piece of 'unexampled cynicism,'[21] though on grounds of policy he was against raising the question at that time. By the thirties it had become one of the dominant themes in German propaganda and a crucial point in European politics.

[17] Stresemann, II. 503; *cf.* II. 159, 221.
[18] I. F. D. Morrow, *The Peace Settlement in the German Polish Borderlands*, 1936, p 191.
[19] M. M. Ball, *Post-War German-Austrian Relations, the Anschluss Movement*, 1937, pp. 8, 10, 29.
[20] M. Hoffmann, *War Diaries and Other Papers*, trans. E. Sutton, 1929, I. 245.
[21] In an anonymous article in the Press. Stresemann, II. 159.

III. National Self-determination and Nazi Ideology

The clue to the understanding of German policy after 1919 lies in the fact that the disappearance of the great non-national Habsburg Empire had released forces of pan-Germanism that had been latent since 1848, when the Bohemian Germans had failed in their attempt to detach themselves from Vienna and Prague. Not only the Austrians and the Bohemian Germans, but German communities all over Central and Eastern Europe now began to be conscious of their national ties, and from the remotest corners of Europe heard the call of the *Volk*. The new tendencies of German policy, while not confined to any one section of the nation, found their strongest expression in the National Socialist Party. Indeed, the National Socialist movement was in part a movement of the *Auslandsdeutsche* back to allegiance to the Reich, which they had forgotten so long as they had been privileged groups, but now needed to support them in face of the Slav revival.

The key-note of the new German policy is struck in the opening sentence of *Mein Kampf*, in which Hitler says that a fortunate predestination decreed that he should be born on the confines of Germany and Austria, whose fusion was to be the most important task of his lifetime, though, as he rapidly goes on to explain, only as a preliminary step to the conquest of those foreign lands necessary for the living space of a great and united German community.[22] Because it stood in the way of a pan-Germanic union, he regarded the survival of the dynastic empire of the Habsburgs as a disaster for the German people, and welcomed its dissolution.[23]

The first article in the programme of the National Socialist Party was 'the unification of all Germans to form a Great Germany on the basis of the right of self-determination enjoyed by nations.' The appeal to this principle was particularly effective for propaganda directed towards the Western democracies, who could not forget that it was supposed to be their own principle in international affairs.

[22] A. Hitler, *Mein Kampf*, ed. of 1935, p. 1.   [23] *id.* pp. 11–14.

Doubtless large sections in Germany also had their moral indignation aroused by the feeling that the rights of self-determination, which had been lavished so generously on lesser breeds, such as Czechs or Poles, should have been refused to the Germans. 'Self-determination,' declared Hitler at his trial in 1924, 'Yes, but self-determination for every negro tribe: and Germany does not count as a negro tribe.'[24]

We should be careful, however, not to take this propaganda at its face value. Self-determination for all nations was no more the general aim of what were to prove the dominant forces in German political life after 1919 than before 1914. 'The much misused "right of self-determination",' wrote a German student of the national question in 1923, 'is really a term of propaganda and a purely theoretical pretension.'[25] It is significant that *Mein Kampf* may be read from cover to cover and hardly any mention of self-determination be found. Hitler's dominating ideas are throughout those of power politics, and where in the international interests of the state it seemed desirable to abandon, either temporarily or permanently, some section of the German people, he did not hesitate to advocate such a policy. Thus, for the sake of an alliance with Italy, he was prepared to sacrifice the Southern Tyrol.[26] An even more remarkable example was the complete closure enforced on the Polish 'Corridor' question after the signature of the German-Polish declaration of January, 1934.[27] It is possible, of course, that the former, like the latter abstention from agitation, was intended to be only a provisional measure, to cover the immediate exigencies of German policy, but to come to an end as soon as German power was sufficient to permit of a bolder course.

A survey of Hitler's speeches leaves one with the impression that the general absence of the appeal to self-

[24] Baynes, I. 83.
[25] M. H. Boehm, *Europa irredenta: eine Einführung in das Nationalitäten-problem der Gegenwart*, 1923, p. 311.
[26] *Mein Kampf*, pp. 710–11.   [27] Morrow, p. 481.

determination in *Mein Kampf* correctly reflects his attitude to this principle. Were it not that his policy constantly, and even systematically, contradicted his professions, one would be struck by the elements of realism in Hitler's approach to the national question. More than once he frankly recognises that owing to the way in which the European peoples are distributed territorially it is impossible to draw up any system of frontiers which will coincide with national divisions,[28] from which he draws the admirable conclusion that it is all the more necessary 'that people who have had the misfortune to be torn away from their national kindred should not be oppressed and maltreated.'[29] In the Peace Speech of 17th May, 1933 he said: 'Our boundless love for and loyalty to our own national traditions makes us respect the national claims of others and makes us desire from the bottom of our hearts to live with them in peace and friendship. We therefore have no use for the idea of Germanisation.'[30] At the same time he professed to recognise the rights of the independent nations of Europe. 'We live,' he said in 1935, 'in the belief that the happiness and the achievements of Europe are indissolubly connected with the existence of a system of free, independent national states.'[31] On the basis of these declarations he claimed that National Socialist Germany had no aggressive purposes against any other European nation.[32] All this is beyond cavil. Indeed, one may begin to wonder whether Hitler does not go a little too far in his criticism of the principle. In September 1938, he launched a frontal attack on it. 'In 1918 under the watchword "the right of the peoples to self-determination",' he declared, 'Central Europe was torn in pieces and was newly formed by certain crazy so-called "statesmen." Without regard for the origin of the peoples,

[28] Baynes, II. 1235, 1428–9. (Speeches of 21 May 1935 and 18 March 1938).
[29] *id.* II. 1235.
[30] Baynes, II. 1047; *cf.* II. 1061, 1158, 1218. (27 May 1933, 30 January 1934, 21 May 1935.)
[31] *id.* II. 1234 (21 May 1935); *cf.* II. 1280 (7 March 1936).
[32] *id.* II. 1252 (11 September 1935).

N.S.N.S.D.

without regard for either their wish as nations or for economic necessities Central Europe at that time was broken up into atoms and new so-called states were arbitrarily formed.' He continued—and now the point of the speech begins to appear—'To this procedure Czechoslovakia owes its existence,'[33] and concluded, inconsequently enough, with a demand for self-determination for the Sudeten Germans.[34]

The truth is that to find any common ground between the professions of Hitler on the national question and the actual policy of Germany is impossible. Except where it was to the direct advantage of Germany his arguments are consistently hostile to the principle of self-determination, yet German policy was only too ready to use self-determination as a principle of disintegration. The positive aims of Nazi foreign policy were revealed with the proclamation of the doctrine of *Lebensraum*.[35] But in *Mein Kampf* Hitler had already exposed his attitude towards the principle of national self-determination. He had expressed scorn for the 'League of oppressed nations', and its German supporters. The belief that Germany should align herself with the other 'oppressed nations' and struggle for her rights in their van was, he said, puerile: as a policy directed towards the power of the German state it was chimerical.[36] Rosenberg in *The Myth of the Twentieth Century* summed up the National Socialist policy with equal frankness: 'We want to support nationalism as a force and other internal values for national regeneration only in those nations whose fateful development, we believe, will not come into conflict with the evolutionary tendencies of the German nation ... We know that under the principle of self-determination utterly valueless national elements could ask for freedom. But all this does not concern us, or only in so far as a far-sighted German policy can expect an increase of German strength from their exploitation.'[37]

---

[33] *id.* II. 1517 (26 September 1938).   [34] *id.* II. 1522.
[35] *id.* II. 1586, 1597 (16 March 1939, 1 April 1939).
[36] *Mein Kampf*, pp. 744-5.
[37] Quoted in E. Beneš, *Democracy To-day and To-morrow*, 1939, p. 173.

If Versailles has led to the charge that the principle of self-determination was in the main merely a weapon of war for the Allies, to be given only a very limited scope when the war was ended, the events of 1939 proved finally that German policy was far more consciously insincere in the use it had made of the appeal for self-determination. The last shreds of the mask of international idealism were now dropped, and the grim visage of power politics again dominated the scene that in reality it had never left. The diplomatists and propagandists had done their work, and now the generals could take over the task.

PART II

The Theory

VI. Introduction to
a Reconsideration of the Theory
of Self-determination

I. The need for a New Definition
of Self-determination

WE HAVE NOW traced the history of the idea of national self-determination up to the outbreak of war in 1939, and are perhaps in a better position to see it in its true proportions. In 1919, and in the following years, this might have seemed the age of the triumph of self-determination, and at least some of its distresses attributed to that fact. A closer examination suggests that the half-century before 1914 witnessed rather a regression than a steady progress of the principle of self-determination, and that the outbreak of war in 1914 was due to the conflict of the interests of the great powers rather than to the strength of the movement for self-determination. The Versailles settlement, as we have seen, was characterised by a failure to apply self-determination logically and systematically, and in the following years it made no fresh advances in Europe. It follows that it is not possible to describe the renewal of war in 1939 as the result of the collapse of a world order, or even a European order, based on self-determination; there was no such order to collapse. This judgment, however, only eliminates one possible line which criticism of the principle of self-determination might take, to substitute another. If self-determination received only a limited application in the peace treaties, it is possible that this was not primarily because of the insincerity or ill-will of the representatives of the chief powers concerned with drawing them up—though most of these certainly had other interests which could not easily be reconciled with a universal acceptance of the principle—but because in the nature of things it could not be applied consistently.

Such a verdict would be even more devastating than the proof of a simple inadequacy in application, and in its ultimate implications far-reaching; for the principle of self-determination was no mere incidental factor in the settlement after the war. World opinion regarded it, along with the principles embodied in the League of Nations, as the moral foundation of the peace. Nor were self-determination and the League system isolated from one another. They were intimately associated in the mind of their most powerful advocate, President Wilson, and in their practical working-out were not easily separable. Although the statement is not true without qualification, on the whole it may be said that the League was the expression of a *status quo* attitude to international affairs, and that, given the popular idealism of 1919, this would not have been accepted if it had not been believed that in the main substantial justice had been done in the territorial settlement, at least in Europe. Now, by substantial justice, world public opinion understood national self-determination, which in this way may be said to have provided a moral basis for the League system in international affairs.

A second assumption involved in the connexion between the League and self-determination lay in the idealistic interpretation of national policies which both implied. The recognition by the League of Nations of the full national sovereignty of its members was only reconcilable with the principle of international order through the belief that the principle of self-determination was in itself a limiting factor which would prevent national sovereignty from being pushed to a point at which it could menace the rights of other nations.

These two assumptions were, unfortunately, neither of them justified. The gradual realisation of the extent to which self-determination had not been put into practice, and perhaps could not be, played a large part in undermining the moral foundations of the League. The further discovery that the League of Nations itself provided no guarantee of national independence involved the collapse of the only dyke that had stood, however weakly, between the independent nations of the world and the onrush of power politics. Western civilisation became slowly aware that it stood on a quicksand, that it had, not an inadequate basis for its international order, but no basis at all. The logical conclusion was the renewal of the Cyclopean battle of empires, in which the nations were to be uprooted, tossed about helplessly at the mercy of the gigantic powers at strife, and laid low.

Is it to be concluded from this unhappy experiment that the ideas of nationalism and national self-determination must henceforth be rejected in their entirety and relegated to the scrap-heap of discarded illusions? Before we can draw this conclusion, it will be necessary to examine the theoretical implications more carefully. We have already suggested that what was taken for self-determination was to a large extent not self-determination at all. Moreover, so long as the idea has not lost its power over opinion throughout the world we cannot afford to dismiss it from consideration. But the need for a thorough re-examination and radical revision of its theoretical basis and practical implications can hardly be questioned. One of the chief protagonists of the principle of self-determination urged this need. 'The principle of self-determination itself,' wrote President Beneš, 'would need very detailed and precise explanation. It was misused and continues to be misused in an incredible degree. Everybody gives to it the interpretation that serves his political interests and aims. Post-war political experiences will force political science as well as practical politicians to proceed to a real and complete revision on this matter.'[1]

So I ask, for the second time: What is self-determination?

[1] Beneš, p. 121, *n.*

It was defined above as, in general terms, the right of a nation to constitute an independent state and determine its own government for itself. This apparently simple and straightforward description, as might be surmised from the difficulties that have been encountered in its practical application, contains a host of unrealised implications. A whole political philosophy lies behind it, and it cannot be safely employed as a basic premise of our thought about the relations of nations and states until we have explored its intellectual hinterland.

II. Self-determination not an Absolute Right

As soon as we examine the definition of self-determination just given we find that it takes for granted a number of political principles on which there is in fact by no means general agreement. We may begin by asking, since self-determination is assumed by this theory to be a right, what kind of right is understood? Is it a right to self-determination where and in so far as circumstances permit, and subject to limitation by the competing claims of other rights? Or is it an absolute right, knowing no qualification? In practice there can be no doubt which is the most appropriate description of the methods of the treaty-makers at Paris. Practically every one, including Wilson himself, recognised that self-determination could only be applied with due regard to circumstances. But they are to be criticised for not having made this plainer in their public utterances. It is difficult to find any public statement of the right of self-determination which is adequately qualified. Public opinion, which grasps only broad principles, was undoubtedly not conscious of the limitations that would be placed on its practical realisation at the Peace Conference.

At the same time, it must be admitted that, however inevitable the limitations on the scope of its practical application may have been, the introduction of qualifications into the theoretical principle of self-determination was not an easy task. We may argue, of course, that it was not reasonable to interpret it as meaning that every tiny splinter of nationality should share in the self-determination afforded to the larger units, regardless of geographical situation, inter-mixture with other nationalities, or any other factors. But however unreasonable it may have been, the fact remains that most nationalities did expect, in so far as it favoured their own claims, a ruthless application of what they understood by self-determination. Every nation claimed it as an absolute right for itself. As a general principle, we have only to put it in a negative form to see how difficult it would have been for any statesman to have denied that there was an absolute right of self-determination. 'Some nations, or parts of nations, have not a right to self-determination'—could any of the Allied leaders have said this? It is difficult to find any who did. It is therefore not a work of supererogation to discuss the theoretical problem raised by the claim that self-determination is an absolute right, for this is the form in which it was normally put forward. The first issue raised by this claim is whether a collective entity, such as a nation, can be said to have any absolute rights at all.

This is not the place for a discussion of the fundamental problems of political philosophy involved in every theory of political rights, but the major difficulties in the attribution of an absolute right to any organised body must be briefly indicated. The basic questions it presents to the political theorist are—first, whether there are rights of any kind, and, secondly, whether these rights can be attributed to a collectivity, such as a nation. It will be necessary to deal with these points in a perhaps unduly dogmatic form. In short, my view is that there *are* rights, for if there were none it is difficult to see what meaning could be given to the general conception of right, lacking which the whole ethical foundation of political thought would disappear, and we should be left to the rule of force alone, without any basis for criticism other than its success or failure in maintaining itself as simple force. Machiavelli, Hobbes, and Hitler were on the whole willing to accept this alternative;

we may, perhaps, be excused for not reproducing the objections to it here. The rights which we derive from the general conception of right are, however, not absolute, but are susceptible of, and indeed demand compromise, whenever they come into practical conflict with one another, as experience proves that they constantly do.

Secondly, it is one thing to recognise rights, and another to attribute them to a collective body such as a nation. Before allowing that there is a right of national self-determination, we should have to admit that the nation is a self, capable of determining itself, moved by a General Will, that is, and not merely a combination of individuals, moved by the wills and striving to achieve the desires dictated by a section or sections of their people. Now the General Will, in so far as it is identified with the good will, may be an ideal: it is never an actual fact. At best, in the most democratic of nations, it has to be identified with the will of the majority if it is to mean anything practical. Further, even if we accept the idea of a nation as a single self with a single will, can it have rights as such? There is no space here to do more than state, without arguing, my own point of view, which is that rights are rights for individual, though not isolated, men and women, or they are not rights at all. Political philosophers have constantly attempted to erect systems of thought attributing absolute rights to some political entity or other; equally constantly the attempt to assert these absolute rights in practice has led to a practical denial of individual rights and the enthronement of the principle that might is right. On this ground I should be prepared to reject any theory which asserted the absolute right of the nation, whether to self-determination or to anything else.

It must not be thought that this is a mere piece of abstract argumentation of no practical importance. On the contrary, one continually meets the assertion, put forward in as absolute a form as possible, 'We are a nation: therefore we have a right to this or to that.' It is not unimportant to draw attention to the inadequacy of the deduction.

III. The Meaning of Nationality in the Theory of Self-determination

A second difficulty in the way of accepting the conception of the right of self-determination arises from the problem of finding a definition for the nation. There is no object in conceding rights, whether absolute or not, to an unidentifiable possessor. Yet this definition is something that no theorist of nationality has been able to provide in objective terms. Central European nationalists have sought in vain for some invariable, positive, eternal symbol of the difference of their nations one from another.[2] Language, religion, traditions, territorial contiguity, natural frontiers, economic interests, race—extensive exceptions can be found to every proposed test, except the subjective one. The best we can say is that any territorial community, the members of which are conscious of themselves *as* members of a community, and wish to maintain the identity of their community, is a nation.

The most effective criticism of this view comes from traditionalist thinkers like Burke and Charles Maurras. 'It is not our will that has made us French,' writes Maurras. 'We have not willed our nationality, we have neither deliberated nor even accepted it . . . the *patrie* is a *natural society*, or, which comes absolutely to the same thing, a *historic* one. Its decisive characteristic is birth. We no more choose our *patrie*—the land of our fathers—than we choose our father and mother.'[3] This argument appears convincing until we reflect that by it every child of immigrant parentage is denationalised. That the great majority will remain members of the nation in which they were born and bred is undoubtedly true, but it is also true that if the historic society is in most cases the operative cause, it is not the

[2] The difference between English and French writers, who have regarded nationality as primarily a subjective fact of the individual's political or social consciousness, and German and Central European writers, who have concentrated on the search for objective tests, has been pointed out many times, e.g. *Nationalism*, p. 35, *n.* 1.

[3] C. Maurras, *Mes idées politiques*, 1937, p. 252.

criterion of the individual's nationality, the only certain test of which is his own feelings,—that is, essentially a subjective test.

One other point needs to be emphasised before we can continue the argument. The definition of the nation, as the term is used in the theory of self-determination, is essentially political. The nation is a community that is, or wishes to be, a state. Before we can pass any verdict on the tenability of the theory we must therefore examine the relations, in idea and in fact, of the nation and the state.

IV. *The Consequence of the Identification of the Nation and the State*

In modern times the term 'nation' has commonly been employed in the sense of the political state. At the same time, as was pointed out at the beginning, the word 'nation' was used long before self-determination was thought of, and used very largely in a non-political sense. A nation was a community of language or culture which might, or which might not, possess common political ties or aspirations. The double significance of the term 'nation' is the foundation of the distinction drawn by Meinecke between *Kulturnationen* and *Staatsnationen*, from which he further derives a series of hybrid forms. He writes: 'There are culture-nations and state-nations; there are national states in the political sense, and national states in the national-cultural sense; among the national states in the political sense, and also among those that are both political and cultural nations, we have to distinguish the ancient and modern types. Finally, we have always to keep clearly in mind that in historical reality these different forms merge into one another.'[4]

In its subtlety and complexity, Meinecke's analysis comes much closer to reality than the naïve attempts of other thinkers to fashion a single simple pattern of a nation, because it allows for the interaction of the idea of cultural nationality and the political conception of the

F. Meinecke, *Weltbürgertum und Nationalstaat*, 6th ed., 1922, p. 15.

nation, without which the modern nationalist movement could never have developed. It would be an understatement to suggest that these two different conceptions of the nation merely exercised an external influence on one another. The critical moment in the history of nationality was when the hitherto distinguishable, if not entirely separate, ideas of the cultural nation and the political state moved together, and merged in one single idea. It was this combination that gave birth to the modern principle of nationality, which, in the words of a French critic, 'demands that state and nationality should coincide. It is only willing to recognise one kind of state, which is the national state; it traces its frontiers, not by the courses of rivers, the direction of mountains, or the chances of war, but according to races, or rather nationalities.'[5]

The prevailing tendency to assume the desirability, or even the inevitability, of identifying the political state with the cultural nation may be illustrated from a discussion of the subject by Ernest Barker. He accepted the definition of the state as 'a juridically organised nation,'[6] the identity of state and nation as both an ideal and a fact. 'In these days of national states,' he wrote, 'we may identify nation and state. In the act of doing so we have to confess that a nation may be conceivably, and indeed has often been actually, something different from a state, and that it may seek, under such conditions, to vindicate its liberty against the state in which it is included. But its effort in such a case, is directed, after all, to the achieving of an identity between nation and state—primarily for itself, but secondarily, and in consequence, for the state from which it secedes, and which it reduces, by its secession, to a basis more purely national.'[7]

The view represented by this quotation is so widely held that it demands careful consideration. It admits that the nation is not necessarily the same as the state in fact, but

[5] R. Johannet, p. 19.
[6] E. Barker, *Reflections on Government*, 1942, p. xiv.
[7] E. Barker, *Reflections on Government*, p. 8.

implies that in this case it is entitled to endeavour to make itself so. Self-determination, on this basis, is the process by which a cultural nation becomes a political state, and also that by which a political state becomes a cultural nation. Until the reappearance of latent nationalities like the Welsh and the Breton, the application of the principle in Western Europe—where states had already to a considerable extent achieved the ideal of a common culture—was only to confirm the existing order of things. But in Central and Eastern Europe, in the nineteenth century, most cultural nations were not yet states. The theory of self-determination involved an effort on the part of these cultural nations to become state-nations.

The result of this theory, therefore, is to confront us with two different and contradictory lines of approach to the nation state. Once the ideal identification of cultural nation and political state has been accepted, the state in its own defence tends to act as though it were a single and united nation from the cultural point of view, and if in fact it is not this, it must endeavour to make the facts correspond to the ideal, regardless of the rights or liberties of those among its citizens who do not belong to the majority nation. On the other hand, every nation, or fraction of a nation, which is not a national state must seek to become one. In other words, 'Just as the nation readily passes from the area of social expression into the political form of a state, so a state which is based on will must necessarily seek to make itself co-extensive with a nation if it is to be true to its basis.'[8]

This is no merely theoretical consideration: it is an accurate reflection of the facts of the contemporary world. The facility with which a nation can pass from the one line of action to the other may be illustrated by the case of the Czechs, as represented by Masaryk. In a lecture of 1916 on Small Nations, he protested against the view that the state was the only social entity which counted. 'To-day,' he said, 'we are forced to acknowledge the existence of *nations* and we are obliged to make a distinction between states and

[8] Barker, *National Character*, p. 129.

nations . . . We Slavs very keenly discriminate the state from the nation.'[9] One cannot deny the sincerity of this statement, but it must be taken along with the fact that the whole endeavour of his life's work was to enable his own nation to become also a state. And when Czechoslovakia had been created, despite its large minorities, the Czech leaders thought and spoke of it as a nation state.

The assumption behind this whole line of thought is that state and nation are potentially one and the same kind of thing. If cultural and political nationality were disparate there would be no possibility of equating them, as this theory demands. Every separate national culture must, on this theory, be a state in embryo, and the ideal of every state should be to embody a single culture-nation. Multinational states are automatically ruled out. Finally, except in the rare cases where nation and state already fully coincide, the two tendencies we have described, moving in contrary directions, are bound to come into conflict. They have been the source of endless domestic disputes and international strife.

In historical fact, cultural unity has usually followed on and not preceded political unity. The cultural nation was more the creation than the creator of the political state in France and England, in the United States, and the British Dominions. The same verdict, as has been shown above, would apply to a good many of the medieval nations, which were welded together out of the most diverse materials—so diverse, indeed, that in some cases they fell to pieces again. But the process by which in the past the state evolved a common national consciousness was generally a slow, and what might be called a natural process. The modern belief in the identity of nation and state, with its corollary that unless a state is also a cultural nation it is no legitimate state, has provided a strong incentive to hasten the process, in so far as it can be done by governmental action. This results in an attempt by the state to compel all its members

[9] Masaryk, *The Problem of Small Nations in the European Crisis*. 1916. pp. 11–12.

to identify themselves culturally with the ruling nation. It is an important element in the development of totalitarianism. As a result of the belief that the political state must perish unless it can achieve cultural unity, all the democratic and national rights of minorities are swept away.

The opposite view is that the nation is prior to the state. Modern nationalism starts as a rule with the existence of the cultural nation, and from this deduces its right to constitute an independent state. Even such a sound student of the national question as Auerbach accepts this view. 'It is the nationality which makes the state;' he writes, 'and not the state which makes the nationality . . . A nationality is only perfect when it has created a state in its image and for its use.'[10] The principle of self-determination is indeed commonly taken in theory—practice is, of course, very different —as a bar against the operation of the process in the reverse direction. The initiative, it is assumed, must come from the nation as a cultural unit. The state is not allowed to have any nation-creating right or capacity. If it is not a nation to begin with, it has no rights at all. In the words of a writer who appeals to the principle of self-determination on behalf of the Magyar nation and who fails to see that he is by implication condemning the whole history of the Hungarian state: 'In place of the brutal phrase of Bluntschli: without a state, no nationality, it is necessary to say rather: without a nationality, no state.'[11]

The effect of the modern belief in the superiority of the claims of the cultural nation over those of the political state is illustrated by the verdict of Auerbach on the pre-1914 state of Hungary. The Magyars, he says, are making a mistake in trying to found a united nation on the bodies of other nationalities which are still alive and must therefore first be destroyed. Such a state, he declares, would to-day be an artificial and monstrous counterfeit, fashioned on the

[10] B. Auerbach, *Les Races et les nationalités en Autriche-Hongrie*, 2nd ed., 1917, pp. xxii–xxiii.
[11] Antal Ullein-Reviczky, *La Nature juridique des clauses territoriales du traité de Trianon*, 1936, 2nd ed., p. 24.

pattern of older political creations which did not have to deal with such deep-seated ethnical or national antagonisms. The time has gone by when unconscious and plastic masses of humanity could allow themselves to be moulded into nations by the hands of despots.[12] One may agree that this is a correct judgment on the facts, but it is rather a harsh description of the process that produced the French and English nations.

With the passing of the initiative from the political state to the cultural nation, the idea of nationality launches a general offensive all along the line on the world of states. Only those cultural nations that are not politically conscious—and this for the modern theory of nationality is as good as denying that they are nations at all—are content in the absence of political independence. If a nation is subject to some state other than its own national state it claims national emancipation. When it has achieved freedom from alien control it agitates for the union to its own political state of any members of its cultural or linguistic community who still remain under foreign rule. If it is a nation-state, and has no *irredenta*, it still does not rest. The idea of the political nation now takes control. There may be minorities to suppress, or territories to which some historical claim is possible. Nor does the process of identifying the nation and the state stop at this. Triumphant nationalism almost invariably tends, wherever it has the opportunity, to swell into imperialism, as the nationalism of the French Republic passed into the imperialism of Napoleon.

The development of nationalism into a principle of aggression is stimulated by the conception of national culture as something inherent in the members of a nation and present in them wherever they may go, as opposed to the older territorial idea of the state, which made the actual physical extent of country occupied the essential element which defined and therefore limited the political community. The theorist who perhaps brings out this change best is the German historian, Karl Lamprecht. The nation

[12] Auerbach, p. 485.

is for him a *Soziale Psyche*, created by habit and economic forces, which derives in the beginning from its physical setting, but takes wings when it has evolved into the form of the modern nation-state. He draws the picture 'of a state and of a national society which are no longer limited to the soil which formerly exclusively supported them and principally supports them to-day; the picture of a state and of a nation which aim to spread themselves through the entire world.'[13] The fact is that in being poured into the mould of the state the nation acquires all the characteristics of the state as a power-organisation, and this is the ultimate result of the identification of cultural nationality with political statehood.

V. Self-determination becomes National Determinism[14]

It can hardly be denied that we have now reached something very different from the theory of self-determination as it found expression in the American Revolution and in the first period of the French Revolution. Then it had been a simple corollary of democracy. In British and American thought it had perhaps not changed fundamentally by 1918. 'In reality, of course,' wrote Professor Zimmern, 'English people when they invoke the principle of Nationality mean the principle of Democracy.'[15] A similar political conception of the nation prevailed during the nineteenth century in France, Emile Ollivier, for instance, writing: 'Civilisation has consisted in destroying the primitive groupings in order to constitute by free affiliation conventional groups much more solidly cemented than those born out of mere chance . . . It is the principle of liberty substituted in international relations for geographical and historic determinism.'[16]

[13] Quoted in C. Andler, *Le Pangermanisme philosophique* (1800 à 1914), 1917, p. 139.

[14] This very useful phrase is used to convey this distinction in C. A. Macartney's *National States and National Minorities*, p. 100.

[15] Zimmern, *Nationality and Government*, 1918, p. 50.

[16] E. Ollivier, *L'Empire libéral*, 1895, I. pp. 168–9.

In Central Europe the nation came to possess very different attributes. The idea of the culture nation, as we have seen, acquired priority over the political conception of the nation. Nationality was regarded as an objective rather than a subjective fact. National self-determination no longer implied an element of choice on the part of individuals: it was decided at birth. Strictly speaking, indeed, it ceased to be self-determination at all. The individual did not determine his nation; rather, the nation determined the individual. An interesting illustration of the change was provided by the German attitude towards the annexation of Alsace, which was justified on grounds of nationality, yet grounds far removed from anything that the West could have recognised as self-determination. 'We Germans who know both Germany and France', wrote Treitschke, 'know better what is for the good of the Alsatians than do those unhappy people themselves . . . We desire, even against their will, to restore them to themselves.'[17] The principle of national determinism found its complete development in Nazi nationality policy. An effective illustration of it was provided by the laws on nationality proposed by the Nazi leader in Czechoslovakia, Henlein, in 1937. Every member of the state was to be enrolled in organisations representing the nationality 'into which he was born'. Any one who in any way enticed any one else into (*a*) declaring themselves of a nationality other than their own, or (*b*) leaving an organisation which used their own language or entering an organisation which did not, was to be punished.[18]

The general trend towards the substitution of national determinism for self-determination obtained something like official international recognition in a decision of the Permanent Court of International Justice, which, appealed to for an interpretation of the Polish Minorities Treaty, upheld the Polish contention that 'the question whether a

[17] H. W. C. Davis, *The Political Thought of Heinrich von Treitschke*, 1914, pp. 110-1.
[18] E. Wiskemann, *Czechs and Germans*, 1938, pp. 257-8.

person does or does not belong to a racial, linguistic or religious minority . . . is a question of fact and not solely one of intention.'[19] It must be admitted that in a less blatant form the same distortion of the original principle of national self-determination was present in the Versailles settlement. It was to be seen, for example, in the American belief in the possibility of determining national divisions by objective tests, and in the general reluctance, which was not only a result of practical difficulties, to have recourse to plebiscites. The newly emancipated nations exhibited it in their anxiety to claim as part of their own nation, without taking the risk of obtaining a popular expression of opinion, any population which might conceivably be regarded as affiliated to their own. Thus the Serbs had no hesitation in incorporating Croats, Slovenes, Dalmatians, Macedonians, and Montenegrins in their national state. The Czechs took in Slovaks and Ruthenes. The Poles included, and presumably hoped to assimilate, Ukrainians and White Russians, and would have added the Lithuanians if the Peace Conference had been willing. And from this list, of course, recognised minorities are excluded. There was much 'national determinism' and little democratic self-determination in all this.

It is possible to argue that the practical difficulties which ensued may have arisen not from the principle of self-determination, but from national determinism, which may be regarded as a perversion of true self-determination. Its result has been that in current political practice as well as in theory, in history as well as in logic, the principle of self-determination has been reduced to a denial of both national and democratic rights, and forced into a complete self-contradiction.

VI. *The Survival of the National and Democratic Ideals*

Our discussion cannot be left with this purely negative conclusion, however. National self-determination is a formula

[19] Kaeckenbeeck, p. 326.

which sums up a great historical movement. The practical realisation of the formula may have been inadequate, or even disastrous, but the force of nationalism behind it cannot be disposed of so easily. Nationality and democracy are still living ideas, and while this remains true the demand for self-determination, in some form or other, is likely to survive. It is no use our saying that self-determination is always perverted, that it is illogical and impracticable, that we do not like it. The positive demand is there. We may attempt to override it or destroy it, but before doing so should ask whether we do not run the risk of destroying our civilisation in the process. The alternative is to attempt to discover some means of satisfying it, without converting it into national determinism or perpetuating the trend towards world chaos with which it has been associated in recent years.

VII. The Idea of the Nation State

A DISCUSSION of the territorial settlement after the last war led to the conclusion that the principle of self-determination had proved inapplicable in fact. It seems in addition to have been self-contradictory in theory. Now if self-determination has meant anything in the past, it has meant the creation of nation states and the assertion of national sovereignty. The final point in a historical and analytical survey of self-determination, therefore, must be an examination of the institutional form in which it eventuates, the nation state, and its operative principle, national sovereignty.

I. The Conflict between the Political and Cultural Ideas of the Nation

1. HERDER AND THE GERMAN IDEA OF THE NATION

We are thus compelled to ask once again what is meant by the nation state. In the first place, as I have already said,[1] it evidently combines the cultural and political ideas of the nation. The dualism between the linguistic or cultural, and the political, approach to the national idea can be seen most clearly in the development of German nationalist thought. Its founder, Herder, who more than any one else is entitled to be called the father of nationalism, was almost exclusively concerned with the idea of the nation as a cultural entity. His originality consisted in the vigour and persistence with which he preached the gospel that the natural unit of society, and the only natural unit, was the nation, by which he meant a cultural community based on

[1] Ch. V, § iv.

a common language. Nature, he held, had 'wonderfully separated nationalities, not only by forests and mountains, seas and deserts, rivers and climates, but more particularly by languages, inclinations, and characters.'[2]

From this cultural idea of the nation Herder passed on, but only secondarily, to the idea of the nation as a political unity. His political theory is as simple as possible. The human race is naturally divided up into nations speaking different languages, and each nation should rightfully be a separate and independent state. That is the sum total of it, and if, put thus baldly, it sounds ridiculous, this does not affect its historical importance, for it is the view that has increasingly prevailed in modern Europe. 'The most natural state,' said Herder, 'is *one* nationality with one national character. This it retains for ages.'[3] Again, 'a kingdom consisting of a single nationality is a family, a well-regulated household; it reposes on itself . . . An empire formed by forcing together a hundred nationalities, and a hundred and fifty provinces, is no body politic, but a monstrosity.'[4]

Although Herder develops into an advocate of the nation state, he is not thinking of the modern centralised form of state,[5] nor does he set up one nation as superior to another. There is no chosen people but each must serve in its own way the common good of humanity. Nation, he proclaims, does not fight nation. It is easy to see how little of anything that might be called political thought there is in Herder. This un-political, cultural conception of the nation has been a constant element in German thought. It is strongly expressed, for example, in the writings of Thomas Mann. Taking the word 'nation' in its political sense, he repudiates it as alien to German ideas. 'The conception "nation",' he writes, 'is historically bound up with

[2] Quoted in R. R. Ergang, *Herder and the Foundations of German Nationalism*, 1931, p. 244.
[3] *id.* p. 243.   [4] Ergang, pp. 244–5.
[5] R. Aris, *History of Political Thought in Germany from* 1789 *to* 1815, 1936, p. 243.

the idea of democracy, whereas the word "folk" corresponds to the actual German—that is to say, culturally conservative, non-political, anti-society idea, and our political romanticists, Constantin Frantz and Bogumil Goltz, contended on good grounds that Germany never has been a nation.'[6]

But one can see a political element enter the German conception of the nation and gradually obtain predominance. Schiller still thinks of the greatness of the nation as existing in the cultural and moral field, but for him nations are no longer, as for Herder, at least potentially equal. Every nation has its day, he says in the famous poem of 1801 on German greatness, but the day of the Germans is the harvest of all centuries past. Later writers of the German romantic school, spurred on by the humiliations of the Napoleonic wars, move much farther in the direction of political nationalism. To take only one example, in 1806 Arndt is asking, 'Why should we any longer regard as a higher humanitarianism our miserable German disunity, our so-called humane all and nothing, through which our country has become so much a nothing, the despised of foreigners?'[7] In the course of time, with writers such as Bluntschli and Treitschke, the cultural idea of the nation slips into the background, and the nation becomes a dominantly political concept, the embodiment of the power of the state. Meanwhile, the conception of the nation state, as the expression of the cultural unity of a people, spread from Germany to all the other peoples of Central and Eastern Europe, with the exception, inevitably, of Switzerland.

2. THE WESTERN CONCEPTION OF THE NATION

When we turn to Western thinkers, the picture of the nation as a cultural unity developing into a political one has to be abandoned, and in its place we have to begin from a prim-

[6] T. Mann, *Culture and Socialism*, translated by H. T. Lowe-Porter in *Past Masters*, 1933, p. 210.
[7] Arndt, quoted in E. N. Anderson, *Nationalism and the Cultural Crisis in Prussia*, 1806–15, 1939, p. 80.

arily political ideal. The development that can be traced is in the contrary direction, from political to cultural, and not from cultural to political. This was only natural, because, as has already been said, in their medieval origins, nations like the French, English, Portuguese, and Spanish were built up by the political power of strong monarchies. The Western conception of the nation took definite shape in the second half of the eighteenth century, when thinkers like Burke and Rousseau were coming to regard the nation state as a community held together by something more than the mere authority of government. At the same time as Rousseau was providing what was to be used as one theoretical basis for the modern state, in the form of the free choice of the individuals voluntarily incorporating their wills in the General Will, Burke was teaching that the political community was the product, not of the will of the people, but of their history: it was not made, but grew, and the individual was shaped to his place in it as inevitably as he was born a member of his family.[8]

The modern Western European conception of the nation has largely been a product of the fusion of these two tendencies, combining a measure of free individual choice with a consciousness of the inherited traditions and values of communal life. It has been well described by Professor Toynbee. 'We think of nationality,' he writes, 'in fact, as the will of the living members of the community; only on second thoughts do we realise that this contemporary generation, which monopolises with such assurance the visible scene is but the fleeting incarnation of a force infinitely vaster than itself. It is the will bequeathed by the past that gives its incalculable momentum to the will of the present.'[9] Western thought thus tended to regard the nation as the result of a '*vouloir-vivre collectif*,'[10] the product

[8] The explanation given above represents the dominant trends in the thought of Burke and Rousseau, but their views were much more complex than such a brief summary can convey and they had much more in common than it would suggest.

[9] Toynbee, *The New Europe*, 1915, p. 60.

[10] This phrase is used by H. Hauser.

of a common consciousness which was derived far more from living in common and sharing common ideals than from any racial, linguistic or cultural inheritance. A nation may therefore be built up by a monarchy in the course of time on the most diverse foundations, as were the British and French nations, or it may be constituted by a deliberate act as was Belgium.

This conception of the nation reappears in Mazzini, who belongs to the Western line of development by virtue of his assertion of the democratic right of the Italians to self-government. But the democratic principle is only part of his national ideal; he regards the nation rather as a spiritual unity than as a political construction. In fact, with Mazzini, following on Burke and Rousseau, we witness the expansion of the Western conception of nationality beyond the purely political field. Nationality is for Mazzini more than the expression of democratic will: it is the conscience of the people, 'which, by assigning to them their part in the work of association, their function in humanity, constitutes their mission upon earth, that is to say, their *individuality*, without which neither liberty nor equality are possible.'[11]

The idealistic, humane nationalism of the mid-nineteenth century welcomed the Mazzinian conception of the historic role of the nation. Renan, rather later, laid equally great emphasis on the nation as 'a soul, a spiritual principle,'[12] and, coming to our own time, Sir Alfred Zimmern has written of nationality as subjective and psychological, in opposition to the objective and political fact of statehood. 'I have come to believe in nationality,' he declared in 1915, 'not as a political creed for oppressed peoples, but rather as an educational creed for the diverse national groups of which the industrialised and largely migratory democracies in our large modern States must be increasingly composed.'[13]

In spite of the tendency represented by such thinkers, the

[11] Mazzini, *Faith and the Future*, 1835, reprinted 1850.
[12] Renan, *Discours et Conférences*, 1887, pp. 306–7.
[13] Zimmern, *Nationality and Government*, 1918, p. 57.

political idea of the nation remained the dominant one in the West. When the Portuguese delegate on the League of Nations Commission at Versailles in 1919 suggested that the new organisation would more correctly be called a League of States, Lord Robert Cecil replied that he thought the difference between the words 'nations' and 'states' was a very small one.[14] Similarly the American Institute of International Law, at a meeting to draw up a declaration of the rights and duties of nations in 1916, was able to use the words 'nation' and 'state' interchangeably. On the contrary, a discussion of the same question by the European *Union juridique internationale* produced acute differences of opinion.[15]

During the early years of this century, however, it may be said that while in Central and Eastern Europe nationality was struggling to move out of the field of culture into that of politics, in Western Europe cultural nationality was emerging from its political casing. Dying languages and cultures—Gaelic, Erse and Welsh, Flemish, Breton, Catalan, Basque, Provençal—received a new lease of life and became the foci of new or revived national movements. Among these revivals, the last was the most remarkable illustration of the power of national culture. 'Above the writer,' it has been said with reference to the Provençal movement, 'there is the creator of *patries*. The essential glory of Mistral is to have created a language, and beyond and by means of that language (I dare write the word), a *patrie*. By him and in him, ten million human beings have become conscious of their ethnical unity.'[16] This claim is an exaggeration, but it is a significant indication of the growth of the sentiment for cultural nationality in the West.

The fact is that Western Europe has come to realise what Central Europe earlier discovered, the conflict between cultural and political aspects of the national idea, a con-

[14] Hunter Miller, *Diary*, IV. 414–5.
[15] L. E. Le Fur, *Races, nationalités, états*, 1922, pp. 109–10.
[16] Delteil, *De Rousseau à Mistral*, 1928, p. 183.

flict which was hardly avoidable, for these two aspects of
the national idea arise from motives which are quite distinct. The political ideal of national unity has usually been
the reply to a disunity which involved internal anarchy or
foreign conquest. It is therefore primarily a means to an
end, and that end the maintenance of law and order by the
establishment of a strong and united state. The nation as a
political unit, or state, is a utilitarian organisation, framed
by political ingenuity for the achievement of political, with
which may be included economic, ends. Politics is the realm
of expediency, and the measure of its success is the degree
to which the material bases of the good life—law and order,
peace, and economic welfare—are realised. The nation as a
cultural conception, on the contrary, is normally regarded
as a good thing in itself, a basic fact, an inescapable *datum*
of human life. It belongs to the realm of the activity of the
human spirit, its achievements are in the fields of art and
literature, philosophy and religion.

The distinction drawn here, however much it may be
obscured in practice, must never be lost to mind, for it is
the beginning of all sound thinking on the national question.
It is not denied, of course, that political and cultural
nationalism constantly influence one another, and that they
tend to move together. The association between political
and cultural nationality can be explained on historical,
among other grounds, but the distinctness of the ends proposed for the two developments which both, unfortunately,
are described by the same word, 'nation', is fundamental.
That this is not merely a theoretical differentiation can
easily be shown. French and British Canadians, for example, seemed to have achieved a common political nationality without abandoning their characteristic cultural
differences, though now doubts are beginning to appear.
On the other hand, the various states of Spanish America
have to a large extent preserved the same cultural background although divided into a number of separate political
nations. Many other illustrations of the failure of cultural
and political nationality to coincide might be found, and

where the attempt has been made, in modern times, to force them both into the same mould, the result has usually been disaster.

II. *Nationality Variable and not Exclusive*

The history of the last quarter of a century affords ample evidence of the necessity for revising the conception of nationality that was taken for granted in the theory of self-determination. The essential assumption was that Europe could be allocated between a limited number of nations, of reasonable size, and capable of sustaining states. There was also at Versailles the rather optimistic belief that the peace-makers knew a nation when they saw it. Neither of these beliefs proved true. The ruthless 'either—or' of the theory of the nation state does not allow for the infinite gradations of which the sense of nationality is capable. In attempting to adopt nationality as a criterion of statehood, Western civilisation has chosen a standard which varies from period to period, from country to country, and even from individual to individual. National feeling differs in kind: it may be mainly political, or mainly cultural, or a mixture of both. It differs also in degree. It merges at one end into the strong local sentiment of the Cornishman or the Ulsterman, and at the other into the imperial loyalty that may be shared by members of any of the numerous nationalities of the U.S.S.R.

The whole theory of the nation state is built on the assumption that national loyalties are exclusive, whereas in practice it is found that they are not. It also implies what has been called the dogma of homogeneity, the belief that the whole world can be divided amongst separate homogeneous divisions of the human race, which is patently not true.[17] Nationality, moreover, is never stationary; it is constantly being built up or broken down. 'Nations,' it has been said, 'are living beings which are born and die. They are not during a single year exactly the same as they were

[17] J. Brunhes and C. Vallaux, *La Géographie de l'histoire*, 1921, p. 652.

the year before.'[18] The larger nations of the modern world were formed of the not always completely assimilated debris of earlier nationalities. By a contrary process smaller nations have been created by the breaking-down of the larger political entities. The process of history sometimes moves in the direction of building up larger states, sometimes towards the revival of the claims of smaller cultural groupings. It is rare for the process of consolidation to reach completion. Even of France, which might be considered one of the most thoroughly united national states in the modern world, it could be said, 'In the French Republic several nationalities exist side by side, some almost completely atrophied, as the Flemish and Provençal nationalities, others still easily recognisable, as are the Basque and Breton nationalities, which formerly all coincided with autonomous states, and which, although they have lost their strictly political and administrative independence, have not disappeared.'[19]

Nationality, then, is variable and malleable. Voluntary change of nationality by individuals is common. In addition, whole communities are capable of diverting their national allegiance. This refers, of course, mainly to the less developed communities, not as yet absorbed in any of the larger nations, which may, according to circumstances, become attached to one nation or another, or develop a separate national consciousness of their own. Of the Balkans not long ago it was said that 'the feeling or reality of ethnic or national solidarity, the perception of the connexion of interests and aspirations between members of the same religion, are facts which vary incessantly and are modified from day to day.'[20] In Macedonia, during the Balkan Wars, the local population appeared, to the best of its ability, as

[18] *id.*, p. 610.
[19] Van Gennep, *Traité comparatif des nationalités: I. Les éléments extérieurs de la nationalité*, 1922, p. 21; *cf.* J. Brunhes, *Les conditions de géographie humaine de la société des nations: nationalités, nations, états*, in *Vers la société des nations*, 1919, p. 33.
[20] Brunhes and Vallaux, p. 662.

Bulgar or Serb, according as the fortunes of war favoured one side or the other. In Upper Silesia, after 1918, many of the inhabitants seem to have remained for years uncertain whether they were Poles or Germans, and in no hurry to make up their minds.[21]

Nationality has been truly described as a 'tendential movement.' 'At each moment of its duration,' says van Gennep, 'nationality is never in other than an unstable equilibrium. It is always becoming. This instability is the proof of its internal vitality.'[22] Even Meinecke, who defines the national ideal as the creation of 'an unbroken, living, national community in all its essential conditions,' confesses, 'the task is endless, for simultaneously with the discovery of the means of solving them, the difficulties also grow and increase.'[23]

III. The Validity of the Multi-National State

There are, of course, a number of small states in which political and cultural nationality to a considerable extent coincide. In the Americas, largely free from the historical complexities of Europe, nation states have been built up on a political basis, and in favourable circumstances they have every chance of creating and maintaining their unity by the absorption of immigrant groups. On the proposal of Brazil, the Pan-American Conference at Lima in 1938 resolved that 'The system of protection of ethnical, language or religious minorities cannot have any application whatever in America, where the conditions which characterise the groups known as minorities do not exist.'[24] But in the Old World, where a *tabula rasa* cannot be made of the preexisting complex of cultural nations and political states, there is an evident necessity of abandoning the belief that the nation state is the one and only model for a sound political community. The multi-national state must re-

---

[21] Kaeckenbeeck, p. 130.   [22] Van Gennep, p. 13.   [23] Meinecke, p. 11.
[24] J. P. Humphrey, *The Inter-American System: a Canadian View*, 1942, p. 162.

enter the political canon, from which, as Acton many years ago declared, it should never have been expelled.[25]

Sir Ernest Barker attacked Acton's view. 'Even in 1860,' he wrote, 'it might have been perceived that in a multi-national state the government either pits each nation against the rest to secure its own absolutism, or allows itself to become the organ of one of the nations for the suppression or oppression of others.' He continued: 'The history of the century since 1815, and of the decade since 1914, will teach us that in some form a nation must be a state, and a state a nation . . . An autocratic state might in the past be multi-national, uniting by the one will of the autocrat a number of nations that were merely social groups. A democratic state which is multi-national will fall asunder into as many democracies as there are nationalities, dissolved by the very fact of will which should be the basis of its life.'[26]

In this statement we find the nationalist standpoint expressed by one of its most moderate and reasonable exponents, but historical evidence by no means seems to support his view. The history of the recent past, as well as of the last century, is far from teaching the necessary identity of the political state and the nation in any other sense. We find ourselves indeed forced to the conclusion that in most cases they cannot possibly be made to coincide. The suggestion that only autocratic states can be multi-national hardly allows for the experience of such states as Great Britain, Canada, Belgium, and Switzerland. It is true that a common political loyalty is needed to hold the state together, but this does not necessarily involve the assimilation of the different national cultures included in the state. These democratic states have given evidence of far greater survival value than was possessed by the autocratic Austrian Empire. Soviet Russia, if hardly a democracy, has at least more democratic elements than the Tzarist Empire, and the severest of tests proved its various nationalities to have a strong measure of cohesion. Much more might, of course,

[25] Acton, *History of Freedom and other Essays*, 1907, IX, Nationality (1862).
[26] Barker, *National Character*, pp. 16–17.

be said on the subject of the multi-national state, but our object here is only to register a protest against its condemnation as such, and to insist that it must be accepted among the possible forms of political organisation. The attempt to make the culturally united nation state the one and only basis of legitimate political organisation has proved untenable in practice. It was never tenable in theory.

VIII. The Principle
of National Sovereignty

I. Democracy and Nationality

THE LAST CHAPTER seems to lead to the conclusion, which is confirmed by practical experience since 1918, that the idea of the nation state as the sole basis of political organisation must be abandoned. If this is so, can we still maintain the principle of national sovereignty, which is the expression of the nation state in operation? The one is the institutional form and the other its activating principle and they necessarily stand or fall together. But what do we understand by national sovereignty? The answer to this question involves us in an examination of the relations between the two prime factors in the theory of self-determination, democracy and nationality, for it can be shown that the idea of national sovereignty arose out of the democractic principle of the sovereignty of the people. One of the major sources of democratic ideas was the eighteenth-century belief in the identity of human nature, or, to use the language of the century, in the natural equality of man. When the cosmopolitanism of the Enlightenment was replaced by the nationalism of the romantic movement, and the differences rather than the uniformities in human nature came to be stressed, it was gradually realised that the homogeneity assumed to be necessary for democracy did not exist in any state containing members of more than one nationality. Here we have an explanation in theoretical terms of the growth of the belief that democracy is only possible in a nationally united state. At the same time, a practical reason for the alliance between democracy and nationalism was provided by the fact that both were fighting against the same enemies. The most anti-democratic states of the early nineteenth century, Russia, Austria, and Turkey, were also the chief enemies of national liberties. The quest of liberty, it could thus reasonably be held, was one, and democracy a necessary corollary of national independence.[1]

The belief in the alliance of nationality and democracy is implied in Renan's definition of the nation as '*un plébiscite de tous les jours*.'[2] John Stuart Mill is less epigrammatic, but more explicit in his identification of the two principles. 'Where the sentiment of nationality exists in any force,' he proclaims, 'there is a *prima facie* case for uniting all the members of the nationality under the same government, and a government to themselves apart.'[3] His reason for urging this view is given in the next sentence. 'This is merely saying that the question of government ought to be decided by the governed.' In other words, national self-determination is merely a statement, in different terms, of the principle of democratic, or at least representative, government. Nor is the association between democracy and nationality, as Mill interprets it, one-sided. If self-determination is to him a simple corollary of democracy, on the other hand democratic institutions are hardly possible where the national principle does not prevail. 'It is in general,' he argues, 'a necessary condition of free institutions, that the boundaries of governments should coincide in the main with those of nationalities.' With his supreme capacity for digging deeper than his own principles, and sometimes, it is true, undermining them, Mill proceeds after this to introduce qualifications which completely alter the complexion of his views on nationality, but, as is usually the case, the general statement is remembered and the all-important modifications are forgotten.

The practical politician, though he had also been a

[1] *Cf.* above pp. 41–4.   [2] Renan, p. 307.
[3] J. S. Mill, *Considerations on Representative Government*, 1861, Ch. XVI, Of Nationality, as connected with Representative Government.

student of politics, who was closest to the ideas of Mill on this subject was Woodrow Wilson. The intimate connexion in his mind of self-determination with democracy was shown by his insistence that democracy, or at least 'self-government,' was a necessity for real national independence, and incidentally, therefore, a necessary qualification for membership of the League of Nations. Agreement on a definition of self-government proved difficult to reach, however. The best that Wilson himself could say was: 'I have spent twenty years of my life lecturing on self-governing states, and trying all the time to define one. Now whereas I haven't been able to arrive at a definition, I have come to the point where I recognise one when I see it.'[4] The discussions that followed over India, Japan, and Germany, to name only a few states, suggested that other statesmen were not so sure that he did. A divergence is apparent even in the text of the Covenant, where the English 'self-governing' is equated with the French phrase, '*qui se gouverne librement.*'

There is this justification for the belief in the close connexion of the democratic and national principles, that historically the introduction of representative institutions has regularly either preceded or gone along with the development of nationalist movements. But if democracy has led up to nationalism, it is equally true that nationalism has more often than not been the enemy of democratic institutions. It has gradually become apparent that two different conceptions of liberty are implied in the national and the democratic ideals, and that the theory of self-determination failed to allow for their possible opposition. Liberty, for the nationalist, meant national liberty. The unity and independence of the nation, not the effectiveness of representative institutions, was, from this point of view, the prime test. Parliamentarianism, indeed, was a possible, and, in some cases, an actual source of dissension and national weakness. It brought disunion, and not unity, to Germany, Meinecke observes.[5] Between 1918 and 1939, representative

[4] Hunter Miller, *Diary*, V. 106.   [5] Meinecke, p. 525.

institutions at least appeared to provide an outlet for separatist tendencies in countries such as Yugo-Slavia and Poland. In pre-partition India the progress of representative government went hand in hand with the development of communal hostilities. Many other illustrations of the same point could be provided. It is therefore not surprising that in many countries a cleavage between nationalist thought and the tradition of nineteenth-century liberal democracy appeared. This development was foreshadowed in the French Revolution, which, although it did in fact bring about the extension of many individual liberties, was primarily directed, not to the limitation of the powers of the state, but to their unfettered exercise by a representative assembly, acting in the name of the people. Democratic ideology, in place of resting on the liberties of the individual, became an assertion of the sovereignty of the people, and during the Revolution 'people' came to be synonymous with 'nation'. The result was the substitution of the sovereignty of the nation for the liberty of the individual as the prime end of politics. National sovereignty, which the revolutionaries had assumed to be synonymous with democracy, turned out in practice to be something very different. What have been its consequences?

II. *The Principle of Sovereignty*

To proclaim the nation as sovereign is equivalent to identifying it with the state. For this reason it may be maintained that the modern movement called nationalism rests fundamentally on the political idea of the state, and not on the idea of the nation, in so far as the latter is non-political. Ernest Barker says truly that the real loyalty of the nationalist is not to the nation, but to the state, in which other forms of national society are engulfed.[6] The extreme of national sovereignty is represented in the Fascist doctrine that 'The higher personality is a nation only in so far as it is

---

[6] Barker, *Reflections on Government*, p. 26. *Cf.* G. de Ruggiero, *The History of European Liberalism*, 1927, p. 416.

a state. The nation does not exist to generate the state . . . the nation is created by the state.'[7]

In the early years of the present century an idea began to spread that the tide of sovereignty was ebbing. This trend of thought began, reasonably enough, as the expression of a hope. 'Some would warn us,' wrote Maitland, 'that in the future the less we say about a supra legal, suprajural plenitude of power concentrated in a single point at Westminster—concentrated in one single organ of an increasingly complex commonwealth—the better for that commonwealth may be the days that are coming.'[8] It is difficult to quarrel with this statement, which puts forward the decline of sovereignty as a *desideratum* rather than as a fact.

Political thinkers in England began to believe, not so long after Maitland, that the sovereign state as well as being discredited in theory was also decaying in fact.[9] In France Léon Duguit went farther. The myth of national sovereignty, which had inspired every political constitution produced by the modern world, had, he said, exhausted its creative fecundity. It was incompatible with the facts of national life.[10] 'We do not in the least deny that the notion of sovereignty has been justified,' wrote a Dutch critic, 'we hold merely that among civilised people it is now no longer recognised and that accordingly it must be expunged from political theory.'[11] Influential writers, such as G. D. H. Cole and Harold Laski, emphasised the same trend of thought, of which many other illustrations might be given. There seemed much reason to believe that the principle of sovereignty was losing its effectiveness. From within and

[7] *La Dottrina da Fascismo*, I. 10, 7; quoted in Barker, *loc. cit.*
[8] F. W. Maitland, Introduction to translation of O. Gierke, *Political Theories of the Middle Age*, 1900, p. xliii.
[9] *e.g.* A. D. Lindsay, 'The State in Recent Political Theory', in *The Political Quarterly*, February 1914; Barker, 'The Discredited State', in the same, February 1915.
[10] L. Duguit, *Law in the Modern State*, 1913, trans. H. Laski, 1921, Ch. I, The Eclipse of Sovereignty, p. 15.
[11] H. Krabbe, *The Modern Idea of the State*, trans. G. H. Sabine and W. J. Shepard, 1922, p. 35.

from without, the state was being challenged. Disintegration and chaos was threatened at home, foreign or international interference from abroad. What was not allowed for in the theoretical arguments, however, was precisely what happened: in the reaction against these developments the sovereign state ceased to disintegrate. It reasserted itself, and most of all in those countries—such as Italy, Germany, and Russia—where it had been most threatened. A strong transfusion of nationalism restored its flagging vigour, and sovereignty reappeared in the guise of totalitarianism, more terrible than ever before.

It was in its later manifestations that the full importance of what might earlier have been considered the merely abstract conception of absolute sovereignty appeared. The absolute sovereignty of the state meant the night of the long knives, and Hitler in person as the Supreme Court of the German people. It meant castor oil and rubber truncheons and concentration camps. It meant the Italianisation of Tyrolese and the sterilisation of Jews. It meant the supression of trade unions and the subservience of Churches. It meant the abolition of individual liberties and the oppression of national minorities. The nation state, inflated with the wind of national sovereignty, became a true leviathan, fatal to the domestic liberties of individuals and groups.

The manifestation of the idea of national sovereignty in international relations was equally disastrous. The idealistic prophets of nationality thought that their new principle would inaugurate an age of peace. A nation, Mazzini believed, that claimed independence for itself, could not but recognise the same right in other nations. Experience has shown how little justified was this hope. Nation states were to prove no less aggressive or annexationist than their predecessors. 'International anarchy,' it has truly been said, 'is founded upon the sanctity of the sovereign state.'[12]

[12] R. G. Hawtrey, *Economic Aspects of Sovereignty*, 1930, p. 138.

III. The Opposition of Sovereignty and Self-determination

The attempt, in the theory of self-determination, to make the principle of national sovereignty the basis of the right of statehood has produced curious inconsistencies in practice, as can be seen if we take for examination a conception which is its necessary corollary—the right of secession—first put into effect by the American colonists, soon to be followed by the French revolutionaries in their early plebiscitary annexations. Yet subsequently the Americans, in defence of the Union, and the French, on behalf of the *nation une et indivisible*, were among the strongest opponents of the same right of secession. The Convention decreed, on 16th December, 1792, the penalty of death for any one who attempted to break the unity of the French Republic, or detach any part of it, and the Americans engaged in a bitterly fought war to keep the Southern States in the Union against their will.

Attempts have been made to define the conditions under which a nationality can break away from the state of which it has formed part and constitute a new state on its own. Beside the desire of a majority of the nationality to do so, other requisites, it has been said, are 'governmental capacity', population, territory and natural resources adequate to ensure its economic and political independence, and an *'indiscutable formation historique originale.'*[13] When the Permanent Mandates Commission agreed to the recognition of Iraq as an independent state, it laid down very similar terms as prerequisites—a settled government and an administration capable of maintaining the essential services and internal peace, laws and a judicial organisation affording equal and regular justice for all, adequate financial resources, and the capacity for maintaining its territorial integrity and political independence.[14] Un-

[13] B. Lavergne, *Le Principe des nationalités et les guerres*, 1921, p. 22.
[14] Permanent Mandates Commission, *Minutes of the 20th Session*, 1931, p. 229.

fortunately, these conditions are easier to draw up on paper than to apply in practice. The last one, in particular, is wholly dependent on the international situation and the policy of more powerful neighbours. All the conditions, in fact, are matters of degree, and only in extreme cases would they be beyond dispute. Moreover, such tests have little relevance to national demands for self-determination. A nation fighting for its independence does not draw up a balance-sheet of its qualifications, nor does the state against which it is rebelling normally look at the position from this angle.

The basic difficulty, if we open the door to secession, even to a limited extent, is to prevent it from being flung wide open. On what grounds can we justify the revolt of the American colonists, and condemn the Southern secessionists, other than those of success or failure? How can we approve the movement of the Czechs against the Habsburg Empire, and criticise the secession of the Bohemian Germans? Why was it right for Ireland to claim independence from Great Britain, and wrong for Ulster to claim independence from Southern Ireland? And if the Ulster Protestants were rightly allowed to remain free from Catholic Irish rule, why should not the Catholics of Tyrone and Fermanagh break away from the remainder of the Six Counties? If India was to be free from the British connexion, was not Moslem India justified in demanding to be free from the Hindu connexion? If the Moslems of the Punjab were to be emancipated from Hindu dominance, are the Sikhs not equally entitled to claim their freedom? Need other examples be given? If self-determination means this kind of thing, where, and with what unit, can the process possibly stop?

On the other hand, under the influence of the principle of national sovereignty, the nationalist movement as a whole has accepted the ideology of the absolute sovereign state, and this new form of *étatisme* proved fatal to national liberties, as well as to liberal democracy and any hopes of international peace. In the guise of nationalism, sovereignty, which had seemed to be declining, has emerged stronger and more absolute than ever. It has developed, to use the language of Professor Toynbee, into a 'parochial totalitarianism'. 'This totalitarian parochial state,' he proceeds, 'is an enormity because it is an attempt to confine new social forces which are intrinsically oecumenical in their spirit and operation within the prison-house of a parochial institution which was originally established under quite different social conditions in order to meet quite different human needs.' He concludes that 'A plurality of parochial totalitarian states will assuredly give place, sooner or later, to a single oecumenical totalitarian state in which the forces of democracy and industrialism will at any rate secure, at last, their natural world-wide field of operation.' But it is inconceivable that in a totalitarian dispensation this change could come about by peaceful means: it will be achieved by totalitarian war, and 'the tribulation will be so great that our present Western civilisation will have little hope of recovering from the shock.'[15] Since all this is in essence a result of the monstrous enlargement of the idea of sovereignty first into nationalism and then totalitarianism, any attempt at a remedy must involve a revision of this idea.

The truth seems to be that if we take the right of sovereignty on the one hand, and the right of secession on the other, as absolute rights, no solution is possible. Further, if we build only on sovereignty, we rule out any thought of self-determination, and erect a principle of tyranny without measure and without end, and if we confine ourselves to self-determination in the form of secessionism, we introduce a principle of hopeless anarchy into the social order. The only hope, it seems, must be in a combination of the two principles, allowing each to operate within its own proper field, and recognising neither as an absolute right, superior to the rights of individuals, which are the true end of society. Is such a compromise possible? This is equivalent to asking whether the sovereign rights of the nation are

[15] A. J. Toynbee, *A Study of History*, 1934, IV. 179–80.

necessarily absolute, and capable of no qualifications or compromise.

IV. The True Function of Sovereignty

It seems to follow from these considerations that the possibility of finding a solution for the problem presented by the opposition between the rights of sovereignty and secession depends in the first place on the possibility of limiting the exercise of both rights. Political philosophers have upheld the idea of the sovereign state as the necessary condition of organised human life. This, however, is a defence of the state as an abstract idea, not of any particular state. A community of pirates might satisfy the same description, but we should not recognise its rights or tolerate its existence for longer than could be helped. Legitimate sovereignty is not an automatic attribute of all political power. We must assert that only in so far as it subserves its proper ends, and within the limits dictated by those ends, has the state any rightful claim to allegiance.

Sovereignty, in other words, has its own natural limits. Chief of these is the duty of respecting the liberties, or rights, of the individual, including his right to national liberty. But this also is not an absolute right: it is only to be asserted in the degree in which it is compatible with organised social life. We cannot, therefore, set it up as a specific criterion of the state's right to existence that it must be 'national'. In a century when systematic attempts have been made to destroy the independent states of Europe by spreading internal dissension, the condemnation by Lecky of the use of national divisions for the destruction of existing political entities comes home to us. 'If the policy of disintegration,' he writes, 'is preached as in itself a desirable thing; if the constituent elements of a kingdom are encouraged or invited to assert their separate individuality, nothing but anarchy can ensue. The door will be at once opened to endless agitation and intrigue, and every ambitious, restless, unscrupulous conqueror will find his path abundantly prepared. It is the object of all such men to see surrounding nations divided, weakened, and perhaps deprived of important strategical positions, through internal dissensions.'[16] One could hardly find a better description of the use made of the principle of self-determination by Germany in the years before 1939.

The practical consequences of accepting an extreme nationalist ideology are now evident. Nationalism is in the circumstances of the modern world most often a disruptive force. Its effect in Europe is patent. In south-eastern Asia, it is said, 'It has made each racial group more self-conscious, more prone to assert itself at the expense of other groups, and either tends towards a disastrous break-up of the present mosaic by some vigilant outsider playing upon this grave weakness in the body politic and social, or leads towards the forced assimilation of the weaker minorities by the most powerfully placed group.'[17] Such consequences are inevitable if states are necessarily to be condemned, and a right of secession proclaimed, on the ground that they are not uni-national. We must insist that this view is not valid. The state is a datum given by history. Circumstances, in their infinite variety, may have made here a state like Germany and here one like Switzerland, here a United States of America, or a Great Britain, and here a Norway or an Iceland. One state is not to be condemned for its diversity of language, religion, or descent, nor another for its homogeneity. The state is only to be condemned, and secession approved, where it does not protect and promote, in reasonable measure, the rights of the individual citizens, included among which are their interests as members of a national community.

We are now in a better position to discover what is true and what false in the principle of sovereignty. During the last generation critics of sovereignty attacked the belief that supreme authority could rest in any one centre of society.

[16] Lecky, I. 400.
[17] R. Emerson, L. A. Mills and V. Thompson, *Government and Nationalism in South-East Asia*, 1942, p. 144.

The life of the state was portrayed as a nexus of forces pulling in different directions, held in equilibrium, as it were, by some immanent but intangible principle such as operated in celestial mechanics. It was not said that the assertion of the absolute supremacy of the interests of the state over all other rights or interests was the extreme medicine of the constitution, only to be used in rare cases, or that the field of the state's supremacy should be limited, that it was not co-extensive with human life. Instead, it was bluntly denied that the state had any sovereign rights at all, which was surely unreasonable.

A sounder basis for criticism lies in asking what is in fact the true and original function of the power of the state. This question has already been answered. The prime object of the establishment of a sovereign authority is the preservation of law and order, and the maintenance of the social fabric. It is a defence of society against civil war and anarchy. The true limiting principle of the state's rightful power is derived from a consideration of its ends. Any power which is needed to maintain law and order against the threat of anarchy is *ipso facto* justified. This right may conceivably extend to practically any field of human activity, but it does not normally do so. Except in the rarest circumstances cultural differences present no such threat. It can therefore be maintained that nationality as a fact of the cultural life of society should normally be outside the sphere of political sovereignty. On the other hand, against the threat of internal disorder or political dissolution as such, an appeal can be made to the principle of sovereignty. If sovereignty means anything it at least means that the state has the right of defending itself against those who would disrupt it, except in circumstances in which the authority of the state is itself fatal to those ends which it should exist to promote.

The final conclusion, then, is that the political power of the state as such is not to be condemned: it is to be restored to its original function of the maintenance of law and order. National sovereignty, on the other hand, is irreconcilable with any solution of the fundamental political problems of the modern world. It asserts an uncompromising right of secession on the part of any community that calls itself a nation. If at the same time the state maintains its rights of sovereignty over the dissident nation, there is no resolving the conflict, except by the destruction of the state or extermination of the nation.

IX. What Remains of the Idea of Self-determination?

OUR ANALYSIS has shown that of the three major elements in the theory of self-determination—nationality, democracy, and sovereignty—the last is the prime source of the contradictions to which the general principle has led. The conclusion which seems to be enforced on us is the abandonment of the idea of national sovereignty. The object in this, as I have said, is not to discover a means of weakening government—in the modern world that would be a counsel of despair—but of limiting the scope of its operation. The idea of national sovereignty, as it has been put into practice in the nationalist movements of the last century, has involved setting up as an ideal the identification of the cultural nation and the sovereign state. This seemed a possible policy before the complexity of the national map of the world was realised.

We are in a better position to-day to understand how truly Acton envisaged the consequences of nationalism when he declared it 'the greatest adversary of the rights of nationality.' 'By making the state and the nation commensurate with each other in theory,' he wrote, 'it reduces practically to a subject condition all other nationalities that may be within the boundary.'[1] The most prevalent solutions of the national problem in a world of competing nationalisms, it has been said, are likely to be expulsion, massacre, or economic attrition.[2] And even these, it must be added, are as apt to intensify as to resolve the conflicts of nations.

[1] Acton, p. 297.   [2] *Nationalism*, p. 295.

The principle of the nation state, in its modern development, leads both to national and to international disaster. It is natural for an oppressed nationality to believe, in the words of Sir Lewis Namier, that, 'No people can be at all secure, still less strong, which is not master of its destiny through a state of its own.'[3] This conviction, in which is summed up the philosophy of the nation state, was put in slightly different terms by Dahlmann, who wrote, 'It is possible to be more a *Volk* than a state, but it is not possible to be a *Volk* without being a state.'[4] If by *Volk* we understand cultural nation, we must stoutly controvert the assertion that it is not possible to be a nation without being a state. To take examples, can it reasonably be believed that the national demands of Wales, White Russia, Alsace, or Flanders, must be met by granting political independence? Should French Canada self-determine itself as a separate state? What is the nationality of Cyprus? Can Greenland afford to be without economic links with some larger and more prosperous state? Must the Copts in Egypt claim a self-determination that they do not want from the Arab population in the midst of which they live? In short, are there not geographical, historical, economic, and political considerations which rule out national self-determination in the form of the sovereign state for many of the smaller nationalities of the world? Even if the majority of the members of a nation desire political independence, circumstances may prohibit it, and the mere desire, of however many people, will not alter them. In the words of Burke, 'If we cry, like children, for the moon, like children, we must cry on.'

The right of self-determination, therefore, if it means anything at all, cannot mean an absolute right to complete national sovereignty. The true rights of man are his liberties—political, economic, national, religious—and these may necessitate some degree of separate statehood, or they may not, and such political independence may be

[3] L. B. Namier, *Conflicts, Studies in Contemporary History*, 1942, p. 146.
[4] Dahlmann, *Politik*, quoted in Meinecke, p. 4, *n.* 2.

objectively possible, or it may not. Circumstances, in the end, are the determining factor.

But I have not said whether national liberty, without complete political independence, is possible or not. Here the facts are decisive. Indeed, it is only since the rise of the theory of national sovereignty that any one could have thought of asking such a question. Tyranny and oppression have always been resented, especially in the form of the exploitation of one community by another. But complete political independence has not invariably been considered a necessary condition of the free existence of diverse cultural communities. In the Roman Empire only the Jews seem to have felt much specifically national resentment. During the Middle Ages the inclusion of diverse peoples in allegiance to the same monarchy was accepted as a matter of course.

Before we can finally say whether self-determination in any given case is necessary for the realisation of national rights or not, we must ask first: What are the basic national interests and are they compatible with membership of the state? The opinion might be held that the demand for national self-determination normally begins as a defensive movement. It is more than a coincidence that the unrest of the nationalities should have followed so closely on the rise in the latter part of the eighteenth century of the idea of the unified and centralised state. Self-determination in a separate state, we may say, is necessary where there is an established tradition of independent sovereignty, or where, as the result of a combination of historical influences, the desire for political independence has reached such a degree of intensity that it is not to be satisfied even by the removal of all the grievances from which in the beginning it may have sprung. Self-determination comes into play here, not as the first, but as the last step, not as a panacea for all national dissatisfactions, but as the remedy, to be administered *in extremis*, when all else has failed.

Practical examples give their meaning to all political principles, so to make the purport of my argument clear

I must cite at least a few illustrations. Thus it may fairly be said that the Poles in Germany and in Tsarist Russia, and the non-Magyar peoples in Hungary before 1914, found in the state to which they were subject primarily an enemy. A somewhat different illustration is provided by the Spanish and English colonies in America. Here the home governments were too remote, and also, it may be added, too inefficient in their colonial administration, to carry on government effectively after the colonies had reached a certain stage of development.

In addition it is important to remember that nations have long historical memories, and repentance on the part of the ruling state may come too slowly and too late to justify the maintenance of a political connexion. The Sinn Féin rebellion in Ireland was not against the misgovernment of a twentieth-century British government; it was a revolt in the name of four centuries of history. Where history has dug a ditch as deep as that between the Catholic Irish and the British state, where even the last hope of reconciliation has been thrown away, as it was in the years before 1914, secession is only to be prevented by the maintenance of a rule based on naked force. One solution that has been offered,[5] re-integration of the dissatisfied elements into the state by concession, good sense, and compromise, is out of the question in such circumstances.

Secession, then, can be justified, but only in certain extreme cases. Since it is generally a work of destruction, and a breaking-down of established connexions, it can hardly be a good thing in itself. The mistake that has been made by extreme theorists of national self-determination is in supposing that all nations do, or ought to, put forward the same demands, and that satisfaction cannot be given to diverse national communities within the same state by any measures short of complete political separation.

The political unity which the idea of sovereignty implies can still be justified as a means of preventing political evils —internal anarchy, or military aggression from without. In

[5] Barker, *Reflections on Government*, p. 409.

this sense it must be allowed that political unity is an essential and overriding need, but it must be clearly separated from conceptions of cultural and economic supremacy. The need for political association to maintain law and order, and to ensure efficient defence against attack, may involve associating different cultural communities in the same political nation, as in the British Isles, Switzerland, Spain, Canada and the Soviet Union; or it may involve political frontiers which are dictated by historical or geographical causes, but unrelated to economic requirements. If economic and cultural interests are partially freed from their subjection to politics the consequences need not be as dangerous as they have been in the past. The essential point to remember is that, in drawing political frontiers, political stability must first be aimed at. This is the prime object of political nationalism and any form of national self-determination which produces a state that is not viable, whether because of internal or external weakness, must be regarded as self-contradictory.

To limit the rights of national sovereignty and self-determination is in effect to reverse the process by which cultural and political nationality became allied, and to separate them once again. This may be condemned as flying in the face of history, but in fact what we are doing is calling on a thousand years of history to redress the balance of a century and a half. Nationality developed and national cultures flourished for century after century in the absence of any idea of national sovereignty. The nation state only became a condition of the free development of national cultures when the state began to assert totalitarian claims over the cultural as well as the political allegiance of its citizens. It is not too late to put the clock back, in this respect with profit.

By doing this we shall not be abolishing nations, or even bringing to an end the struggle of nationalities. National communities will always be rising and declining, and this process cannot be prevented from influencing, and being influenced by, political developments. But the economic and military conditions of the present day seem to dictate the creation of larger political groupings, if the influence of cultural nationalism tends in the direction of smaller ones. The attempt in 1918 to found world order on the principle of the nation state, and to endow all states with rights of equality and independent sovereignty they had never enjoyed before, was perhaps the basic reason for its failure. In the name of self-determination, or of the rights of small nations, to return to this policy would be to court a repetition of disaster.

But all this does not mean that the nations of the world must bow to a tyranny worse than any they have known before. The simple solution of self-determination and national sovereignty has shown itself inappropriate to the complexities of the modern world, but the national demands which evolved it still remain to be satisfied. The idea of the nation still provides the 'myth' that is needed for the willing acceptance of government in the modern world. It is still the contemporary answer to the requirement posited by Spinoza: 'A dominion, that looks no farther than to lead men by fear, will be rather free from vices, than possessed of virtue. But men are so to be led, that they may think that they are not led, but living after their own mind, and according to their free decision.'[6] An attempt has been made in this chapter to suggest that it may be possible to meet national demands by something short of absolute national sovereignty. National self-determination, in a sense, would have its place in such a solution, and more truly perhaps than in that of 1919, though, as I have said, in the form of complete political separation, it is only to be resorted to where history has produced national antipathies so great that any form of political connexion is out of the question, and even where this seems to be the case greater forces may intervene to prohibit the desired separation. If we are not thinking in terms of national sovereignty, frontiers become less important. They may correspond more closely to the interests and wishes of populations, and

[6] Spinoza, *A Political Treatise*, Ch. X, § 8.

be less liable to modification on economic, strategic, or other considerations. The debatable areas, many of which are inhabited by peoples who differ from all their greater neighbours, may be dealt with on a system of regional autonomy; economic arrangements may cut across political frontiers; strategic military control may be separated from everyday political government, if the principle of sovereignty is reduced again to reasonable proportions. To quote an international lawyer, 'Independence is not unrestricted liberty for a state to do what it likes without any restriction whatever . . . Independence is a question of degree.'[7] With the abandonment of the conception of absolute national sovereignty, nationalism would no longer be a necessary enemy of democracy. Self-determination in this new dispensation would not mean the objective national determinism of the past but would imply a truer and more subjective conception of nationality. All that is rightly implied in national liberty, all that any nation can have in the interdependent conditions of the modern world, small nations would have in the same degree as great. The right to tyrannise over other nations, the right to a suicidal political or economic isolation, the right to rely on one's own strength alone in a world in arms—these are what would be lost, but they are no rights that a sane world order would tolerate, or a sane nation desire.

Finally, it must be acknowledged that the solution for the problems created by the principle of self-determination in national states is unlikely to be provided within the framework of the nation state itself. There are great extra-European powers which have already taken steps towards a transcending of national sovereignty, and from the experience of these we may possibly gain some indication of the conditions in which a practical solution of the problem we are studying may be found.

[7] L. Oppenheim, *International Law*, ed. Lauterpacht, 1937, I. 236.

PART III

The Contemporary World

X. National Autonomy
in the British Commonwealth
of Nations

I. The Principle of the Multi-National State

OUR ATTENTION has up to the present been concentrated mainly on Europe, but self-determination is not merely a European problem and we cannot appreciate its full scope until we have taken its development outside Europe into consideration. This involves in the first place a discussion of the policies of three great extra-European powers—the British Empire, the United States of America, and the Union of Socialist Soviet Republics. In addition it will be necessary to devote a chapter to the demand for self-determination in those African and Asiatic countries which have little or no European population. Inside Europe it cannot be pretended that the movement for self-determination played much more than a destructive part, whatever hopes there may be for a better manifestation of the ideals it implies in the future. *Europa irredenta* has been a source of disintegration. What has been the effect of the movement for national self-determination elsewhere?

With the now defunct British Empire we enter a field to which the nationalist theories of Europe had little relevance. This perhaps explains the widespread misconception of the nature of that Empire, and the persistence in regarding colonies and dominions alike as a huge conglomeration of territory, overrun and ruled, through some incomprehensible dispensation, by the little English nation. If at some stage in the past this had been true, it gradually lost its validity as the Empire evolved into a Commonwealth. The fundamental fact about the British Commonwealth, on the contrary, is that it is multi-national and that there is no ruling nation, in the sense in which Austrians and Magyars were ruling nations in the Habsburg Empire.

The British state was fortunate in that it lost less of its medieval political heritage than any country in Europe. Politically speaking, in relation to the two fundamental issues of nationality and sovereignty, in spite of exceptions it might be said that the British tradition runs back with no important break to the Middle Ages. Medieval states like England, France, Bohemia, Hungary, were primarily political conceptions; their cultural nationalities developed out of heterogeneous ingredients under the aegis of medieval monarchy. The English nation state, which was thus created, acquired during the Middle Ages non-English elements which have remained distinct to the present day, in the Channel Islands, the Isle of Man, and Wales. In the early modern period, when conceivably a tendency towards compulsory assimilation might have started, another and a stronger nationality was incorporated in the United Kingdom—Scotland, which had its own laws and distinct institutions. The Lowland Scots, who made up the majority of the population, were not so different in language and culture as to make co-operation in the same state with the English impossible, but, especially with the addition of the Highlanders, were sufficiently distinct to prevent the development of a common Anglo-Scottish nation. Finally, in Ireland the United Kingdom included an even less assimilable people. Anglicisation, so far as it occurred in the British Isles, was almost entirely a natural development. Where there was some attempt at compulsory Anglicisation by the state, as in Ireland, it had unfortunate consequences. It was never a deliberate and persistent policy anywhere, and the British Isles have remained the home of four nations—Irish, Scottish, Welsh, and English, as well as a number of smaller sub-nations, the Channel Islanders, Manxmen, and Ulster Orangemen.

The same principle of multiple cultural nationality in a single state has followed the British Empire throughout the world. When Canada was acquired, the Treaty of Peace promised that the French should retain their own language, laws, and religion. Although a scheme of compulsory Anglicisation had its supporters, the permanent trend of British policy in Canada was laid down by its second Governor, Carleton, whose views are expressed in a letter of 1767 to the home government: 'Barring a catastrophe shocking to think of, this country must, to the end of time, be peopled by the Canadian race, who already have taken such firm root and got to so great a height that any new stock transplanted will be totally hid and imperceptible among them except in the towns of Quebec and Montreal.'[1] Pitt's Canada Act of 1791 had to make provision for the growing British population, but it did so without robbing the French Canadians of their existing rights. It is significant of the association between radical democracy and the nation state ideal that the Durham Report should have advocated a policy of assimilation. Deserving all the credit they have been given for the big step they advocated in the direction of self-governing institutions, Durham and his advisers were too much under the influence of the French conception of the *nation une et indivisible* to envisage the possibility of a democratic state containing more than one national culture. Durham indeed only advocated the grant of responsible government on the assumption that a British majority was guaranteed in Canada.[2] The possibility of preserving 'a French Canadian nationality in the midst of Anglo-American colonies and states' seemed to him a 'vain endeavour.'[3] 'I entertain no doubts,' he wrote, 'as to the national character which must be given to Lower Canada; it must be that of the British Empire; . . . that of the great race which must, in the lapse of no long period of time, be predominant over the whole North American continent.'[4]

[1] R. Coupland, *The Quebec Act*, 1925, p. 59.
[2] *Durham Report*, ed. C. P. Lucas, 1912, Vol. I, Introduction, p. 136.
[3] *id.* II. 70.   [4] *id.* II. 288.

And in Buller's appended report on the state of education in Lower Canada it was frankly declared that the great object in view was 'uniting the two races and Anglifying the Canadian.'[5]

The influence of the deeper tendencies of British polity fortunately proved stronger than these ideas, and Canada emerged into independence as a state made up of two nationalities. Moreover, while the sentimental tie of the English-speaking Canadians to Great Britain was naturally far stronger, the French Canadians, in the interests of the preservation of their own nationality, proved anxious for the retention of the British connexion. This was particularly true of the clergy, who had always been the strongest force in French Canadian society.[6]

When, after the conquest of the Boer states in the South African War, the Empire had again to face the problem of a dual nationality in a single state, it already had in Great Britain and Canada precedents for its solution. The South African Constitution, having to cater for different conditions, naturally did not follow the Canadian model. The difficulties, and the possibilities of a breakdown, were much greater. Australia and New Zealand, being colonised mainly from the British Isles, had no problems of nationality comparable to those of the other two dominions, but the comparative success—after initial mistakes and worse—with which New Zealand has managed to find room for the small but growing Maori population, should be recalled in this connexion.

The same problems of the multi-national state, but of a much more complicated kind, were presented in India and Ceylon, but these must be discussed in a later chapter. The failures as well as the successes are instructive. The least that can be said is that national self-determination in the British Empire meant not merely a process of breaking down, but also an attempt at building up, and that the recognition of

[5] *id.* III. 288.
[6] G. Vattier, *Essai sur la mentalité canadienne-française*, 1928, pp. 315–6, 323.

national liberties proved a sounder foundation for the co-operation of different nations than their suppression.

II. *Self-determination by Consent*

Above the association of different nations in a single state there has been the association of independent, self-governing states in a far-reaching commonwealth. When English colonies grew up, in the seventeenth and eighteenth centuries, on the Atlantic coast-line of North America, it was natural that English traditions of local self-government should go with them. New ideas of sovereignty, which had been spreading in Europe in the sixteenth century, began to exercise an influence over English policy during the next two centuries. Out of the struggle against the divine-right theories of the Stuarts emerged the conception of parliamentary sovereignty, and although this stopped short of the extreme absolutism of Hobbes, it was not reconcilable with the idea of a division of authority in the Empire. Consequently, when the American colonies increased in strength and began to grow restive under British control, Parliament, tied to its own legislative supremacy, was unable to respond to the new situation. The British Government saw no *via media* between the sovereignty of Parliament and secession, and forced the American colonies to make the choice between legislative subjection to a parliament in which they were not represented and the assertion of a right of self-determination.

It is seldom that a nation is given the chance to undo its errors and does so, or that it retraces the same ground without making the same mistakes. Britain, having lost one empire in the eighteenth century, found herself with another in the nineteenth. If British policy had been thoroughly imbued with the conception of sovereignty the loss of the American colonies would have made no difference to the treatment of the new colonies; but the persistence of the contrary current of ideas in the British political mind was strong, and despite the influence of the new unifying democratic conceptions, and the legal theory of sovereignty that found expression in the writings of Austin, the memory of the American Revolution was sufficient to tilt the balance against the insistence on British sovereignty over the colonies. The history of Canada, Australia, and New Zealand is the history of a steady accretion of the powers of self-government and a steady decline in imperial control. The culmination of this development came in the report of the Inter-Imperial Relations Committee of the Imperial Conference of 1926, which declared that the self-governing states of the Empire are 'autonomous communities within the British Empire, equal in status, in no way subordinate one to another in any aspect of their domestic or external affairs, though united by a common allegiance to the Crown and freely associated as members of the British Commonwealth of Nations.'[7] The Statute of Westminster of 1931 gave Parliamentary recognition to this equality of status.

The process of evolution of dominion status has been, to all intents, a process of self-determination, though it differs from the European manifestation of the same principle in certain important respects. The dominions are not all culturally united nation states. Canada and white South Africa were each composed of two distinct cultural nationalities. They are *political*, and not cultural, nations, just as is Great Britain itself. Secondly, the self-determination of the dominions has been achieved peacefully, by agreement, and not by war or revolution. Thirdly, almost complete institutional separation—apart from the periodic Imperial Conference, and the symbol of the Crown, now, however, not one crown, but several united in the same person—has been brought about; while more intangible, but powerful, ties remain, which not only prohibit war between Great Britain and the dominions, but strongly influence them to act together in a crisis, as well as in many of the more ordinary occasions of international life.

[7] A. B. Keith, *Speeches and Documents on the British Dominions*, 1918–1931, 1932, p. 161.

The nature of self-determination inside the British Commonwealth cannot be understood without examining these ties. In the first place, it is important to note that the existence of a common imperial nationality is not one of them. Loyalty to the British Commonwealth of Nations, whether in Great Britain, in the dominions, or in the colonies, is something quite distinct from consciousness of nationality. There is really no such thing as a British imperial nationality, in either the cultural or the political meaning of the term. The absence of a single cultural nationality is too obvious to need arguing. The term 'British,' says Professor Zimmern, is 'nationally colourless.'[8] 'The English,' he claims, 'are the people who have most completely solved the problem of nationality, because they have most completely divorced it from politics.'[9] In the political sense a British nationality may be said to exist in the British Isles, excluding Eire. But there is no common political nationality covering the whole British Commonwealth or Empire. The essence of political nationality is the recognition of a single political authority, and common citizenship. Neither of these factors holds for the countries in the British Commonwealth as a whole. It is true that citizenship of the various component parts of the Commonwealth is not necessarily exclusive. On the other hand, rights of migration and residence as between these separate parts are not without definite limits. The resolution moved at the Imperial Conference of 1918 by Sir S. P. Sinha declared: 'It is an inherent function of the governments of the several communities of the British Commonwealth, including India, that each should enjoy complete control of the composition of its own population by means of restriction on immigration from any of the other communities.'[10] It is hardly possible to avoid accepting the definition of the position given by Mr. McGilligan in Dáil Eireànn in 1931;

[8] A. Zimmern, *The Third British Empire*, 3rd ed., 1934, p. 180.
[9] *id.* p. 186.
[10] Quoted in W. K. Hancock, *Survey of British Commonwealth Affairs*, Vol. I, *Problems of Nationality*, 1918–1936, p. 174.

'The essential point is that you have not a single Commonwealth nationality based upon a single law. It is not a single Commonwealth nationality at all, or even a dual nationality. The Irish Free State national will be that and nothing else so far as his nationality is concerned.'[11]

The ties which still hold the British Commonwealth of Nations together are not to be sought in any of the accepted political forms. They can be summed up under three headings: sentiment, influence, and interest. Sentiment is another word for history—the effects of a common cultural and political tradition in holding together, though with no formal ties, all those parts of the Empire populated from the British Isles. Historical tradition has also built up a considerable sentiment of common membership of a great political community in many of the smaller communities— Maltese, Gibraltans, West Indians, and so on. Even of a people with a strong consciousness of its own separate nationality, such as the French Canadians, it could formerly be said by a French observer that they had a strong sense of personal loyalty to the British Crown.[12]

'Influence,' which by no means merely radiates from Great Britain, but which has become to-day a reciprocal process throughout the Commonwealth, is something that cannot be given institutional form, but in spite of Washington's dictum, 'Influence is not government,' as Professor Hancock rightly declares, it is not necessarily an inferior instrument of policy.[13] The third cause of the cohesion of the Commonwealth is interest, which may be analysed under the headings of economy and defence, but before we turn to discuss these aspects it is necessary to conclude our discussion of the development from the British Empire into the British Commonwealth of Nations as a process of self-determination.

It should by now be clear to every one that the states in the British Commonwealth are completely independent and autonomous. How early the right to self-determination had been accepted in the British Commonwealth can be

[11] Keith, p. 241.   [12] Vattier, p. 311.   [13] Hancock, I. 46.

seen if we take what has come to be regarded as the acid test, the right of secession.

As the ultimate stage in the achievement of political independence, the right of secession has naturally been the latest and the most reluctantly recognised. In the discussions leading up to the Irish Treaty, it was at this point that the British Government drew the line in the concessions it was willing to make. At the Round Table Conference on India in 1930, when Mr. Srinvasa Sastri claimed that dominion status implied the right of secession, his view was contradicted by Lord Chelmsford, who declared that the concession of responsible government must be regarded as qualified by the phrase '*within* the Empire.'[14] In South Africa General Smuts made himself the advocate of the view that there was no constitutional right of secession, but in 1929 the South African Assembly, in adopting the report of an Imperial Conference on merchant shipping, did so with the proviso that it should not be taken 'as derogating from the right of any member of the British Commonwealth of Nations to withdraw therefrom.'[15]

During the next ten years British opinion on the right of secession matured rapidly. When General Hertzog returned from the Imperial Conference of 1930 he was able to report that it had taken notice of his claim to the right of secession.[16] In 1933, Mr. de Valera inquired whether punitive measures would be taken if the Free State were to sever the British connexion. The British Government refused to commit itself to an answer to what it called a hypothetical question. The matter was perhaps less hypothetical than it imagined, for in the course of the next few years Eire peacefully seceded, and it can be said that the right of secession for the dominions is now a recognised fact.

[14] W. T. Elliott, *The New British Empire*, 1932, p. 196, *n*. 1.
[15] Quoted in Hancock, I. 275.
[16] *The British Empire*, Royal Institute of International Affairs, 1937, pp. 67–8.

III. Ireland

In the history of the British Empire the right of self-determination had twice been pushed to the logical conclusion of secession, and each time the claim to parliamentary sovereignty was the fundamental cause of the break. When the success of the British treatment of the problem of nationality is under discussion, it is as well to remember that only in one of its constituent parts did the United Kingdom have to face a problem of nationality comparable with the problems of Central Europe and the Balkans, and that there it failed as completely as any state could have failed.

The history of Ireland might almost be regarded as a classic for the study of national self-determination. Practically all the leading complications which have influenced the national problem elsewhere are combined in the history of the struggle of the Irish against the British Government. Differences of economic interest, religion, and descent, bitter historical enmities, the presence of an alien ascendancy, a class division largely coinciding with a national one, and both with the religious cleavage, a minority inside a minority, and an area of intermingled population, a determination on the part of the ruling power to maintain its legislative sovereignty, a revolutionary brotherhood handing down the torch of rebellion from generation to generation, vital strategic interests of the dominant power involved in the territory of the subject nation—all these were factors in the situation. The British Government might conceivably have dealt with the evil before it became incurable by granting a measure of independence, if it had not been for the strength in British society and politics of the Protestant minority in Ireland. All it could produce, however, and that at the cost of an incipient rebellion of the loyal minority, was the Home Rule Act of 1914, which has been described as 'a scheme of provincial autonomy so circumscribed that an Australian colony even sixty or seventy years earlier, would have rejected it with indignation.'[17]

In the subsequent struggle, the British Government could doubtless have suppressed the Southern Irish movement for self-determination if it had been prepared to send a much larger army of occupation, to spend much more money, to adopt an even more ruthlesss policy of repression, and to sacrifice completely its own principles of government. It was not prepared to go as far as this, though it went a long way. Some of the Southern Irish leaders, realising the hard facts of the situation, were willing to compromise to the extent of abandoning the demand for the immediate independence of the whole of Ireland, and accepting for Southern Ireland the equivalent of Canadian dominion status. It subsequently became evident that the possibility of secession was inherent in dominion status, and, under Mr. de Valera, Eire in fact seceded from the British Commonwealth, except for one slight link.

The essential price of the triumph of Irish nationalism was partition. In Ireland, the fatal logic of the nation state, held in check in Canada and South Africa, had triumphed. Except where a community is culturally homogeneous, the principle of the nation state means that the success of a majority in achieving self-determination will involve the assimilation, extinction, or exclusion of the minority. The Ulster Orangemen, with Great Britain behind them, were able to insist on the third of these possibilities. The policy of partition was not welcomed by the British state, which was faced with the same issue in many lands—in Canada, South Africa, Ireland, Ceylon, India, Palestine—and invariably in the first place sought a solution on the lines of the multinational community, basing national unity on political and not cultural nationalism. The Irish Treaty was the first occasion on which this policy had to admit defeat: others were to follow. Ample provision was made in the treaty for a subsequent reunion of Ireland by mutual consent, but

[17] Hancock, I. 94.

the developments of subsequent years were to make such a reunion less and less likely.

Irish patriotism has been described as 'pre-eminently patriotism of place'. 'Armagh, the Glens of Antrim, the "four green fields" are inextricably interwoven with the national sentiment.'[18] On this basis of territorial nationalism, the union of all Ireland was undoubtedly a possibility. There was nothing inevitable in the victory of the tradition of Wolfe Tone over that of Grattan and Flood. British policy, diverging from the sounder lines it had followed in Canada, by supporting the Protestant loyalists at all costs, laid the foundation of partition. Parnell might have prevented it; even as late as Michael Collins and Griffith, the restoration of a united Ireland was not inconceivable. Mr. de Valera was as devoted to the ideal of a united Ireland as any of his predecessors. For Ireland, he said in 1932, the treaty has meant 'the consummation of the outrage of partition, and the alienation of the most sacred part of our national territory with all the cultural and material loss that this unnatural separation entails.'[19] But actually the gulf dug between the Ulster Orangemen and Eire became almost impassable after the treaty, though not necessarily as a result of it. The determination of Eire to be a uni-national state in the cultural as well as the political sense, to associate the Catholic religion as intimately as possible with the state, and to make its own native language compulsory in education and administration, put union with the Protestant counties of Ulster out of the question. If national liberty means anything, the right of Eire to do these things cannot be questioned. But, equally, if self-determination means anything, the right of Ulster to exclude itself from a culturally alien and uni-national Eire must also be acknowledged.

Ulster, then, remains a part of the British Commonwealth. The apparent secession of the rest of Ireland from

[18] Hancock, I. 381.
[19] The Minister for External Affairs, Irish Free State, to the Secretary of State for Dominion Affairs, 5 April 1932; Keith, p. 463.

the British Commonwealth was completed by the proclamation of neutrality in World War II. The principle of the nation state, held in check elsewhere in the British Commonwealth, had achieved an outstanding triumph in Eire. This is the essential reason—not the cause, which is to be traced in a long, unhappy history—why self-determination, which proved compatible with continued co-operation between different cultural nationalities in the other dominions, as well as with membership of the British Commonwealth, proved incompatible with them in Ireland. Yet even this situation is evidently not final.

IV. Self-determination and Defence in the British Commonwealth

The history of the development of the dominions into autonomous communities, reaching theoretical completion in the peaceful secession of Eire from the British Commonwealth, is sufficient evidence of the progress of the right of self-determination in the British political mind since the time of the War of American Independence. But we have yet to ask why, apart from Eire, it has not resulted in the complete disintegration of the British Commonwealth. Since force is obviously not the answer, it must be sought partly in the sphere of sentiment, but also partly in that of interest. An adequate discussion of the advantages to Great Britain and the dominions of their economic relations cannot be provided here. It must be said, however, that the attempt to organise an imperial economic system, in so far as it has been made, has conspicuously failed. The nearest it ever came to realisation was in the Ottawa Agreements, and on these we are bound to accept the verdict that 'The Ottawa policy had thus failed to draw closer the ties that hold the states of the Commonwealth together; instead of goodwill it had bred questionings and consciousness of divergent interests.'[20]

When we turn to imperial defence and foreign policy, the

[20] E. A. Walker, *The British Empire*, 1943, p. 192.

matter is very different. In this field the tendency for the members of the British Commonwealth to act together has been very marked.

After 1918, the dominions made good their claim that no important developments in British foreign policy should be made without their previous consultation and, if necessary, consent. Twice, on the occasions of the Chanak telegram in 1922 and the Geneva Protocol of 1924, dominion influence was thrown into the balance to weigh down the tilting scales of British political opinion heavily on one side. In 1925 the dominions, being unwilling to accept European commitments, were excluded from the Locarno treaties. We must be careful not to draw the wrong conclusions from these examples, however. The first two are illustrations, not of a cleavage in foreign policy, but rather of the growth of a common foreign policy for Great Britain and the dominions. Locarno is the real argument for the belief in a growth of separate British and dominion foreign policies, and if the dangers of the international situation could have been isolated into geographically separate compartments it might have set the precedent for a steady drifting apart. 'As late as 1932,' it has been said, 'a committee of the Ottawa Conference could dispose of the Empire's foreign policy in twenty minutes by recommending in effect that there should be no such thing.'[21] At an unofficial conference of 1933 on Commonwealth relations the 'diversity of interests which render a close-knit common foreign policy impossible' was commented upon, and the conclusion was drawn that 'it is only the mother country's wide interests which give the present semblance of unity to imperial foreign policy.'[22] There was also the fact, however, that Great Britain, conscious of her weakness in man-power and raw materials, needed the support of the dominions and was determined not to involve herself in war without their agreement. Defence was on both sides the prime motive in Commonwealth foreign policy, and the essential factor in defence

[21] Walker, p. 202.
[22] A. J. Toynbee (ed.), *British Commonwealth Relations*, 1934, p. 24.

was British sea-power. So long as that bulwark protected them from invasion, membership of the British Commonwealth was not a limitation on the independence of the dominions, but a guarantee of their survival as independent states. The British navy could not, admittedly, protect Canada against aggression by the United States, but this contingency was fortunately out of the question.

Reliance on the British navy as a first line of defence involved as a corollary a certain minimum degree of co-operation between the several self-governing states of the British Commonwealth. Defence policy for each of the dominions was entirely under its own control, and limited only by voluntary arrangements with Great Britain. The question of national sovereignty was not involved in such agreements, but it was raised by the two questions of independent navies and strategic bases, in both of which is illustrated the incompatibility between modern defence requirements and absolute national sovereignty. In desiring their own navies, the dominions failed to realise that concentration of the fleet was a condition of victory.[23] As regards strategic bases, in relations with Canada, Australia, and New Zealand no problems of sovereignty have been raised. The provision of a naval base in South Africa was settled by the Smuts-Churchill agreement of 1922, by which Great Britain handed over to South African sovereignty the naval base at Simonstown and agreed that its land defences should be entrusted to the Union. South Africa, for her part, guaranteed the use of Simonstown to Great Britain as a naval base in peace and war. General Hertzog contended that this arrangement did not necessarily compromise the neutrality of the Union of South Africa, being of the nature of an international servitude,[24] and though this view was contested, the general opinion seems to be that it was valid, at least in law.

The same problem of strategic bases arose in relations

[23] G. Neuendorff, *Studies in the Evolution of Dominion Status*, 1942, p. 334
[24] *The British Empire*, Royal Institute of International Affairs, 1937 pp. 80–1.

with Eire. Provision had been made in the Irish treaty for the continuance under British control of naval bases in Southern Ireland. This was one of the grievances of Mr. de Valera's party. He promised in 1935 that Eire would never be permitted to be used as a base for attack on Britain, but it is not irrelevant to observe that the regular army of Eire amounted to under 6,000 men and that its naval and air forces were negligible. The promise of Eire to defend her neutrality did not make it any the less necessary for the British Government subsequently to maintain a large army in Northern Ireland for the purpose of combating, if possible, a German air invasion of Eire. Shortly before the war, which was plainly on the point of bursting into flame, actually broke out, the British bases in Southern Ireland were unconditionally given up to Eire. If this was done in the belief that a demonstration of weakness would win the sympathy and support of the Government of Eire in the event of war, it was evidently mistaken. In relation to strategic interests, as in other respects, Ireland offers an illustration of the difficulties involved in the principle of self-determination of the nation state where it is treated as an absolute right and pushed to its logical extreme; and the strategic, like other problems presented by the relationship of Eire to other parts of the British Isles, remained to be solved.

On the whole, however, the British Commonwealth, in so far as concerns Great Britain and the dominions, may be said to have made a notable advance towards a reconciliation of national self-determination with the survival of an association of stable and peaceful states, possessed of a right of secession, but not exercising it, and co-operating, especially for mutual defence, in peace and war. It should be added, perhaps, that many factors which help to maintain the association between the dominions and Great Britain also serve to attract them towards the United States; this is true of economic relations, defence, and the use of a common language.

Finally, it must be repeated that the degree of success

achieved by the British Commonwealth in its treatment of this problem is directly traceable to the general acceptance of two principles—the principle of the multi-national state, and the principle of the divisibility of sovereignty. Where these principles did not apply, where, as in Ireland, the nationalists insisted on the uni-national state and the British Government on its absolute right of sovereignty, no solution was found save secession, which itself left all the major problems—partition, frontier, economic relations, and strategic requirements—unsolved. Both in its successes and its greatest failure the British Commonwealth of Nations has notable lessons to offer to the student of self-determination.

XI. The Policy of the United States in Relation to the Rights of Small Nations

I. The Rise of American Imperialism

THE United States is not normally thought of as an imperial power. Its actual possessions are a comparatively minor aspect of the problem we shall have to discuss in this chapter. But the United States is undoubtedly a great nation, and small nations that lie in the shadow of great powers are liable to come under their influence to a degree which raises the question of national independence, even in the absence of annexation. Two factors operated from the beginning against the development of any general United States policy of conquering and ruling the smaller nations of the American continent. The first was the existence of a vast unoccupied territory to fill and exploit at home: American colonisation had a large part of a continent at its disposal under its own flag. The other factor was of an ideological nature. The revolt of the English colonies in America had been the first successful assertion of the right of national and democratic self-determination in the history of the world. For the United States openly to deny or disregard, in its relations with other nations, a principle which was its very foundation-stone was possible, but not easy. The natural bias of American opinion was necessarily against anything that looked like imperialism, though this did not rule out a considerable and forcible extension of United States territory on the North American mainland.

During the nineteenth century the foreign policy of the

United States was summed up in the Monroe Doctrine. This was in effect a declaration of an American sphere of influence; it took the negative form of warning off European powers from the American continent, rather than of asserting any American right of interference. There were, of course, expansionist elements in United States policy during the nineteenth century. The acquisition by purchase of Louisiana and Alaska, and by force of the northern territories of Mexico, and the immense growth of the United States in wealth and population, encouraged a belief from time to time in its 'manifest destiny' to bring the whole of the Americas under its sway. Opposing influences held this tendency in check, and the policy of annexation was never dominant or indeed seriously prosecuted, except in the continental expansion already mentioned. The Monroe Doctrine, however, grew with the growth of the United States, and it became a doctrine of the paramount interest of the United States in the Western Hemisphere. This doctrine was asserted in its extremest form by Richard Olney, Secretary of State under Cleveland, who declared in 1895, 'To-day the United States is practically sovereign on this continent, and its fiat is law upon the subjects to which it confines its inter-position . . . Its infinite resources combined with its isolated position render it master of the situation and practically invulnerable as against any or all other powers.'[1]

The wave of imperialism with which the nineteenth century closed did not leave the United States unaffected. The juxtaposition of the young American power with the relics of the decadent Spanish Empire, in which open revolt was raging, provided the incentive to war, and the rapid success of American forces left the victors with sovereignty over Puerto Rico and the Philippines, and a rather indeterminate protectorate of Cuba. Even in the hey-day of American imperialism, however, the right of national independence was acknowledged in principle.[2] A treaty was signed with

[1] G. Nerval, *Autopsy of the Monroe Doctrine*, 1934, p. 207.
[2] *Cf.* D. G. Munro, *The United States and the Caribbean Area*, 1934, pp. 7–8.

Cuba in 1903 recognising its independence, although the United States was to retain a naval base in the island, and exercise control over its treaties with foreign powers, public debts, and sanitation. It was also agreed 'that the government of Cuba consents that the United States may exercise the right to intervene for the preservation of Cuban independence, the maintenance of a government adequate for the protection of life, property, and individual liberty, and for discharging the obligations with respect to Cuba imposed by the Treaty of Paris on the United States.'[3]

With the acquisitions of the Spanish-American War the territorial expansion of the United States came to an end except for the purchase from Denmark of the Virgin Islands in 1916. On the whole it is true to say that, apart from the northern territories of Mexico, annexation has never been the aim of United States policy in relation to other American states. The claim that the United States 'has not permanently deprived any Latin-American state of its autonomy or its opportunity for self-development'[4] is strictly true. If this verdict provides an inadequate description of the relations between the United States and other American states, this is to be regarded as evidence, not of the shallowness of American pretensions to international morality, but of the influence of sheer force of circumstances in determining the relations between an overwhelmingly great economic and political power and its small and weak neighbours.

II. *The Policy of Intervention*

A more active stage in the exercise of United States influence was reached in the early years of the twentieth century. What was termed the 'big stick' policy of Theodore Roosevelt, was illustrated in the utilisation of the Panama revolt to provide a new and amenable petty state through which

[3] C. P. Howland, *American Relations in the Caribbean*, 1929, p. 17.
[4] C. H. Haring, *South America looks at the United States*, 1928, p. 9.

the proposed Panama Canal could be driven.[5] It developed into a generalised principle of intervention, which became known as the 'Roosevelt corollary'. 'Brutal wrongdoing,' Roosevelt declared in 1904, 'or an impotence which results in a general loosening of the ties of civilised society, may finally require intervention by some civilised nation, and in the Western Hemisphere the United States cannot ignore this duty.[6] But although the method by which the Canal zone had been acquired undermined Latin-American confidence in its good faith,[7] Sumner Welles claims that in all its other dealings with American governments the Roosevelt administration scrupulously respected their sovereignty, and that the label of a 'big stick' policy is a misnomer.[8]

The real wave of intervention came with President Taft's policy of 'active intervention to secure for our merchandise and our capitalists opportunity for profitable investment'[9] —'dollar diplomacy' it was called by its critics.

We need not trace the many consequent interventions of the United States in the internal affairs of the Caribbean and Central American states. A more idealistic trend in American policy appeared with the administration of Woodrow Wilson. The ideal of self-determination was one which Wilson evolved in relation to American problems before he came to apply it to Europe. His address at Mobile, Alabama, in October, 1913, is famous as the first proclamation of the new attitude towards the other American states. It was a declaration of the abandonment of economic imperialism. 'States that are obliged,' said Wilson, 'because their territory does not lie within the main field of modern enterprise and action, to grant concessions are in this condition, that foreign interests are apt to dominate their domestic affairs, a condition of affairs always dangerous and apt to become intolerable. What these states are going

[5] Dexter Perkins, *Hands Off: a History of the Monroe Doctrine*, 1941, p. 235.
[6] Dexter Perkins, pp. 238–9.
[7] Sumner Welles, *Naboth's Vineyard: the Dominican Republic*, 1844–1924, 1928, pp. 917–18.
[8] *id.* p. 919.   [9] Quoted in Haring, p. 8.

to see, therefore, is an emancipation from the subordination, which has been inevitable, to foreign enterprise, and an assertion of the splendid character which, in spite of these difficulties, they have again and again been able to demonstrate.'[10] This speech was followed by a change of policy towards Mexico. In his third annual Message to Congress, of December, 1915, Wilson declared that 'All the governments of America stand, so far as we are concerned, upon a footing of genuine equality and unquestioned independence.'[11] In relations with the greater American states, he believed, like his closest adviser, Colonel House,[12] that the time had come for an equal partnership, but towards the smaller states of the Caribbean he favoured the continuance of a more paternal policy aimed at the establishment of stable governments.

An explanation of the Wilsonian policy on less altruistic grounds would stress the changing requirements of American financial interests. 'The antagonism to violence has increased,' it has been pointed out, 'as the non-concessionary investment, representing bona-fide capital, has come to predominate over that depending upon special contracts of exploitation. The shoe-string type of promoter . . . often prospered through revolutions.[13] We find, moreover, a new principle emerging at this time. A Memorandum of 1915 by Lansing, the argument of which was accepted by Wilson, proposed the extension of the Monroe Doctrine in the form of a definite Caribbean policy. While disclaiming any idea of domination in the territories of other states, it proclaimed the necessity of aiding the peoples of Central America and the Caribbean in the establishment and maintenance of 'honest and responsible governments'.[14] Thus, declares its latest and most authoritative historian, 'the spirit of Monroeism had by 1915 been deeply charged with an

[10] A. Alvarez, *The Monroe Doctrine: its Importance in the International Life of the States of the New World*, 1924, p. 554.
[11] Baker and Dodd, I. 408. [12] Seymour, I. 196.
[13] B. H. Williams, *Economic Foreign Policy of the United States*, 1929, p. 136.
[14] Perkins, pp. 268–9; *cf.* the speech of Secretary Hughes in 1923, *id.* pp. 333–5.

assumption of a right of control, of superior power, of hegemony, over the other states of the New World.'[15]

The policy of intervention in Central America was continued, and perhaps even intensified, under President Coolidge. It produced an increasing resentment among the Latin-American states, which, while not unaware of the protection afforded by the Monroe Doctrine from the danger of European conquest, were inclined to look upon it as too often a mere cloak for United States imperialism. Since the attack on Mexico, declared a former President of Honduras, the Monroe Doctrine, instead of being regarded as a guarantee of independence by the Latin-American states, had been considered as a menace to their existence.[16] A Mexican writer described it in 1916 as 'a myth which serves as a cloak to the following natural fact: the ambitions of a powerful people who pretend to exercise their hegemony over a group of weak peoples, giving to their domination the insincere appearance of unselfishness and benevolence.'[17] These are only two of many similar expressions of opinion which might be found. By 1928 the hostility of Latin America to United States interventionism had reached a high pitch, which was manifested at the Havana Conference in a 'slashing attack upon the policy of the United States.'[18]

The awkward fact was that intervention was necessarily one-sided: it was a monopoly of the United States. It was exercised, moreover, mainly, if not exclusively, in the interests of the American investor, and it provided no safe basis for a permanent régime because it was always liable to change with a change in the American presidency.[19]

---

[15] *id.* p. 316.   [16] Alvarez, p. 242.   [17] *id.* p. 312; *cf.* p. 353.
[18] Perkins, p. 338.
[19] H. F. Guggenheim, *The United States and Cuba: a Study in International Relations*, 1934, p. 208.

III. *The Abandonment of Intervention*

Opinion in the United States has always been sensitive to charges of imperialism, and it has been said with evident truth that 'the American people have never responded with enthusiasm to the idea of a general tutelage over the Latin-American republics.'[20] American statesmanship met the challenge of the Havana Conference in a constructive way and with remarkably little delay. The need to free the Monroe Doctrine and American policy from their accretion of interventionism was clearly put in a Memorandum by the Under-Secretary of State in 1928.[21] This Memorandum was accepted as the basis of his policy by the new Secretary of State, Henry L. Stimson, in 1929, and by 1930 the Roosevelt corollary had been specifically repudiated. The right of intervention had not so far been abandoned, but it had been divorced from the Monroe Doctrine.[22]

A further step was announced in a speech by President Roosevelt in December, 1933. 'The maintenance of constitutional government in other nations,' he said, 'is not, after all, a sacred obligation devolving upon the United States alone. The maintenance of law and the orderly processes of government in this hemisphere is the concern of each individual nation within its own borders first of all. It is only if and when the failure of orderly processes affects the other nations of the continent that it becomes their concern: and the point to stress is that in such an event it becomes the joint concern of the whole continent in which we are all neighbours.'[23] This was a repudiation of the whole policy of unilateral intervention, whether it took the form of the imperialism of Theodore Roosevelt or the paternalism of Woodrow Wilson. It was put into the form of a convention on non-intervention at the Pan-American Conference at Montevideo, and in June, 1934, this was ratified unanimously by the Senate.[24] Nor were these

[20] Perkins, p. 373.   [21] Perkins, p .243–4.   [22] *id.* p. 344.
[23] C. L. Jones, *The Caribbean since 1900*, 1936, p. 477.
[24] Perkins, p. 346.

declarations mere pious aspirations. A few months before the Conference the United States marines had been withdrawn from Nicaragua. In 1934, the military occupation of Haiti came to an end, certain limitations on the sovereignty of Cuba were abandoned, and in 1935 financial intervention in Nicaragua, Haiti and Salvador was restricted.[25] Finally, a protocol signed at the Buenos Aires conference of 1936 declared that intervention 'directly or indirectly, and for whatever reason' was 'inadmissible'.[26]

It may seem that our tale is now ended. Manifest destiny, paramount interest, the policy of the big stick, dollar diplomacy, Wilsonian paternalism, anti-revolutionary intervention—all have passed. The United States has abandoned, apparently, all its direct or indirect attempts to infringe the political sovereignty of the lesser American states. Is there then any remaining problem involved in the maintenance of the right of national independence, or self-determination, in the Americas, it may be asked. Why, indeed, have we troubled to go into this question if its interest is purely historical? The answer is that the whole problem of self-determination has now expanded beyond its traditional political framework. We have so far omitted those aspects of American relations with other nations which are the crux of the whole matter. There are, first, the actual possessions of the United States, Puerto Rico and the Philippines, to be treated. But of far greater importance are the economic relations between the United States and the little states of the Caribbean and Central America, and the whole issue of continental defence.

IV. The Independence of the Philippines and Puerto Rico

The imperial policy of the United States towards the Philippines hardly comes within the scope of this chapter. All that need be said is that the recognition of the right of

[25] *Survey of International Affairs, 1936,* p. 808; *Survey, 1938,* I. 665, *n.* 1.
[26] Perkins, p. 347.

the Philippines to self-government had always been implicit in American policy. Under Wilson the administration made rapid—according to its critics, too rapid—steps towards this goal. In his annual Message to Congress of 1920 the President declared that the time had now come for granting the islands their promised independence. [27] The Republican administrations which followed did not implement this proposal, but during the 'thirties' the hostility of the Farm group to Philippine competition in the American market, [28] and the tendency of American policy towards isolation, [29] led to the passing of an Act conferring independence on the Philippines in two stages. For ten years a Commonwealth Government was to function, with certain reserved powers in the hands of the United States, after which the Philippines were to have complete independence, except for the possible retention by the United States of strategic bases. [30]

Puerto Rico, with a population of now nearly two millions, of which 73 per cent were classified as white in 1930, [31] had expected on annexation to become a state of the United States. There seems to be general agreement now that its real problem is not political, but social and economic. All we need say from the political point of view is that neither the Philippines nor Puerto Rico can legitimately be cited as evidence of any United States intention permanently to exercise direct political control over other nations.

V. Economic Relations with the Caribbean and Central America

While the discussion is kept on strictly political grounds, as I have already said, we cannot appreciate the real nature of the relations between the United States and the smaller American nations. The basic facts of American imperialism

[27] G. L. Kirk, *Philippine Independence: Motives, Problems and Prospects*, 1936, p. 48.
[28] *id.* p. 95.   [29] *id.* p. 127.   [30] *id.* p. 123.   [31] Jones, p. 191.

are not political, but economic, not the product of the will of the government, but of the commercial and financial activities of its citizens. The movement for territorial aggrandisement was comparatively short-lived. Its motivation had been mainly economic, and while some small groups of individuals profited from it, other groups suffered economic injury. In the colossal trade of the United States the part that could be played by small colonial possessions, either as markets or as sources of raw materials, was insignificant. In any case, direct political control was not necessary for the maintenance of predominant economic influence in the Caribbean and Central American area.

Already in 1881 a consular report described Cuba as 'commercially a dependency of the United States, while still remaining a political dependency of Spain.'[32] Between 1900 and 1929 the value of Caribbean trade with the United States was multiplied approximately eight times. The United States capital investment in the Caribbean, which was $300,000,000 in 1912, became $2,517,000,000 by 1933.[33] Even more striking evidence of the economic dependence of the Central American and Caribbean countries on the United States is given by the percentage of their total trade which was conducted with the United States. The figures for 1927 were; Honduras 77, Cuba 71, Panama (1925) 71, Nicaragua 61, Santo Domingo 48, Guatemala 47, Haiti 43, Costa Rica 41, Salvador 34.[34] Finally, it must be remembered that while this trade was a matter of life or death for all the little nations concerned, it was, except perhaps for the trade of Cuba, trivial in comparison with the total volume of United States trade.

Such a high degree of economic dependence could not but have political consequences. 'In the case of the Caribbean relations with the United States,' one writer says, 'there is fortunately little conflict between the political and economic aspects of integration. The historical and geographical influences on the area's development are such as to create legitimate economic sinews for the political em-

[32] Howland, p. 7.   [33] Jones, pp. 9–10.   [34] Howland, p. 281.

brace in which the United States holds it. Accordingly, that embrace need be neither costly to the United States nor stifling to the Caribbean.' He continues, however: 'Unhappily, it has so far in a large measure been both.'[35]

The relations of the United States with the Central American and Caribbean countries, in fact, provide a striking illustration of the problem involved in the conflict between imperialism and national independence in an area in which actual annexation has been slight and even military intervention comparatively limited. The natural consequences of American capital investment in tropical or sub-tropical districts such as the Caribbean and the Philippines was the development of these as great raw-material producing areas. The greater part of their productivity was devoted to a small number of products, which were exported almost exclusively to the United States. Any change in the direction of United States trade was bound to have decisive repercussions on the prosperity of the islands, as more responsible elements on both sides have recognised. Thus Sumner Welles wrote in 1928: 'The United States protective tariff has constituted necessarily a natural obstacle to the effective development of the natural resources of many of the American republics . . . This obstacle is the chief and greatest hindrance to the rapid development of real prosperity in the smaller republics of the continent, and the removal of this obstacle would do infinitely more to promote the creation of stable governments in those republics where the United States has frequently felt itself called upon to exercise its police power, than all the myriad discourses which have been declaimed by American statesmen emphasising the benefits conferred upon those nations by the Monroe Doctrine.'[36]

Trade, when it is of so exclusive a nature, breeds consequences similar to those of colonial possession. Puerto Rico, where the American flag flew, and which did 95 per

[35] J. Polk, 'The Plight of Puerto Rico', in *Political Science Quarterly*, LVII, No. 4, December 1942, p. 483.
[36] Sumner We'les, p. 930.

cent of its total trade with the United States,[37] offered the most acute example of these responsibilities. The large investments of American capital in the island made it in effect a tributary state. 'This ghastly spectacle of wealth drained from a starving people into the richest country on earth is sanctimoniously entitled in the official reports, "a favourable trade balance",' said one study of conditions in Puerto Rico.[38] An American journalist described Puerto Rico as marked by 'misery, disease, squalor, filth'. It had, he said, the highest infant mortality in the world, and a peasantry with an average income of less than 1*s*. 8*d*. a day.[39] 'The plain fact is,' said another critic, 'that, under American, as under Spanish control, the people of Puerto Rico live at a desperately low standard of life and there is no early prospect of change in that condition.'[40] The solution for such conditions was clearly not in the concession of political rights, but in drastic economic reforms, and the other economic dependencies of the United States presented a challenge which was fundamentally the same. Old-fashioned territorial imperialism, outside the North American Continent at least, is also not in accordance with the traditions of national policy. The end of the Second World War therefore saw an independent State of the Philippines in 1946; Puerto Rico became self-governing in 1952; and Hawaii a state of the Union in 1959. The political issue was settled in this way. The economic difficulties were greater but the degree of success of the United States in improving social conditions in the countries which came temporarily or permanently under its control should not be underestimated. It is clear that the American government and people have become conscious that economic power, like political, brings with it responsibilities, which are not fundamentally different in kind from those of Great Britain in its former colonial Empire or of the Soviet Union in its more backward republics.

[37] Polk, p. 486.
[38] B. W. and J. W. Diffie, *Porto Rico: a Broken Pledge,* 1931, p. 203.
[39] J. Gunther, *Inside Latin America,* 1942, p. 336.   [40] Jones, p. 189.

VI. *Strategic Interests of the United States*

Besides economic relations, there is a second factor binding the Central American and Caribbean states to their over-mighty neighbour, which up to the present we have only briefly mentioned. This is the strategic interest of the United States in the area. From the very beginning there was a definite strategic element in the conception of the Monroe Doctrine. It has grown with the growth of United States interests. For the naval defence of the United States, and therefore of the whole American continent, the route through the Panama Canal has become the essential life-line. A necessity for the southern defences of the United States is control of the Gulf of Mexico and the Caribbean Sea.[41] The key to both is the island of Cuba, and for this reason the exclusion of any dangerous influence from Cuba was a permanent object of United States policy. 'The news of the cession of Cuba to any foreign power,' declared Secretary Clayton to the Spanish Minister as long ago as 1849, 'would, in the United States, be the instant signal for war.'[42] Existing foreign interests in the Caribbean offered no threat to American interests, for the French forces there were unimportant and early in the twentieth century the British West Indies fleet was withdrawn. Gradually the United States has secured possession of what must now be considered an impregnable system of bases. Soon after the treaty of 1903 a base was obtained on the Windward Passage by agreement with Cuba. In 1914 Nicaragua leased the Great Corn and Little Corn Islands to the United States. In 1917 the Virgin Islands were purchased from Denmark. In 1928 by a treaty with Colombia the use of a number of islands as naval and air bases was obtained. Finally, the protective belt was completed in 1940 by the British concession, on a ninety-nine years' lease, of a series of bases from the Bermudas to British Guiana.

[41] *Cf.* Rear-Admiral Chester, quoted in Alvarez, pp. 402-3.
[42] Alvarez, p. 44.

In its latest phase American strategy has witnessed the fulfilment of the conception of continental defence which lay, as an embryo, in the Monroe Doctrine of 1823. The United States no longer relies, as it largely—though no doubt unconsciously—did throughout the nineteenth century, on the British navy to maintain the integrity of the western hemisphere, and the form which the new scheme of continental defence has taken is highly significant. Although the primary intention of the Monroe Doctrine, the preservation of United States military security, still remains at the heart of American policy, in application it has become a collective and multilateral policy.[43] The Pan-American Conference at Lima in 1938 put this in the form of a declaration that 'In case the peace, security or territorial integrity of any American republic is thus threatened by acts of any nature that may impair them, they proclaim the common concern and the determination to make effective the solidarity, co-ordinating the respective sovereign wills by means of the procedure of consultation.'[44]

VII. The Reconciliation of United States Interests with the Rights of Small Nations

From this brief account of American economic and strategic relations it can be seen that the United States, like other great powers, has either had to be content with the bald assertion of its imperial destiny or to find some other means of reconciling its economic and strategic interests with the rights of the lesser nations which come within its sphere of influence. This is essentially the problem of national self-determination presented from another angle.

The extent of American political control in the Caribbean and Central American area has varied from time to time. In 1920 it could be said that 'several of the Caribbean countries are in fact no longer independent and belong almost, if not quite, in the category of the British crown colonies, so far as

[43] *Survey of International Affairs*, 1938, I. 686.
[44] Perkins, p. 315.

their relationship to the United States is concerned.'[45] Another writer declared, in 1936, that 'The connexions of the United States and the Caribbean have now become so intimate that only in a technical sense can they be spoken of as "foreign relations".'[46] Panama has been described as 'a sovereign nation only in so far as her sovereignty does not clash with the ideas of the elder statesmen of the State, War and Navy Buildings at Washington.'[47] A book of 1928 could say: 'To-day we control the political destinies of Mexico, Central America and other nearby Latin regions as effectively as if we exercised a formal protectorate over the entire area.'[48] The extent to which this situation has been modified during the last forty years has already been explained.

The policy that is followed in the Caribbean by the United States is far-reaching in its repercussions, for it does much to determine the future of relations with the whole of Latin America. The Caribbean republics—excluding perhaps Haiti because it is Negro, and French rather than Spanish in its connexions—are the test case for United States policy for the whole of Latin America.[49] Already the lines on which a solution may be found are emerging. The political independence of all Caribbean and Central American communities that are capable of constituting and working effective governments is recognised. This would exclude, of course, such a tiny community as that of the Virgin Isles, with a population of only a few thousand. So long as major public interests of the United States are not threatened, a policy of non-intervention is followed. If intervention becomes necessary, the United States endeavours to associate itself with other American states before it takes action, so that the intervention can be presented, at least in form, as a joint one. In matters of economics and

[45] G. H. Blakeslee (ed.), *Mexico and the Caribbean*, 1920, p. 202.
[46] Jones, p. 467.
[47] Quoted in W. D. McCain, *The United States and the Republic of Panama*, 1937, p. 253.
[48] Haring, p. 7.   [49] Haring, p. 114.

defence the wealth and power of the United States has been recognised by a correspondingly greater assumption of responsibilities.

Tradition prohibits the United States from forming alliances, but the same object may be secured under more than one designation. Relations with the small states might be stabilised by treaties negotiated separately between each nation and the United States. Such a system of treaties has in fact appeared. Negotiations with Panama in 1926 produced a plan for the control by the United States, if necessary, of the whole territory of the republic in the event of war, and for Panama to consider herself in a state of war whenever the United States was. This agreement was not ratified by Panama,[50] but in 1936 a treaty was signed for the joint defence of the Canal, and a further agreement of 1942 disposed of all outstanding questions between the two countries. Of considerable significance for the future was the agreement of 1942 between the United States and Nicaragua. By this the United States was to extend credits and to make specific supplies available to Nicaragua, to send agricultural experts to assist in the improvement of Nicaraguan agriculture, to aid in the construction of a road from the Atlantic to the Pacific, and to bear two-thirds of the cost of completing the Pan-American Highway through Nicaragua. The shifting of the emphasis from political sovereignty to questions of common economic and strategic interest is obvious.

It is not too much to say that in the course of the 'thirties the attitude of the United States towards the small nations of the American continent was given a new orientation, based on a positive recognition of their national rights and interests. The conception of state equality was left where it belongs, in the field of law. The right of national self-determination for the small states ceased to be a formula, overridden continually by the private imperialism of American big business, and became more of a reality. The results were a vindication of the new line in American policy. The

[50] Howland, pp. 217–18.

threat of pan-Hispanism, and the attempts at Fascist and Nazi infiltration on the American continent, largely failed. In the early 'thirties, if the United States had been involved in a great war the attitude of Latin America would have been at best uncertain. Ten years later, immediately the threat to the United States developed, the little states of Central America and the Caribbean, recognising the logic of the situation and their community of interest with the United States, at once aligned themselves with her in the war, to be followed by most of Latin America. This was the kind of imperialism that under modern conditions succeeds: and a basic element in that success was the recognition of the right of self-government.

XII. National Self-determination in the Theory and Practice of the Soviet Union

I. *The National Question in Tsarist Russia*

MASARYK, who perhaps understood the spirit of Russia as well as any external observer, described the Tsarist empire as Byzantine rather than Slav.[1] It was essentially a supranational, dynastic empire, though built round a national Muscovite state. Great Russian national sentiment, however, became stronger and more aggressive in the latter part of the nineteenth century; the Polish rebellion of 1863 provoked a fear of the nationalism of the subject nations; and, as a result of these two developments, wherever in the great empire the presence of national agitation was suspected it was mercilessly repressed, and russification encouraged by a combination of threats and favours.

The chief effect of the policy of russification appears to have been the stimulation of national consciousness in the border provinces of Russia, but national resistance presented little real danger to the unity of Russia up to 1917. Revolutionary movements in the Tsarist empire were overwhelmingly social and political in inspiration. National minorities in the Baltic provinces and Transcaucasia seized the opportunity presented by the revolution of 1905 to put forward demands for autonomy, but nothing came of these manifestations; there was little separatism before the complete collapse of the Imperial government in 1917,[2] and

[1] Masaryk, p. 383.
[2] E. Haumant, *Le Problème de l'unité russe*, 1922, p. 116.

even then most of the nationalities were demanding autonomy and not complete independence. Military disaster
and social revolution each played its part in the break-up of
Tsarist Russia: the motive of national self-determination
was a consequence rather than a cause, except in Finland
and Poland. With the total collapse of central authority in
Russia in 1917, of course, the proportions of the national
question immediately changed. Poles and Finns staked out
their claims for independence. The other nationalities at
first demanded no more than autonomy in a Russian
federation.

The Kerensky government proclaimed as its object the
establishment of 'a durable peace on the basis of the rights
of nations to decide their own destiny.'[3] All sections in the
confused struggle which ensued attempted to win the support of the minority nationalities. The Whites were too
wedded to imperialist ideas to achieve much success. The
Bolsheviks, on the other hand, were equipped in advance
with a theory on the national question which facilitated
their approach to the problem of self-determination. This
was the work of two men—Lenin and Stalin—and the
direction of communist policy on nationalities mainly
followed their ideas, with the analysis of which we must
therefore begin.

II. *The National Theory of Lenin and Stalin*

At the root of all communist theory, of course, are the
writings of Marx himself; but part of the strength of the
communist movement has lain in its capacity for change,
which is still far from exhausted and which has often outrun
the adaptability of its disciples. In the beginning Marxism
was the enemy of nationalism. National differences, it
seemed to Marx and Engels when they wrote *The Communist Manifesto*, were rapidly disappearing before the
growth of international capitalism. The workers, the dis-

[3] Temperley, I. 183.

inherited of bourgeois civilisation, had no fatherland: to conduct their struggle against the bourgeois international successfully they must recognise this fact and form a strong workers' international. In so far as, at this early stage, Marx recognised the existence of nations, he adopted a thoroughly Western political point of view. When, for example, there was a proposal to align the German-speaking Alsatians with the German instead of the French section of the First International, he protested against the attempt to substitute 'an artificial contrivance of arbitrary lingual connexions' for 'the actual state and national connexions.'[4] Towards the lesser nationalities of Europe Marx was distinctly hostile. He had all the German contempt for the Slavs. Movements such as those of the Czechs and Irish seemed to him unprogressive and counter-revolutionary.[5] But as his hopes of immediate revolution in the advanced nations of Europe— Germany, France, or Great Britain—receded, he came to look with greater favour on national movements in the more backward countries, not as a good thing in themselves, but as a step towards the proletarian revolution. By 1872 he was prepared to admit that 'special regard must be paid to the institutions, customs, and traditions of various lands.'[6] In 1875 he emphasised the national setting of the class struggle. Socialism must achieve its victory first of all in particular countries.[7] With these later tendencies of Marx's thought in mind, the national theories of Lenin and Stalin appear less as a remarkable breakaway, and more as a natural development of Marxist thought.

German and Western European socialism had on the whole tended to ignore or underestimate the force of nationalism, regarding national movements as merely a by-product of the victory of capitalism over feudalism, and therefore essentially reactionary. Lenin did not deny that nationalism was normally associated with the rise of the middle classes to power, or that the nation state was the

[4] S. F. Bloom, *The World of Nations, a Study of the National Implications in the Work of Karl Marx*, 1941, p. 19.
[5] *id.* pp. 38, 41, 201.　[6] *id.* p. 92.　[7] *id.* p. 88.

characteristic political form of the capitalist period.[8] But he refused to jump from this to the unduly *simpliste* conclusion that therefore all nationalist movements were to be condemned. He divided the nations of the world into three categories in this connexion. In the West, he said, are advanced capitalist countries, where the progressive national movements of the bourgeoisie long ago ended, and where purely oppressive régimes prevail. In Eastern Europe, and especially Russia, bourgeois democratic and nationalist movements were now in progress: these the party should support. Thirdly, in colonial areas, such as the whole of Asia, where bourgeois nationalism had as yet hardly begun, its appearance should be encouraged.[9] In a polemic against Rosa Luxemburg, Lenin protested against the view that so long as capitalism existed the right of self-determination was illusory.[10] He criticised her condemnation of the separation of Norway from Sweden, which she described as 'merely a manifestation of peasant and petty-bourgeois particularism.'[11] Lenin argued more realistically that there was a democratic content in the nationalism of every oppressed nation, and that in this respect it should be supported, in spite of its bourgeois character.[12] Similarly, he saw in the victory of the Serbs and Bulgars in the Balkan wars the destruction of Balkan feudalism and the creation of a more or less free class of peasant landowners, which, inasmuch as it represented a step forward, was to be applauded.[13] It was on these grounds, he pointed out, that Marx towards the end of his life had favoured the Irish nationalist movement.[14] In all this, of course, it must not be assumed that national freedom was an end in itself; but it was desirable as a step towards the future proletarian revolution.[15]

Lenin's support of national revolutionary movements was

[8] V. I. Lenin, *Selected Works*, 1936, IV, 250–1 (*On the Right of Nations to Self-Determination*, 1914); *cf.* J. Stalin, *Marxism and the National and Colonial Question*, 2nd ed., 1936, p. 13.

[9] Lenin, V. 275–6 (*The Socialist Revolution and the Right of Nations to Self-Determination*, 1916).

[10] *id.* IV. 252–3. [11] *id.* IV. 426, *n.* [12] *id.* IV. 267; *cf.* IV. 420, V. 268.

[13] *id.* IV. 424, *n.* [14] *id.* IV. 279. [15] *id.* V. 271.

particularly relevant to the Russian situation. Under his influence the second Congress of the Russian Social-Democratic Labour Party, in 1903, adopted as a clause in its programme 'The right of self-determination for all nations forming part of the state.'[16] Not the nationalism of the lesser nations in the Russian Empire, but the nationalism of the Great Russians was the real enemy, Lenin held.[17] This was the 'canker' that was poisoning the whole political atmosphere and strengthening reaction throughout the empire.[18] and this was the nationalism he opposed, not the democratic defence of the fatherland, as it was seen, for example, in the French revolutionary war, or in the campaigns of Garibaldi.[19] Aggressive nationalism was the enemy, not defensive.

The kind of democratic nationalism which can be found in Lenin's writings did not, of course, involve support of the war of 1914. 'Are we enlightened Great-Russian proletarians impervious to the feeling of national pride?' he asked in 1914. 'Certainly not! We love our language and our motherland; we, more than any other group, are working to raise its labouring masses.'[20] But a Tsarist triumph would have the opposite effect. In the first World War, Lenin claimed, the nationalist element was represented only by the Serbian struggle against Austria, a factor of no real significance in the general European war, which was a conflict of rival imperialisms.[21] As an old opponent of Tsarist imperialism, when the Revolution broke out Lenin could consistently appear as the advocate of liberation for the minorities in the Russian Empire. 'If Finland, if Poland, if the Ukraine break away from Russia, there is nothing bad about that,' he declared in a speech of May, 1917. 'Anyone who says there is, is a chauvinist.'[22]

We have said enough to indicate the general trend of Bolshevik thought on the national question, as it was represented by Lenin, and up to 1917. The leading specialist of

[16] Stalin, p. 294.   [17] Lenin, IV. 266.   [18] *id.* IV, 290.   [19] *id.* V. 273, *n.*
[20] Lenin, *Collected Works*, 1930, XVIII. 100.
[21] Lenin, *Selected Works*, V. 132.   [22] *id.* V. 310.

the Communist Party on the question was his colleague Stalin, in whose writings a more elaborate treatment of the whole problem can be found. The first point to be noted in Stalin's study of the national question is the more systematic, and at the same time rather more realistic approach. He begins with an attempt to decide what kind of thing a nation is, and his answer is far truer than any of the attempts to define it by a single characteristic. He rules out the racial or tribal conception of the nation at the outset. 'A nation,' he writes, 'is not a racial or tribal, but a historically constituted community of people.'[23] This means that in effect he accepts the political, Western interpretation of the basis of nationality. At the same time, he does not identify the nation with the state.[24] 'A nation,' his definition runs, 'is a historically evolved stable community of language, territory, economic life and psychological make-up, manifested in a community of culture.'[25] There is no single distinguishing feature. This is probably as true a definition as one could reach for Central and Eastern European conditions, though it does not take into its scope such Western nations as Switzerland or Canada. Understanding the nation in this sense, he proclaims its right of self-determination. 'It has the right to arrange its life on the basis of autonomy. It has the right to enter into federal relations with other nations. It has the right to complete secession. Nations are sovereign, and all nations are equal.'[26]

With this last sentence we may seem to be going almost too far, but taken by itself it gives a false impression. All that Stalin writes on this question must be read in the light of the dominating principle of socialist progress. As Lenin put it in 1916, 'The various demands of democracy, including self-determination, are not an absolute, they are a *particle* of the general democratic (at present general socialist) *world* movement. In individual concrete cases a particle may contradict the whole; if it does then it must be rejected.'[27] There are two important qualifications to Stalin's

[23] Stalin, p. 5.   [24] *id.* pp. 5–6.   [25] *id.* p. 8.   [26] *id.*, p. 19.
[27] Lenin, *Marx, Engels, Marxism*, 1934, p. 147.

principle of self-determination. It follows from what has just been said that national rights do not include the right to the maintenance of petrified forms and reactionary institutions. 'Take, for instance,' says Stalin, turning to the part of Russia he knew best, 'the Transcaucasian Tatars, with their minimum of literacy, their schools controlled by the omnipotent mullahs, and their culture permeated by the religious spirit . . . It is not difficult to understand that to organise them into a national cultural union would be to place them under the control of the mullahs, to deliver them to the mercies of the reactionary mullahs, to create a new stronghold of spiritual enslavement of the Tatar masses to their worst enemy.'[28]

The second important qualification of the right of self-determination was brought out in the Bolshevik attack on the national programme adopted by the Austrian Social Democratic Party at Brünn in 1899. This proposed to divide the nationalities in the Austro-Hungarian Empire into separate units, each with its own national autonomy, based on cultural connexions, that is, on personal nationality, and not on territorial contiguity. Stalin criticised this project as 'an absolutely unjustifiable substitution of national autonomy for self-determination of nations.'[29] The distinction he drew between this brand of national autonomy, which he condemned, and regional autonomy, which he advocated, shows the essentially political nature of his conception of self-determination. Regional autonomy, he said, 'does not deal with a fiction deprived of territory, but with a definite population inhabiting a definite territory.'[30] It is the opposite of a narrow particularism. It helps small nations to 'cast off the shell of isolation peculiar to small nationalities.'[31] Of course, within autonomous regions there are bound to remain minorities, but what these want is not to be attached artificially to similar minorities elsewhere, but 'real rights in the localities they inhabit.'[32]

[28] Stalin, p. 49; *cf.* pp. 10, 33. [29] *id.* p. 31. [30] *id.* p. 57.
[31] *id.* p. 49. [32] *id.* p. 58; *cf.* Lenin, IV. 420, *n.*

III. The Right of Secession

When the disintegration of the Tsarist empire began, in 1917, the Bolsheviks were not afraid to put these principles into practice. To mark the breach with the past, they ceased to call the new Soviet state by the old national name of Russia. Feeling that the right of self-determination was not sufficiently explicit, and wishing to outbid the Western democracies for the support of subject nations, they now substituted for it the right of secession. Stalin therefore drew up a Report on the National Question in 1917, on the basis that 'The oppressed nations forming part of Russia must be allowed the right to decide for themselves whether they wish to remain part of the Russian state or to separate and form an independent state.'[33] Following on this, the All-Russian Party Conference resolved that 'the right of all nations forming part of Russia to secede freely and form independent states shall be recognised.' 'The Party demands wide regional autonomy, the abolition of tutelage from above, the abolition of a compulsory state language, and the determination of the boundaries of self-governing and autonomous regions by the local population itself, based on economic and social conditions, the national composition of the population, and so forth.'[34] As a first step, the right of Finland to independence was recognised. The right of secession did not, of course, imply that a nation had necessarily to secede. Stalin explained that he personally would be opposed to the secession of Transcaucasia. 'But if, nevertheless, the peoples of Transcaucasia were to demand secession, they would, of course, secede, and would not encounter opposition on our part.'[35] He summed up the Bolshevik national programme in four propositions: '(*a*) The recognition of the right of peoples to secession; (*b*) regional autonomy for peoples which remain within the given state; (*c*) specific laws guaranteeing freedom of development for national minorities; (*d*) a single, indivisible

[33] Stalin, p. 63.   [34] Stalin, p. 269.   [35] *id.* p. 64.

proletarian collective body, a single party, for the proletarians of all the nationalities in the given state.'[36]

So far we have been concerned with theory, and its practical implications are clear and unmistakable. But the Bolsheviks were to find in applying the right of secession as many difficulties as Wilson in the application of the right of self-determination, though their greater dialectical experience may have enabled them to reconcile irreconcilables with greater skill than was exhibited at Versailles. In addition, their theory was better balanced, in so far as the right of secession had as its counterpart the principle of proletarian unity. But the opposition between national and socialist interests was bound to come to the surface sooner or later as a result of practical developments.

The Bolsheviks, then, when they went to Brest-Litovsk, were armed with the principle of the right of secession. Lenin had disclaimed the intention of retaining even the Ukraine by force. 'The Russian worker,' he declared, 'having no confidence even for a single moment in the Russian or Ukrainian bourgeoisie, now defends the right of the Ukrainians to separate and does not impose upon them his friendship.'[37] Trotsky, as Commissar for Foreign Affairs, issued proposals for an armistice on 22nd November, 1917, based on a general recognition of the right of self-determination. The Soviet delegates at Brest-Litovsk found that this idealistic scheme did not coincide with German plans for the future of Eastern Europe. One party wished to break off negotiations, but Lenin believed that in the interests of the Communist Revolution peace was the first necessity, at whatever cost. 'There is not a single Marxist,' he wrote in his *Twenty-one Theses for Peace* in January, 1918, 'who, while adhering to the foundations of Marxism and socialism, would not say that the interests of socialism are above the right of nations to self-determination.'[38] Consequently, he was not prepared for a rupture of the negotia-

[36] *id.* p. 66.
[37] Quoted in W. R. Batsell, *Soviet Rule in Russia*, 1929, p. 292.
[38] Wheeler-Bennett, Appendix III, p. 390.

tions for the sake of the nations that the Germans were in effect annexing.

By accepting German dictation the Bolshevik leaders obtained peace, but they were alarmed at the unexpectedly rapid disintegration of the former Russian Empire. One after another the non-Great Russian nationalities, partly of their own volition and partly under German influence, asserted their independence. The right of secession assumed a different aspect when it meant the encirclement of Russia by a ring of hostile states, largely under foreign control. As long as German expeditionary forces remained in Poland, Finland, and the Baltic provinces, in the Ukraine, the Crimea, and Transcaucasia, the Soviet government was powerless. The defeat of Germany restored their freedom of action, for it involved the removal of these troops, and left the new republics to stand or fall by their own resources. The Western powers were sympathetic to their independence—some of them even favoured the establishment of an independent Ukraine—but were not prepared to commit themselves to their support.[39] The civil war in Russia immensely complicated the situation. As most of the new states had socialist governments, it was difficult for them not to regard the Bolsheviks as their enemies. The Soviet Government, for its part, protested that the border governments were controlled by counter-revolutionaries, and that the principle of national independence was merely put forward to deceive the masses.[40] The Bolsheviks, in fact, having recognised the right of secession of the border nationalities of Russia on national grounds, found that they were being used as bases for military and political action against the Soviets. Stalin at a later date argued that 'The right to self-determination cannot and must not serve as an obstacle to the exercise by the working class of its right to dictatorship. The former must give way to the latter. That, for instance, was the case in 1920, when in order to defend the power of the working class we were obliged to march on

[39] *Cf.* Hunter Miller, *Diary*, IV. 227; d'Abernon, II. 108.
[40] Stalin, p. 73.

Warsaw.'[41] And he did not forget that Pilsudski had first marched on Kiev.

Again, in distinction from the ideas which were influential at Versailles, the Bolsheviks, even while they advocated a policy of self-determination, had never believed in small states. Lenin held that in modern times small nations had lost their significance and had become merely parasitical, fostering the imperialism of the great powers.[42] 'The advantages of large states,' he wrote, 'both from the point of view of economic progress and from the point of view of the interests of the masses, are beyond doubt.'[43]

A further motive came into play when it was realised by the Bolsheviks that in giving up the border states they were not only providing bases for possible—and indeed actual—military attacks on Russia, they were also abandoning some of the empire's most valuable material resources. Russia, declared Zinoviev before the Petrograd Soviet in 1920, has renounced the policy of exploitation, 'but we cannot do without the petroleum of Azerbaijan or the cotton of Turkestan. We take these products which are necessary for us, not as the former exploiters, but as older brothers bearing the torch of civilisation.'[44] This has rather a familiar sound. The situation was put more tactfully by Stalin. The border regions, he pointed out, which abounded in raw materials, fuel, and foodstuffs, were also the most vulnerable from a military point of view. 'They are not in a position to defend their independent existence without the military and economic assistance of Central Russia; just as Central Russia is not in a position to preserve its military and economic power without the assistance of the border regions.'[45]

The Communist government, in other words, was forced to recognise that as a practical policy national self-determination, or the right of secession, was incompatible with the military and economic interests of Soviet Russia. At the

[41] *id.* p. 168.   [42] Lenin, *Marx, Engels, Marxism,* p. 149.
[43] Lenin, V. 270.   [44] Batsell, p. 117.
[45] Stalin, pp. 117–18; *cf. id.* p. 78.

same time the right of secession was too useful a weapon
against the great capitalist empires to be abandoned in
principle. There was nothing fundamentally inconsistent in
the belief that secession from a capitalist empire was justified
as a first step towards economic freedom, whereas secession
from a communist state for the purpose of establishing a
bourgeois nationalist régime was a retrograde movement;
but it is difficult to deny that so far as the Soviet state was
concerned the right of secession had become a mere form
of words. In theory, of course, the Communist Party continued to proclaim it. As late as 1936 the new Constitution
reserved to all constituent republics the right of secession.
The theoretical guise of the right was perhaps wearing a
little thin by now, for at the Extraordinary Congress of
Soviets called to discuss the draft constitution three qualifications were introduced by Stalin himself. He declared:
'So that the right to leave the Union shall not be an ephem-
eral right it is necessary (*a*) that the Republic should not
be surrounded on all sides by territories of the Soviet
Union, but should lie on its boundaries, because in the
opposite case it would be impossible for her to leave the
Union; (*b*) that the population of the Republic should not
be less than a certain minimum, because in the opposite
case she would not be able to defend herself against the
attacks of imperialist beasts of prey; (*c*) that in the population one nationality should form a compact majority.'[46]

But, however it was defined, the truth was that the right
of secession was a theoretical right and no more. If it retained any value, apart from propaganda purposes, it was
solely as a sop to the *amour-propre* of the nationalities in the
Soviet Union. There is perhaps more in this suggestion than
may seem at first sight: In effect what Moscow was saying
to the minority nations was: 'You have the right of secession: this is an inherent right which we recognise in you by
virtue of your national status. In fact, however, military and
economic considerations make it impossible for you to
exercise the right. Nevertheless, we formally proclaim it, as a

[46] Article 17, quoted in W. E. D. Allen, *The Ukraine*, 1940, p. 319.

sign of your equal partnership in the Union.' This is, after all, not such an unreasonable attitude. The strongest criticism one might make would be that in the event of a sharp cleavage of interests between the Russian Soviet Republic and any other of the Union republics—such a cleavage as developed between North and South in the great American Union—the right of secession might become a provocation towards civil war. In fact, however, the preponderance of the R.S.F.S.R. over the other republics, taken separately or together, is so great that such a danger seems remote.

IV. Soviet Autonomy

The proclamation of an abstract right of secession did not go very far towards a solution of the problem of subject nationalities. The Soviets had recognised the independence of Finland and Poland, in both cases with more extended frontiers than would have been accepted had not the need for peace been so urgent; and treaties recognising their independence were negotiated with the Baltic and Transcaucasian states. But it was soon apparent that the simple right of self-determination was not by itself a satisfactory means of reconciling the interests of a great state and small nations which had long been integral members of its economic and political system. 'So-called independence of a so-called independent Georgia, Armenia, Poland, Finland, etc.,' wrote Stalin in 1920, is merely a means of concealing their dependence on foreign imperialists. If any of these nations decided by a majority to secede, he admitted its right of self-determination should be theoretically respected. 'But the question here is not of the indubitable rights of nations, but of the interests of the masses of people, both in the centre and in the border regions.'[47]

The acceptance of secession in practice was only a temporary measure. With the movement for Ukrainian independence, the Transcaucasian states, and the backward Asiatic peoples, the Red Army in due course dealt satis-
[47] Stalin, pp. 79–80.

factorily. But having brought the nationalities back into the Russian imperial orbit, the problem was what to do with them. The Communists, by virtue of their earlier revolutionary experience, were acutely conscious of the strength of national feeling. 'The proletariat of the nations which have been oppressing nations,' wrote Stalin in 1920, 'must exercise special caution and pay special attention to the survivals of national sentiment among the toiling masses of oppressed or non-sovereign nations.'[48] As was said above, Lenin and Stalin both interpreted the nationalism of the minority nations as primarily a reaction against Great Russian nationalism. To check its development into dangerous forms, the first essential was therefore for the Great Russians to give up the attempt to dominate the other nations, and to recognise instead the principle of national equality.[49] This was not merely a pious aspiration: to realise it in practice a Commissariat of Nationalities was set up in the early years of the Revolution under Stalin. While it served to propagate communist ideas among the non-Russian peoples, it also acted as an arbitrator between them, and protected the interests of national minorities.[50] National interests were further recognised by the establishment in 1920 of a Soviet of Nationalities as one chamber of the Russian 'Parliament'.

In the field of positive institutions, however, the most important development was the creation of a federal system of republics in what remained of the former Russian Empire. This was the communist alternative to self-determination. The Federation of the seven Union Republics, finally enacted in January, 1924, was the crown of a widespread system of autonomy. 'Soviet autonomy,' Stalin wrote, 'is not a rigid thing fixed once for all time; it permits of the most varied forms and degrees of development. It passes from narrow administrative autonomy (the Volga Germans, the Chuvashes, and the Karelians) to a wider, political

[48] *id.* p. 86.   [49] *id.* p. 157.
[50] A. Yarmolinsky, *The Jews and other Minor Nationalities under the Soviets*, 1928, p. 152.

autonomy (the Bashkirs, the Volga Tatars, and the Kirghiz); from wide political autonomy to a still wider form of
autonomy (the Ukraine and Turkestan); and finally from
the Ukrainian type of autonomy to the supreme form of
autonomy—contractual relations (Azerbaijan).'[51] It was on
the basis of such an organisation that the Communist Party
prided itself that it had found a solution for the national
question.

Such was the formal expression of the Soviet theory of
nationality. In its analysis of the national problem and
proposals for its treatment the communist system has a
great deal of value, not the less because the suggestions it
offers do not fundamentally conflict with the conclusions
forced upon us by a study of practical developments in the
Western empires. It remains to ask what success attended
the Soviet Russian treatment of the problem of national
self-determination in practice.

The first point to be noted is of course that all constitutional arrangements in the U.S.S.R. must be read in the
context provided by the supremacy of the Communist Party.
No local bodies are allowed to function in any way dangerous to its interests. Party members are expected to take the
lead right through the system, and as, especially in the more
backward areas, it was often difficult to find an adequate
supply of native party members, sometimes a large proportion of Great Russian communists had to be used. It is
only fair to state, though, that strenuous efforts were made
to obtain a supply of competent party members from among
the minority nationalities. Again, the pervasive influence of
Moscow must be interpreted in the light of the fact that, at
least during the earlier years of the new Union, central
pressure was consistently applied to suppress tendencies towards 'Great Russian chauvinism'. This pro-minority bias
of the central power must be borne in mind in estimating
the significance of the watch kept over Great Russians and
other nationalities alike by the Communist Party.

In discussing the national policy of the Soviet Union it

[51] Stalin, p. 81.

must be remembered that Russia had been relieved of its most restive minorities, the Poles and the Finns. It is hardly to be conceived that any policy would have succeeded in reconciling these to the rule of Moscow. It must also be remembered that Great Russians and Ukrainians between them constituted practically three-quarters of the whole population, and that they were not merely confined to their homeland, but also scattered throughout the whole Union. A considerable proportion of the urban working class in the Ukraine, White Russia, Azerbaijan, and Turkestan was Great Russian.[52] Thus the dictatorship of the proletariat might be not very dissimilar in practice from the predominance of the Great Russians. Indeed, in Azerbaijan, Turkmenistan, Tajikistan, Bashkiria, the Tatar Republic, Kazakstan, and the German Volga republic only a minority of the members of the Communist Party, the real ruling power, belonged to the local nationality, in the Ukraine and White Russia slightly over half, and only in Armenia and Georgia did they predominate greatly.[53] A further great advantage is that in the non-Russian districts, intermarriage is common; it forms a bond of union between the nationalities, and is producing a class which readily accepts Russian leadership.[54]

The Communist régime, as I have said, in practice denied the right of all-round self-determination, and turned the right of secession into a pious protestation, but it did not on that account believe that it could leave the national question to settle itself. Much energy and thought continued to be devoted to its solution. Wherever, as frequently occurred, nationalities overlapped, there was an elaborate system of minority legislation.[55] As far as possible an attempt was made to sort out the peoples of Russia on ethnographical grounds. In the Ukraine, for example, seven 'National Minority' regions and 366 'National Minority' village

[52] J. Maynard, *The Russian Peasant and other Studies*, 1942, p. 385.
[53] *id.* p. 386.   [54] E. S. Bates, *Soviet Asia*, 1942, p. 180.
[55] H. Kohn, *Nationalism in the Soviet Union*, 1933, p. 69.

Soviets were set up.[56] In Tsarist Russia the administrative divisions had been based on strategic and political considerations. The administrative map of communist Russia, says a hostile critic, 'has a kind of nightmare resemblance to the historical-ethnographical map of primitive Russia'[57] —a recognition of the rights of the smaller communities which was not achieved, of course, without opposition from the larger national groups.[58] In thus dividing up the country the Communists were in fact paying homage to the social democratic principle of cultural autonomy which they had condemned so bitterly in pre-revolutionary days. But their divisions were always territorial, and not personal, and they did not abandon the principle of regional autonomy, which was embodied in the federation of Union Republics, theoretically equal members of the Soviet Union, though under these republics there was created a mosaic of subordinate authorities, with the most varied powers and constitutions.

V. *The Marches of Russia*

In the border territories Moscow went even farther than conditions seemed to demand in granting autonomous privileges. A series of borderland republics was set up, with the object partly of checking tendencies towards separatism by the timely grant of concessions, and partly of attracting kindred populations on the other side of the frontier towards the Soviet Union. Such republics were the Autonomous Republic of Karelia, bordering on Finland, the White Russian Socialist Soviet Republic, next to Polish White Russia, the Moldavian Autonomous Republic, to exercise attraction on Bessarabia, the Tajik Socialist Soviet Republic, which was of use for propaganda purposes in Afghanistan, and in which Soviet literature was said to pay particular attention to Indian grievances,[59] the Kirghiz Socialist Soviet Re-

[56] Allen, p. 373.   [57] Batsell, p. 123.
[58] D. Tutaeff, *The Soviet Caucasus*, 1942, p. 71.
[59] Bates, p. 106.

public, and the Buriat-Mongol Autonomous Republic, on the frontiers of Mongolia.

Outside Russian territory proper, yet connected with it, were the three nominally Chinese states of Sin-kiang, Tannu-Tuva, and Outer Mongolia. These should not be omitted from any study of the Soviet attitude towards the question of self-determination. Social revolutions were carried through in Outer Mongolia and Tannu-Tuva under Russian auspices, and the structure of these republics has been largely Sovietized. Army, foreign trade, and all relations with the outside world are under Soviet control, but Mongol nationalism also has held Chinese influence in check.[60] Sin-kiang has a Chinese governor and is occupied by a Chinese army.[61] The U.S.S.R. assisted the Chinese against the Turki Moslem movement in Sin-kiang, for fear of its spreading to Russian Turkestan,[62] but Soviet forces withdrew when the rebellion had been crushed.[63] The most important influence operating on the province was the economic connexion with the U.S.S.R. resulting from the construction of the Turksib Railway. As a result of the opening up of communications on the Russian side of the border, it could be said in 1940, 'Sin-kiang, like Outer Mongolia, has inevitably become economically a province of the Soviet Union.'[64] Since then Chinese pressure has done much to redress the balance.

The peculiar significance of Outer Mongolia and Sin-kiang is that in them Russian and Chinese spheres of influence meet, and overlap. The small Tuva Republic after having been practically an autonomous Soviet Republic,[65] subsequently became an electoral district of the Soviet Union. Outer Mongolia and Sin-kiang are larger, however, and had strong traditional Chinese connexions. Soviet policy seemed to be to accept the suzerainty of China *de jure*

---

[60] G. F. Hudson and M. Rajchman, *An Explanatory Atlas of the Far East*, 2nd ed., 1938, p. 95.
[61] *id.* p. 98. [62] *id.* p. 99.
[63] O. Lattimore, *Inner Asian Frontiers of China*, 1940, pp. 200–1.
[64] *id* p. 199. [65] Bates, p. 91.

in these areas, but to ensure that they were under friendly governments, to develop their natural resources and their trade with the Soviet Union, and to endeavour by means of education and propaganda to secure a Russian orientation in the minds particularly of the younger generation. This was a realistic policy and appears in Outer Mongolia to have achieved a considerable degree of success.[66] It is all the more significant in the curious way in which it echoes, in a Soviet setting, some tendencies in the British Empire, and the methods employed by the United States in Central America and the Caribbean. One observer specifically compared the relations between Russia and Outer Mongolia to those which existed between the Indian Princes and the British Government.[67]

It is evident, of course, that none of the autonomous republics inside the Soviet Union have anything approaching the total independence of the British dominions. Moreover, the underlying aim of Russian policy has been to achieve their closer integration in the Soviet system. Alongside the national divisions of the U.S.S.R. there is a system of economic regions which does not coincide with them. Thus the Ukraine is divided into two regions, one agricultural and one industrial; White Russia is part of an economic region which has its capital at Smolensk in the R.S.F.S.R.[68] The economic powers of the autonomous republics are obviously limited by the existence of these economic regions. Financially, they are limited by the absence of an independent budget and of power to borrow.[69] Moscow controls directly Defence, Foreign Affairs,[70] Foreign Trade, Railways, Com-

---

[66] On the relations between Soviet Russia and Outer Mongolia, Tannu-Tuva, and Sin-kiang I derived useful information from *Soviet Asia* (Oxford Pamphlets on World Affairs, No. 62), by V. Conolly 1942.

[67] J. Levine, *La Mongolie: historique, géographique, politique*, 1937, p. 234.

[68] Maynard, p. 390.   [69] *id.* p. 397.

[70] Changes in the machinery for conducting foreign affairs resulted in the separate representation in the United Nations of White Russia and the Ukraine. There is no reason to believe that this change reflected any alteration in the control of foreign policy.

munications, Water Transport, Heavy Industry, while the Union Republics have Commissariats for Food, Light Industry, Timber, Agriculture, State Farms, Finance, Internal Trade, Internal Affairs, Justice, and Health.[71] The scope of the autonomous republics and provinces is considerably smaller. It varies because each autonomous unit has its own constitution, taking into consideration its special features,[72] but a common feature is that decrees and regulations of autonomous republics are liable to suspension by order of the Union republic in which they are included, and acts of lesser authorities may be entirely rescinded.[73] It should be noted that the Constitution of 1936 increased the elements of centralisation in the U.S.S.R. But the Kremlin, as is now clear, was by this date so acutely conscious of being on the brink of a life-and-death struggle for existence that national defence must have been the overriding motive of all its acts. A permanent tendency cannot be argued from these developments. The federalist implications in Soviet polity will become manifest only if and when the régime acquires a sense of security such as it has only recently begun to show.

VI. *National Culture in the Soviet Union*

Constitutional arrangements are, however, only the formal aspect of the problem. It is more important to know how they are applied in practice. On the question of the actual as opposed to the formal treatment of the problem of nationality in the Soviet Union information is scanty and often contradictory. Certain generalisations appear safe, however. It may be said that control of military and economic policy, of foreign trade and of general foreign relations, has been kept firmly in the hands of the central authority. On the other hand, the languages and cultural activities of the minority nationalities have received every encouragement. Even dormant nationalities have been aroused to life. 'To the White Russians,' it has been said, 'nationhood came

[71] Constitution of 1936, Articles 77, 78.   [72] Article 92.   [73] Article 82.

as an almost unsolicited gift of the Russian Revolution.'[74]

From the beginning of the revolution the Communist Party made energetic efforts to win over the minorities, even more in Asiatic than in European Russia, by abandoning the Tsarist policy of russification and by promoting national cultures and languages. The appeal of Lenin and Stalin to the Mohammedans of Russia may be taken as typical. 'Mohammedans of Russia,' they proclaimed, 'Tatars of the Volga and Crimea, Kirgiz and Sartes of Siberia and Turkestan, Turks and Tatars of Transcaucasia . . . your beliefs and customs, your national institutions and culture, are hereafter free and inviolable.'[75] Later Stalin wrote: 'I have little faith in this theory of a single, all-embracing language . . . The socialist revolution has not diminished, but rather increased the number of languages, for, by stirring up the profound depths of humanity and by pushing them into the political arena, it awakens to new life a number of hitherto unknown or little known nationalities.'[76]

These aims were not incompatible with the main Communist programme, nor did they involve any abandonment of the ideal of proletarian unity. Culture was to be 'proletarian in content and national in form'. In 1930, writing on deviations on the national question, Stalin said: 'The period of the dictatorship of the proletariat . . . is a period in which national culture, socialist in content and national in form, blossoms . . . Only if the national cultures develop will it be possible to secure the real participation of the backward nationalities in the work of socialist construction.'[77]

The pride of the Russian Communists in their work for native languages may be judged from a typical rhapsody on the cultural achievements of the régime among one obscure people. 'When the Udmert Autonomous Region was established (in 1920) only 22 per cent of the population was

[74] D. S. Mirsky, *Russia: a Social History*, 1931, p. 278.
[75] Batsell, pp. 108–9; *cf.* the proclamation to the Kalmyks, *id.* p. 168.
[76] Stalin, p. 210.   [77] Stalin, p. 261.

literate, and only 10 per cent of these were Udmerts. Before the Revolution the Udmerts received no instruction in their own language . . . There was no national press except the church missionary press . . . A national press has been organised, and during the past ten years about 300 publications, mainly text-books, have appeared. Belletristic talent is encouraged; forty-seven Udmert writers have already created much of literary value.'[78] The same writer complained that the work of converting all administrative bodies to the use of the local language is still far from complete, but he admitted that the courts of justice and a majority of the smaller governmental organisations used the native language of the masses.[79] Thus the Communist state, at least for a time, abandoned the conception of an official language. If Russian was still widely spoken it was as a matter of convenience in a multi-national state, but uniformity of language ceased to be an object of policy.[80]

An influence which works indirectly in favour of russianisation must be mentioned, however. Whereas most of the native peoples were exempt from service in the Tsarist Army, service in the Red Army became compulsory on all citizens of the Soviet Union.[81] The Red Army is perhaps the most powerful educational influence in the whole Soviet system and it naturally tends to spread the Great Russian language and culture. Moreover, in 1938 Russian became a compulsory second language in all non-Russian schools.[82] A minor point to be noted concerns the actual alphabet used for the minority languages. Soviet supporters have claimed that 'the greatest achievement in the cultural reconstruction of the national districts' was the adoption of the Latin alphabet for the languages of Soviet Asia.[83] It was said to be more adequate phonetically, and much simpler in use than the Russian Cyrillic script. In 1940, however, this step was reversed.[84]   These were merely indications of the way in which the wind was blowing. The

[78] A. Ruisakov, *The National Policy of the Soviet Union*, 1932, pp. 58–9.
[79] *id.* pp. 63–4.   [80] Kohn, p. 93.   [81] Conolly, p. 21.
[82] Maynard, p. 393.   [83] Ruisakov, p. 56.   [84] Bates, pp. 158–60.

massive revival of Great Russian patriotism reached its climax in the struggle against the German invaders, and the successful conclusion of that struggle was a triumph for patriotism in the Soviet state. The question inevitably arises: Does all this mean a return to the Russian imperialism of the past? Will the encouragement that was offered to the minority national cultures in Russia fall into perspective as a mere historical episode, a temporary retrogression in the ruthless march of Great Russian imperialism?

No certain answer can be given to these questions, but it must be said on the other side that this policy of reviving the patriotic spirit in the Soviet Union, though partly perhaps a reaction from earlier communist excesses in the opposite direction, was primarily a deliberate measure undertaken in view of the need for defence against the threat of German aggression. Now that the threat has been removed, though the official attempt to delete the history of Russia from the records except as a tale of proletarian oppression may never be revived, it is not to be expected that the belief in national cultural freedom, which has been so marked in the policy of the Soviet Union and which is prominently expounded in the writings of Lenin and Stalin, will have completely vanished. The nationality policy of the Soviet Union is all the more likely to survive because, despite some notable examples to the contrary, on the whole it proved itself in the hard testing-time of war.[85]

VII. *The Attack on National Economic Inequality*

If the Soviet Union has achieved a considerable degree of success in dealing with the national problem, this is to be attributed to more than its national cultural policy. It attacked also one of the roots of the demand for national self-determination—the economic inequality of nations in-

[85] A decree of the Praesidium of the Supreme Soviet of October 1945 withdrew electoral privileges from four autonomous republics and one autonomous region, probably for disloyalty during the war with Germany.

side a single political system. 'A series of republics and peoples,' declared a Party Resolution of 1923, 'who have not seen, or have almost not passed through, the stage of capitalism, who have almost no proletariat of their own, and who, consequently, have remained backward, are unable fully to utilise the rights and possibilities given to them by this principle of equality of nationalities; they are unable, without effective and unceasing external assistance, to raise themselves to the highest degree of development, and to place themselves on an equal footing with the nationalities which have already advanced in this respect. The reasons for this actual inequality lie not only in the historical past of these peoples, but also in the policy of Tsarism and of the Russian bourgeoisie which always aimed to convert the boundary regions into markets for raw products where the manufacturing central regions could exercise their exploiting methods.'[86] They recognised that this inequality could not be overcome without long-continued effort. As a Resolution of a Party Congress in 1921 declared, 'any mechanical transplantation to the Eastern border regions of the economic measures of Central Russia, which are suitable only for a higher stage of economic development, must be rejected.'[87] But the conclusion drawn was not that the backward nations must be left in their condition of backwardness, but that since national inequality rested on economic inequality, the remedy was to be found not merely in a stimulation of backward cultures, but in the removal of the economic roots of their backwardness.[88] As a Resolution of the Twelfth Party Congress proclaimed, the more advanced regions must come to the help of the backward ones. 'This aid must first of all be expressed by taking practical measures to organise industrial centres in the republics of the formerly oppressed nations, and in attracting the greatest possible number of local workers to these industries.'[89]

The economic development of the undeveloped areas of

[86] Batsell, pp. 639–40.   [87] Stalin, p. 277.   [88] Ruisakov, p. 19.
[89] *id.* p. 20; *cf.* Stalin, pp. 94, 101, 115, 142, 156.

the U.S.S.R., and the exploitation of unused raw materials, was undertaken with amazing energy and success. Commenced for the reasons given above, it was continued on grounds of military security. Along with the new industries a new industrial proletariat was built up, which as well as including many Russian immigrants—voluntary or compulsory recruits—drew also upon native sources. In normal circumstances such industrialisation in backward areas means a rise in the standard of living. Even if, under the Spartan conditions of the Five Year Plans, this did not come about, at least the prospects of future improvement were evident. The Soviet Union was to be no Habsburg Empire with a comparatively rich industrial and financial centre in striking contrast with miserably poor agricultural provinces. The minority nationalities had the evidence of economic progress on a gigantic scale in their own homelands and under their own eyes. If the Soviet Union eventually proves to have dealt successfully with the problem of uniting the most varied nationalities in a single great federation, that success will have to be attributed in no small measure to the steps it took from the very beginning to bring the 'subject nations' into the full stream of industrial development, and so to remove the source of economic inequality and exploitation.

VIII. *Nationalist Opposition in the Soviet Union*

Before drawing any conclusions as to the success of the Russian alternative to self-determination, however, it is necessary to consider the case of certain nationalities in which national opposition appeared. It must be premised that of the history of the lesser nationalities, especially in Soviet Asia, little is known. It was not to be expected that the chiefs and mullahs would watch the crumbling of their authority without some resistance. All one can say is that the destruction of reactionary authorities and the establishment of the Soviet system seems to have been successfully carried through without arousing any concerted national resistance on the part of these peoples. A chapter entitled 'Traitors' in a work of popularisation on Russian Asia speaks of a 'pan-Mongol' movement in the Buriat-Mongol A.S.S.R. in 1937. Fortunately, it says, 'the workers and peasants caught them out,' and a veil is drawn over the sequel.[90] Soviet authority does not seem anywhere to have been seriously challenged.

Transcaucasia, with its somewhat more advanced populations, presented a more difficult problem for the Communist régime. It holds fragments of many different peoples in its valleys. Its five main groups are divided into over forty sub-divisions, of which twenty to twenty-five are indigenous.[91] Movements for autonomy had appeared in this area in 1905–6, but when the February revolution broke out in 1917 separation was not at first thought of in any part of the Caucasus.[92] The three largest groups, Georgians, Azerbaijans, and Armenians, however, elected assemblies, which, in the chaos of civil war, were easily led in the direction of separatism.

After its re-conquest of Transcaucasia, the Communist government faced the failure of the policy of self-determination, in practice withdrew the right of secession, and applied the alternative policy of regional and cultural autonomy. In the Northern Caucasus, one autonomous republic, six regions, and one district were set up, as part of the R.F.S.S.R. In Transcaucasia three Soviet republics, which were first federated into the Transcaucasian Federated Republic, and subsequently formed into separate Union republics, were established. Under them there are three autonomous republics and two autonomous provinces. That this apparently complex and unwieldy territorial solution has worked is shown by the absence of serious disturbances since it was founded.[93]

[90] G. D. R. Phillips, *Dawn in Siberia*, 1942, pp. 164–172.
[91] I. Bowman, *The New World*, 1924, p. 452.
[92] Z. Avalishvili, *The Independence of Georgia in International Politics*, 1918–1921, pp. 1, 3.
[93] Yarmolinsky, p. 154.

On the northern frontiers of European Russia two minor national problems appeared—in the provinces of Eastern Karelia and Ingria, bordering Finland. By treaty with Finland the Soviet Government had promised autonomy to Eastern Karelia, and an autonomous republic was consequently set up. But the Karelian situation seems generally to have been handled rather badly by the Soviet Union, probably through inability to decide between two possible objectives. The territory was desired for strategic reasons, but this element in the situation was naturally not given much publicity until the war with Finland in 1940. One possible method of stabilising the situation was to attempt to sever all ties between Karelia and Finland, where irredentist designs were not absent, as was shown by the help Finnish Activists gave to the Karelian rebellion of 1921, though the Finnish Government maintained a correct attitude.[94] This involved emphasising the differences between the Karelian people and language and the Finnish people and language. The alternative was to attempt to use Eastern Karelia as a bait to attract the population on the other side of the Finnish frontier, which involved a stress on similarities rather than differences. The Finnish tendency prevailed up to 1935. Then, in consequence of the shift to a strictly defensive policy, the Finnish communist leaders of Eastern Karelia were accused of nationalist deviations and put on one side, and the Karelians set up as a nationality in their own right. A partial return to the earlier policy appeared in the establishment of the Finnish Karelian Republic, by the incorporation of additional territory after the war with Finland. The source of this second tendency was now, however, not so much any hope of expansion, as the presence of a potentially hostile, and certainly unfriendly, régime in Finland.

In addition to Karelia, the irredentism of less responsible elements in Finland appears to have affected the Ingrian population of some 150,000 in the neighbourhood of Leningrad. The fantastic conception was actually put forward of

[94] *Survey of International Affairs, 1920–1923*, p. 246.

an independent Ingria, linking Finland and Estonia, in which the great Russian metropolis of Leningrad was to be permitted to enjoy the status of a free city.[95] The only result of this fantasy appears to have been the deportation by the Soviet Union of many unfortunate Ingrians from their homeland for reasons of security.[96]

Finally, we come to the one really great national problem of Russia, the Ukraine. Although there has never been an independent state in the Ukraine, except in 1918–19, plans for one have occasionally been put forward by politicians who hoped in this way to destroy the power of the Russian Empire. The Germans, after the defeat of Russia in 1917, planned to establish the Ukraine as a separate state under German protection, and to use it as the granary for Central Europe. For a year or so a series of nominally independent governments succeeded one another in Kiev. None of them secured any real popular support from the Ukrainian people. 'The difficulty in the Ukraine,' wrote General Max Hoffman, 'is simply that the Central *Rada* has only our rifles behind it. The moment we withdraw our troops their authority will collapse at once.'[97] The general population was indifferent or hostile to its self-appointed leaders,[98] and when the Red Army eventually captured the Ukrainian capital it was with Ukrainian regiments.[99] The Bolsheviks, while they professed their willingness to grant independence to the Ukraine if it were desired by a majority of the workers and peasants, never seriously contemplated separation. Lenin put as the alternatives, whether the Ukraine should be united with Russia or whether she should remain independent, but added, 'and in the latter case what *federal* relations shall be established between this re-

[95] This plan is mentioned in an article in *Contemporary Russia* (Vol. I, No. 1, October 1936, p. 51), a periodical which appeared from 1936 to 1939, nominally for the study of Russian and Eastern European questions, but in fact, judging by its contents, for the purpose of advocating the partition of the Soviet Union.

[96] E. Ammende, *Human Life in Russia*, 1936, p. 130.

[97] Wheeler-Bennett, p. 316.   [98] Allen, p. 280.   [99] *id.* p. 281.

public and Russia.'[100] The issue was settled in 1920 by the Ukraine entering into a military and economic union with the R.F.S.S.R.

Having successfully dealt with the not very strong movement for separation, the Soviets now began to apply their policy of stimulating national culture in the Ukraine. 'It is obvious,' Stalin declared in 1921, 'that the Ukrainian nation exists, and it is the duty of communists to develop its culture. We must not go counter to history.'[101] A policy of vigorous Ukrainisation was therefore followed for the next ten years. Despite the fact that many serious students challenged the view that Ukrainian was distinct from Great Russian,[102] its use in schools and in the press was consistently encouraged.

An alteration in the policy of Moscow towards the Ukraine is said to have resulted from the struggle over collectivisation. Soviet policy was also doubtless influenced by the knowledge that Germany, reviving her plans of 1917, was counting on Ukrainian separatism as one of the cards in her hand against the Soviet Union. Moscow took its measures of defence in time. Accusations of separatism played a large part in the trials of March, 1938.[103] It had been clear from the beginning of the Soviet régime that national liberties would not be tolerated if they appeared to be in any way dangerous to the safety of the state. Throughout the history of Soviet Russia, it may be said, both the right of self-determination, and any measure of national cultural autonomy, have invariably been subordinated to the economic policy and the military security of the Union.

[100] Batsell, p. 104.   [101] Stalin, p. 110.
[102] A. Meillet, *Les Langues dans l'Europe nouvelle*, 1918, pp. 257–8; Haumant, pp. 35–6.
[103] Maynard, p 399.

IX. *The Success of the Soviet Alternative to Self-determination*

Precise and reliable information about the Soviet Union is still in all fields difficult to acquire. In spite of this, it is perhaps justifiable to draw some provisional conclusions from this discussion of Soviet national policy. It is clear that for all the nationalities now included in the Soviet Union the right of self-determination, if it means a right of secession, is a formula devoid of meaning. The interesting question is to ask whether the Russians have been able on any other basis to deal satisfactorily with the problem of 'subject nationalities'. In his speech on the admission of the Soviet Union to the League of Nations, in September, 1934, Litvinov said: 'I will make so bold as to claim that never before have so many nations co-existed so peacefully within a single state, never before have so many nations in one state had such free cultural development and enjoyed their own national culture as a whole and the use of their own language in particular. In no other country are all manifestations of race and national prejudice so resolutely put down and eradicated as in the Soviet Union.'[104]

An equally high testimonial was given by a historian of nationalism, who declared that in the Soviet Union we have the only multi-national state in which the national question fails to dominate state policy and public life.[105] The study of American and British imperialism suggests, however, that in this field Soviet development is in line with what has been happening elsewhere. As the authors of *Nationalism* write, 'Soviet Russia seems to be moving towards a pattern, familiar in Great Britain, and elsewhere, of a major nationalism comprising within itself minor nationalisms which are active mainly in the cultural field.'[106] The emphasis during the years of war was naturally on loyalty to the Soviet Fatherland, but there is still no reason to believe that this

---

[104] *Documents on International Affairs, 1934*, 1935, p. 104.
[105] Kohn, p. 113. [106] *Nationalism*, p. 80.

major loyalty is incompatible with the existence of lesser loyalties to nations inside the Union, and with the survival of their cultural nationalities.

It will be worth while, in conclusion, to summarise the main features of the Soviet solution. In the first place, self-determination, in spite of what I have said, may be allowed to have had a certain place in the Soviet plan, for nationalities which, for historical reasons, were irreconcilable, and were also territorially separable—the Poles and the Finns. At the same time, the history of relations between the Soviet Union and the Finns shows that strategic interests have to be taken into account. Secondly comes the theoretical right of secession. This is merely a form of expression for the principle of national equality. Thirdly, the power of elements in any minority populations which are naturally antagonistic to the Soviet régime—such as feudal landowners, priests, or bourgeoisie—is destroyed. Fourthly, linguistic or cultural and economic inequality are treated positively by measures designed to stimulate national culture and promote economic advancement.[107] Fifthly, control of the main strings of economic and political power is kept firmly in the hands of the Soviet authorities, but that does not mean the absence of considerable local activity. In the central institutions of the U.S.S.R. the multi-national nature of the state is recognised in theory by the existence of the Soviet of Nationalities, elected by the constituent and the autonomous republics, the autonomous provinces and national regions, and having equal rights with the Soviet of the Union.[108] The establishment and maintenance by a minority of a new social order has obviously involved merciless repression throughout the Soviet Union; but at least an outline has been sketched for the separation of nationality from sovereignty, which may be completed in happier days.

Finally, the nations of the U.S.S.R. are bound together,

[107] Equal rights, irrespective of nationality, are guaranteed by the Constitution of 1936.
[108] Constitution of 1936, Articles 35, 37.

and their national aspirations prevented in fact from developing into secessionism, in two ways. In so far as communism has succeeded in establishing a generally accepted ideal for the progress of the whole Union, this is a spiritual bond uniting all its peoples. It is a new form of patriotism, and not the worse because it is directed to internal progress rather than to foreign conquest. At the same time, the Soviet Union is rapidly becoming—perhaps has already become—an economic nexus from which no part can be severed without severe injury both to the part and the whole, and a vast defensive structure, the parts of which are equally necessary to one another from the strategic point of view. Economic and military inter-dependence from above, local self-government, cultural autonomy and national equality from below—that is the ideal scheme, however many faults there may be in its present realisation, which the U.S.S.R. seems to be striving to achieve.[109]

[109] An article on 'The Nationalities Policy of the Soviet Union' in *Social Research* (Vol. II, No. 2), New York, May 1944, by Erich Hula, gives a verdict which appears to be very similar to my own.

XIII. Nationalism outside Europe

I. National Self-determination in Non-European Countries and the Policies of the Imperial Powers

As HAS BEEN seen, the idea of nationalism was a product of Western conditions, but, with the extension of European influence throughout the world, Western political ideas, self-determination among them, inevitably spread in its train. To a certain extent this was an unexpected and even an undesired development. The general assumption at the beginning of the process of European conquest was that peoples and civilisations so different from those of the West would continue to retain their traditional political characteristics even after European had replaced native rulers. The influence of the West proved impossible to limit in this way, and the progress anticipated by Macaulay, in a famous passage,[1] is now evidently not only in the British, but in all colonial territories.

The first point of importance, then, in the consideration of extra-European attempts to achieve national self-determination, is that they are everywhere to be attributed to European influence. Because it appeared under the influence of Western rule, nationalism in Asia and in Africa tended to follow the lines of political cleavage imposed by the West. The Arab national movement, for example, split

[1] 'It may be that the public mind of India may expand under our system till it has out-grown that system; that by good government we may educate our subjects into a capacity for better government; that, having become instructed in European knowledge, they may, in some future age, demand European institutions. Whether such a day will come I know not. But never will I attempt to avert or to retard it. Whenever it comes it will be the proudest day in English history.' *Speech on the Government of India*, 10 July, 1833.

up into Egyptian, Syrian, Iraqui, Jordanian, Libyan, Tunisian, Algerian, and Moroccan nationalist movements.[2] In the Malayan countries of South-East Asia and the East Indies, separate nationalist movements have appeared in the possessions of British, Dutch, and Americans, despite considerable homogeneity of race and culture.[3] On the other hand, in British India, where there are distinctions of every conceivable kind, in the beginning a united national movement appeared, under the influence of a common rule. European conquest, as well as spreading the Western ideal of national self-determination, was the stimulant which provoked national spirit into action. It may be asked how it was, given the strength of the colonial powers and the marked political and economic weakness of their subject populations, that the demand for national independence stood any chance of success. The answer is partly that some of these empires, having accepted the idea of self-determination in principle, could not wholeheartedly deny it to their own subjects, but above all, that outside as inside Europe, subject nations found their opportunity in the rivalries of their rulers. The break-up of the Habsburg Empire under foreign attack is paralleled by that of the Ottoman dominions. The rivalry of Russia and Great Britain gave Persia and Afghanistan their chance of remaining independent and developing into national states. British influence assisted in the temporary loosening of Chinese control over Tibet. During the Second World War Japan appealed, with varying success, to anti-European national movements in Thailand, Burma, the Dutch East Indies, and the Philippines, while Russian, Chinese, and Japanese hostilities between them provided the opportunity for a nascent Mongol nationalism.

The proclamation of war aims in the first World War, including a right of self-determination, was also a powerful influence. It did not occur to the Allied governments that the propaganda they employed against the Central Em-

[2] *Cf.* G. Antonius, *The Arab Awakening*, 1938, p. 100.
[3] Emerson, Mills, and Thompson, p. 17.

pires would affect their own empires fundamentally, or that by proclaiming the principle of self-determination they had laid the axe at the roots of their own colonial domains. But after 1918 they could only keep other nations in political subjection at the cost of moral inconsistency, except in so far as it could be maintained that they were unfit for self-government. This meant the development of a new situation, to which they had to adapt themselves. In practice three methods of dealing with the national demands of colonial populations were evolved—assimilation, strongest in the French Empire and the Soviet Union, self-determination, which the British and Americans have laid down as their aim, and suppression, the chosen policy of the Italians and Japanese.

II. *Nations and States*

With the defeat of Italy and Japan the type of imperialism that relied purely upon suppression became a thing of the past, but the pressure for rights of self-government continued. Will the national movements of Asia and Africa be able to consolidate the gains they have made? This is equivalent to asking whether nation states such as the theory of self-determination requires can be set up outside Europe and the countries populated from Europe. Are nation states a practical potentiality of the many non-European countries newly converted to nationalism? Do the Chinese and the Indians constitute nations, in the sense in which the Welsh or the Norwegians do? Is there a single Arab nation? Are tribal countries like the Congo or Nigeria nations? Is there a nation capable of self-determination in the South Arabian peninsula? The only way of attempting to answer these questions is to discuss the problems of different countries in turn, taking them in the various categories into which they fall.

1. CHINA
Beginning our analysis with the larger nations and working

downwards, the first problems we have to consider are those of the great civilisations of China, India, and the Arab world. Can China constitute a single nation state? It was regarded by Sun-Yat-Sen as a unique form of nation, a race-nation.[4] The Chinese word *Min*, which appears in *Kuomintang*, is closer to the German *Volk* than to the English *People*.[5] The Chinese have a common language, a common civilisation going back for thousands of years, a homeland that they have inhabited for as long, and a tradition of imperial unity. Until China experienced the influence of Western democratic ideas there was no explicitly national conscience, but although there are great differences in spoken language and physical characteristics between the inhabitants of the various parts of the great Chinese domain, there can be no real doubt that the Chinese are a single people. If a people so numerous, inhabiting a territory so extensive, is capable of being a nation state, China is one. In China proper there can be no problem of self-determination, except that of size.

The non-Chinese provinces of the former empire present a different picture. The decline of Manchu authority in the nineteenth century involved a relaxation of Chinese rule in the outlying portions of the empire, and the new situation was recognised, when the republic was set up, by the establishment of a federative structure, including Chinese, Mongols, Tibetans, Manchus, and Moslems, and symbolised by the five-barred flag. The dynamic of the nationalist movement, however, operated against this federal tendency, and the secessionist activities of provincial war-lords led the Kuomintang to adopt a policy of stricter centralisation, in so far as its power allowed. Between 1927 and 1931 the five-barred flag was abandoned and an attempt to recover Chinese control over the dependent nations initiated. Opposition was encountered from Tibetans, Mongols, and the Moslem Turkis of Sin-kiang.[6] Subsequently the Japanese invasion altered the context of the whole question.

[4] P. M. A. Linebarger, *The Political Doctrines of Sun-Yat-Sen*, 1937, p. 62.
[5] *id.* p. 228.   [6] Hudson and Rajchman, p. 52.

With the removal of the Japanese from the mainland of Asia it recovered its importance. The Chinese were faced with the demand for self-determination in their turn, and the rivalry of Russian and Chinese influences came in to complicate the problem.

2. INDIA

India, unlike China, is a sub-continent riddled with internal national divisions. Here all that unites China—languages, race, common civilisation, tradition of political unity—is absent. The problem of India, says Tagore, is the problem of the world in miniature. 'India is too vast in its area and too diverse in its races. It is many countries packed into one geographical receptacle.'[7] Even among the Hindus there is the barrier of caste. 'When we talk of Western nationality,' again to quote Tagore, 'we forget that the nations there do not have that physical repulsion, one for the other, that we have between different castes.'[8] If France could not properly be a united nation before the system of privileged orders of the *ancien régime* had been abolished, it might be asked, how can India with its far profounder divisions of caste be one? Race, language, religion, and to a certain extent territorial situation, all separate the Moslems from the Hindus. Their whole history deepens the gulf between them. 'Their past,' it has been said, 'is a past of mutual destruction.'[9] The closer the prospect of self-government came to India, the bitterer became the rivalries between the Hindu and Moslem communities. Only the Westernised, educated Indians were capable of envisaging a nation which would override the traditional Hindu-Moslem differences. These were intensified by the association of the religious ideologies respectively with Hindi and Urdu.

'So long as authority was firmly established in British hands,' declared the Simon Commission, 'and self-government was not thought of, Hindu-Moslem rivalry was con-

[7] Rabindranath Tagore, *Nationalism*, 1917, p. 114.   [8] *id.* pp. 123–4.
[9] B. R. Ambedkar, *Thoughts on Pakistan*, 1941, p. 30.
N.S.N.S.D.

fined within a narrower field.'[10] In the Indian states, where the national movement made less progress, there was less communal friction. But in British India the history of the last twenty years before independence was one of increasing friction between the religious communities.[11] It is interesting to see the way in which the problems created by the attempt to put the theory of national self-determination into practice reappear in the most diverse environments, and on the most varying scales. The growth of Moslem demands has been compared to the rise of the Sudeten movement in Czechoslovakia—with the claim to separate nationhood, denial of national unity, atrocity charges, demand for partition, and frontier disputes.[12] The sequence of events is well put by E. I. J. Rosenthal. The great leader, on the Moslem side, of the struggle for Indian self-government was Mohammad Ali Jinnah. In the effort to win mass support the religious factor had to be called on. Growing mutual fear divided the Moslems and Hindus, until Jinnah and his Moslem league came to seem more a defensive force against growing Hindu dominance than against an obviously decaying British rule. In 1940 Jinnah demanded a separate Moslem homeland, and the last step was taken when, in August, 1942, a resolution of the All-India Moslem League asserted the right 'of 100 million Moslems in India to establish sovereign states in zones which are their homelands and where they are in the majority.' Self-determination for Moslem India—that is, *Pakistan*—was proclaimed as the goal.[13]

The next step was an appeal by Mr. Jinnah, the leader of the Moslem League, to the Sikh community to join the Moslems in the demand for self-determination. He was only willing to offer the Sikhs minority rights, whereas they required a partition of the Punjab and strongly resented the plan of the Moslem League for incorporating them against their will in a new Moslem political community. The dis-

---

[10] Report of the Simon Commission, 1930, I. 29. [11] Ambedkar, p. 180.
[12] B. Prasad, *The Hindu-Muslim Questions*, 1941, p. 72.
[13] E. I. J. Rosenthal, *Islam in the Modern National State*, 1965, p. 202.

pute between Hindus, Moslems, and Sikhs, like similar disagreements in Europe, was over the size and nature of the community that had the right to self-determination.

The national problems of India are so acute and on such a large scale that they exhibit with a high degree of magnification the peculiar difficulties involved in the theory of self-determination. For the Congress Party nationality was essentially political and territorial, but, given democratic institutions and the existence of a large Hindu majority, this was a basis which the non-Hindu communities did not feel they could safely accept; nor indeed were all the Hindus themselves prepared to accept it. In an acute analysis of Congress ideas V. V. D. Savarkar declared, in December, 1939: 'The whole Congress ideology was vitiated *ab initio* by its unwitting assumption that the territorial unity, a common habitat, was the only factor that constituted and ought to and must constitute a nation. This conception of a territorial nationality has since then received a rude shock in Europe itself . . . All nations carved out to order on the territorial design without any other common bond to mould each of them into a national being have gone to rack and ruin . . . Cultural, linguistic, historical and such other organic affinities proved stronger than the territorial one.'[14]

But in India, as elsewhere, a theoretical demonstration of the inapplicability of the idea of the nation state was from the point of view of practical politics ineffective. The demand for national independence was a fact which, wherever it existed, was not to be argued away. Nationalist ideology was so strong, India so great and populous, and the resources of Great Britain so comparatively limited, that the conclusion had to be drawn that the maintenance of British rule was no longer a policy capable of being enforced. It must be emphasised, moreover, that the difficulty was essentially a political one. The nations of India already had, and had always had under British rule, complete freedom of religion, language, and culture. This, indeed, has so much

[14] Quoted in Ambedkar, pp. 134–5.

come to be taken as a matter of course that no credit is given
for it, and it is forgotten that it is not a universal experience
in the history of conquest and domination. But alien rulers
cannot expect to maintain their sway on the strength of the
bad things they have not done in the past, and the demand
now was for the political right of self-government. The real
problem was for Indians to agree on what form this should
take. India is composed of many communities, some of
which, always distinct in their culture, are rapidly becoming politically conscious of their separate national identities
A solution which subjected large blocks of Sikhs to Moslems,
or Moslems to Hindus, had little prospect of being a peaceful or permanent one. Even between different Hindu
peoples—Sikhs, Bengalis, Rajputs, Madrasis, Marathas,
and so on—there are strong antipathies. 'The Hindu provinces,' again to quote Dr. Ambedkar's clear-sighted
analysis, 'have no common traditions and no interests to
bind them.'[15]

The first step towards a solution of the national problem
in India, as elsewhere, had to be recognition of the fact that
self-determination, if it is to be applied at all, must be
applied, so far as is possible, to real self-conscious communities. Wherever a separate community inhabits a
distinct region, it should automatically be entitled to regional autonomy, with powers varying in accordance with
its size and separateness. This would not be possible, of
course, without extensive changes in provincial boundaries,
but there is nothing sacrosanct about these. In their latest
form, they were largely the result of the chance circumstances in which territory passed under British rule. 'The
existing provincial boundaries,' the Report of the Simon
Commission says, 'in more than one case embrace areas and
peoples of no natural affinity, and sometimes separate those
who might under a different scheme be more naturally
united.'[16] Thus it held that a strong case had been made
out for the creation of a separate Orissa province.[17] Con-

[15] Ambedkar, p. 6.   [16] *Report of Simon Commission*, II. 24.
[17] *Report of Simon Commission*, II. 50–1. It has been urged that the fate of

gress itself formerly declared in favour of linguistic provinces,[18] but clearly language is only one among many
considerations to be taken into account, such as race,
religion, economic ties, geographical contiguity, balance
between town and country, and between coastline and
interior.[19] And it must not be forgotten that the most important factor of all is the wishes of the people themselves,
in so far as they are ascertainable.

No possible modification of provincial boundaries, however, could eliminate the problem of minorities. The
establishment of *Pakistan* still left millions of Moslems in
Hindu territory,[20] and also placed an appreciable number
of Hindus under Moslem rule. The only lasting solution, it
has been said, is their transfer;[21] but if such a policy is
conceivable in parts of Europe, it can never be complete
with the far greater numbers involved in India. Another
danger in the path of self-determination inside India is
irredentism. The fact must be faced that even on a basis of
partition national homogeneity is not attainable in India.
This is not a purely negative conclusion: it has one very
important positive implication. If the establishment of more
or less united nation states, which was the main justification
for the partition of India into separate sovereign states, was
not in fact going to be achieved by it, then the case for a
complete separation became distinctly weaker.

The problem of the future of Indian government is far
too complex for an adequate survey in this place, but from
all that has been said the conclusion seems to emerge that
India can neither be united nor divided. There is nothing
paradoxical or impractical in this verdict. The policy

---

the Curzon partition of Bengal in 1905, which created a new Moslem
state out of Eastern Bengal and Assam, is a warning against tampering
with provincial divisions; but its reversal in 1911 seems to be rather a
proof of the more advanced political consciousness of the Hindus, and
of the strength of the pressure they could then bring to bear as compared
with the Moslems, than of any inherent defects in the idea itself.

[18] Ambedkar, pp. 21–2. [19] *Report of Simon Commission*, II. 25.
[20] Ambedkar, p. 112. [21] *id.* p. 110.

logically to be followed was neither to partition India nor
to attempt to treat it as a united nation state; but on the one
hand to divide it into autonomous provinces, and these
where necessary into smaller self-governing entities, and on
the other to unite the provinces or states under a federal
government for those functions in which separation would
have harmful results. It has even been suggested that the
provinces into which India might be divided should have
been as independent as the British dominions, except for
central control over defence, customs, currency, and
foreign relations. [22]

I do not pretend to have made other than a partial and
introductory analysis of the Indian question, but for the
study of self-determination the problems India presents are
too relevant to be omitted from consideration. The unity of
India has been destroyed by nationalism. This, if it represents the facts, is not necessarily a bad result, but it remains
to be seen whether any peaceful and stable settlement is
possible on the basis of self-determination.

3. THE WORLD OF ISLAM

The Indian sub-continent presents in its acutest form the
problem of the conflict between a religious ideology and the
claims of the national state. Religion and politics have been
the source of endless conflict in European history, but there
is a difference. Christianity was always prepared to render
unto Caesar what was Caesar's, though there was frequently
dispute about what that was. For Islam everything was
God's. Just because Islam was never a Church, there could
be no secular state. On the broadest level, the universal
brotherhood of all Moslems was not reconcilable with the
claims of the national state; within the Islamic state, a non-
Moslem could not be a member of the community. Of
relations between the Moslem majority and non-Moslem
minorities, a Pakistan educationalist observes, 'We possess
common nationality, which is a legal concept, but we are

[22] In an address by Sir Firoz Khan Noon to students at the Aligarh
Moslem University, 24 August 1942.

not the same nation, which is a sociological concept. We are *not* one nation, and yet we are citizens of the same State.'[23] This is why patriotism is compatible with Islam, but nationalism, unless every member of the state is a Moslem, is not.[24] There is thus a political as well as a religious source of difficulty. Compared with Pakistan, in the Arab world of the Near and Middle East religious problems are far less difficult, but political divisions are greater. As T. E. Lawrence wrote, 'A first difficulty of the Arab movement was to say who the Arabs were. Being a manufactured people, their name had been changing in sense slowly year by year. Once it meant an Arabian. There was a country called Arabia; but this was nothing to the point. There was a language called Arabic; and in it lay the test.'[25] The only possible definition of the Arabs is linguistic, including all those people who speak Arabic. They are divided between a number of states. At the Islamic Conference of Jerusalem, in December, 1931, the Arab members proclaimed a pan-Arab goal in the form of a declaration that: '1. The Arab lands are a complete and indivisible whole . . . 2. All efforts in every Arab country are to be directed towards the single goal of their complete independence, in their entirety and unified . . .'[26] In fact, however, the Arab states of the Middle East have shown singularly little tendency towards fusion. Arab Congresses have tended to bring together groups of discontented Arabs, but not the Arab kings or their ministers.[27] Even now Arab nationality as a whole seems likely to remain within the field in which it already exists, that of language, culture and political alliance, and unlikely to be translated into terms of the single nation state. The last thirty years have only confirmed the trend towards division in the Arab world. Even the rudiments of unity lasted no longer than the struggle against Ottoman dominion or foreign rule.

[23] Cited in Rosenthal, p. 219.   [24] *id.* p. 65.
[25] T. E. Lawrence, *Seven Pillars of Wisdom*, 1926, Ch. II.
[26] *Survey of International Affairs*, 1934, p. 107.
[27] E. Monroe, *The Mediterranean in Politics*, 1938, p. 234.

The successor states to the defunct Ottoman or European Empires, and other Moslem states, stretching in a belt from Morocco to Indonesia, can be classified in terms of their movement away from the Islamic ideal and towards the national state in which religion and politics are separate spheres. Turkey has advanced farthest in this direction. The abolition of the caliphate by Kemal Atatürk, his substitution of the Western Swiss Civil Code for Islamic law and establishment of a secular education, the assertion in the Turkish Constitution that 'Sovereignty belongs to the nation without conditions and restrictions,'—all seem to indicate that Turkey is the complete nationalist state. Yet it can be said that 'Islam is still a problem in Turkey after forty years.'[28] Tunisia, though in a less ruthless way, has moved almost as far in the same direction. The extensive kingdom of Saudi Arabia and the smaller sheikdoms have hardly yet begun to experience the pressures of nationalism on Islam. We may be sure, that as they do, so the western national state will emerge and religion be thrust back into a more limited field of action.

This will not solve the nationality problems of the Arab world.

Though the Arab population of this extensive area is united in religion, there are enclaves which differ from it in important respects; such are the Christian Lebanese, the Druse, and the Kurds. The Maronites of the Lebanon are Arab-speaking and have in the past made their contribution to Arab nationalism, but they are Christian in religion. The Jebel Druse of Syria have traditions of independence and in their mountain fastnesses considerable capacity for defending it. The Kurds, numbering in all some three millions, about half in Turkey and the rest divided between Iran, Iraq, and Syria, present a more difficult problem. In Syria and Iraq local autonomy for the Kurds would be desirable, though it is not clear how this might react on the Turkish policy of assimilation. Finally, there are the Jews of Israel. How can their presence be reconciled with awakened Arab

[28] Rosenthal, p. 312.

nationalism? Will their history, in the territory they have conquered, be like that of a former kingdom of Jerusalem, the crusading state which survived for generations in the heart of Islam but always as a beleaguered garrison, saved by repeated infusions of blood from the outer world? Or will Israel become one more in a mosaic of Near Eastern nation states? The latter becomes more likely as both Arabs and Jews move away from the state founded on religious ideology and towards one based on nationalism.

4. SMALL NATIONS

Besides the greater non-European peoples of the Old World there are also many smaller national units, some of which we have already mentioned. Many of these can hardly be considered capable of standing by themselves as independent, sovereign states. Nationalism was apt to be regarded in the nineteenth century as a phenomenon peculiar to the greater peoples. German, French, or Italian nationalism was recognised, but not Welsh or Alsatian. This was because what came later to be known as the right of national self-determination was identified with the establishment of a sovereign state, and of this the smaller nations were obviously incapable. If we accept the view that all nations, however small, have cultural and political rights, though in varying degree, we can recognise that even the smallest national communities are entitled to protection for their culture and, wherever they are sufficiently separate, to regional autonomy, even if they are not in the nature of things able to constitute absolutely independent states.

The island of Malta, though it is more properly considered as part of Europe, may conveniently be taken in illustration of this point. The Maltese are a distinct people, with a separate language of their own, but Italian influence, especially through the Church and the law-courts, has naturally been great on the island. It reached its height by 1933. The British administration had made no efforts to counteract this Italian influence, and the grant of a Constitution seemed to the Italian party the first step towards the secession of Malta from the British Empire and its attachment to Italy. What saved Malta for the British, and incidentally for the Maltese, was the adoption at this time of a new course by British policy. An energetic attack was begun on Italian influence in the island, but instead of endeavouring to replace it with British, a belated attempt was made to revive the apparently dying Maltese nationality, which met with immediate and great success. To the disgust of the Italian Government, and Italianate elements in Malta, the Maltese language was introduced into the lawcourts and administration. Maltese culture was encouraged, social barriers between British and Maltese were reduced, and there was an effort to improve the economic prosperity of the island. This policy was destined to be completed in due course by the establishment of self-government. Even so far as it had gone by 1939 it was justified by success, not the least of the reasons for which may have been the consideration in the Maltese mind that under the British Crown there was a future for Maltese nationality: as an integral part of a Fascist Empire there was none.

Intermediate between a national community as small as that of Malta, and the great nation-civilisations, are nations such as the Thais, Filipinos, Burmese, Iranians, Afghans, Tibetans, Ethiopians, and others.[29] These have a more or less preponderant nucleus of homogeneous population, which on grounds of language, race, or political traditions can be regarded as belonging to a single nation, and may therefore be considered to possess the capacity for constituting nation states. Other small nations are still tribal, and whether such peoples can develop into nation states is a subject to be discussed in the next section.

5. TRIBAL PEOPLES: *Africa*

Most of Africa and part of Asia, is still basically tribal. Among recognised states, Afghanistan and Saudi Arabia

[29] The influence of changing Western ideas of nationality, and the decline of the territorial conception of the state, is shown in the substitution of the names Iran and Thailand for Persia and Siam.

show that where the tribes are sufficiently closely related there is a reasonable prospect of their fusion into a single nation, given a period of strong, centralised government. Ethiopia illustrates a different aspect of the problem. It has a tradition of independence going back for two thousand years, and the ever-present tribal and feudal rivalries have been prevented from destroying the state by an unreliable but constantly reappearing loyalty to the national Church and the king or Negus, just as they were in the monarchies of medieval Europe. But round the Ethiopian nucleus is a ring of conquered provinces, inhabited by tribes that differ in race, language and religion from the ruling Amharic stock, and greater in total numbers. The possibility of fusing these non-Amharic tribes into a national union with the Ethiopians must still be doubtful. There are also, of course, many tribal peoples in Asia, Africa, the East Indies, and the islands of the Pacific, which have not even the pretence of a central monarchy to hold them together. Where the tribal population is comparatively small and assimilable, it does not constitute a serious barrier to the formation of a nation state. Thus the Highland clans merged into the Scottish nation.

The acid test of the possibility of passing from tribalism to nationhood is provided by Africa, all the more because when it was partitioned between the European powers they ignored ethnological facts and paid scant attention to the natural divisions and affiliations of the population.[30]

Lord Hailey wrote in 1939 that in Africa 'our political divisions mean little or nothing to many natives.'[31] 'The absurd national boundaries which now cut tribes in half,' he added, 'are as embarrassing in an economic as they are in a social sense.'[32] Dr. E. H. Carr concluded, only twenty-five years ago, that the arbitrary divisions of Africa ought to give place to 'an administrative patchwork based on the self-determination of the tribal unit.'[33]

These were very reasonable opinions at the time. The

[30] Van Gennet, pp. 186–7. [31] *International Affairs*, 1939, XVIII. 194.
[32] *id.* p. 197. [33] E. H. Carr, *Conditions of Peace.* 1942, p. 66.

conclusion to which they lead, that the partition of Africa into nations based on the previous political divisions is not viable, remains to be disproved; but it is at least not so self-evident now as it may have seemed a generation ago. The seeds of nationalism had been sown earlier, and they had driven deeper roots into African soil than was then generally appreciated. The Confederation of Fanti chiefs, formed for defence against the Ashanti, has been called the first nationalist movement of the Gold Coast. The date was 1871 and it is difficult to believe that it had a predecessor anywhere in Africa south of the Sahara. Even in Egypt the revolt of Colonel Arabi against foreign influence only dates from 1879. Generally speaking, in the years between the two World Wars, European consciousness of the possibility of political rights for the undeveloped countries was satisfied by the system of mandates under the League of Nations. Such Negro agitation as developed before the Second World War took forms which on the surface mostly appeared unrelated to any demand for national self-determination. There were revolts sparked off by local grievances, and African churches, often of a millennial character, adopted attitudes which easily assumed a political form. Demands for independence were largely inspired from outside, especially America, and were pan-African in nature. They reached their climax in the Pan-African Congress of 1945, held at Manchester, which proclaimed as its goal a United States of Africa. More significant developments were taking place within Africa. A small sector of educated Africans which was growing up provided the nucleus for nationalist parties. The nature of these was dictated by the limits of the authorities against which they were agitating. The nationalist movements were thus given territorial boundaries which, like the frontiers they followed, paid little heed to tribal divisions. Nationalism was once again to be seen as primarily a political movement based on a pre-existing state, even though one imposed artificially by alien rule.

The present combinations and permutations of tribalism

and nationalism in the nearly thirty new independent states of Negro Africa are too numerous and involved for any attempt to discriminate between them here. In Kenya the greater size of one tribe, the Kikuyu, and the general use of a single language, Swahili, may have eased the first steps towards nationhood. At the opposite extreme stands Nigeria, with over 50 million people divided between some 250 tribes, including the large, progressive and aggressive tribe of the Ibos in the East, the rival Yoruba of the West, and a huge and populous Northern territory, Moslem in religion, culturally backward and ruled traditionally by its Emirs. The optimistic belief that the antagonisms between these great sections of Nigeria could be attributed exclusively to the Machiavellian British policy of 'divide and rule' has suffered a severe shock since Nigerian independence was achieved in 1960. Yet, in spite of the strength of separation and the coups and counter-coups with accompanying murder to which it led, even such an artificial 'nation' as Nigeria showed more tenacity of life than might have been expected. The fear of tribalism is doubtless one reason why in so many African states there has been a trend to the single-party system. This in turn has led to the charge, frequently only too well founded, of corruption—not a unique feature of parliamentary institutions in Africa, as students of eighteenth-century British politics will be aware. There is another feature of African nationalism, as indeed of the new nationalisms everywhere, which calls for attention. This is the role of the army, which in country after country has stepped in to take over or prop up a tottering new state. These military coups are reminiscent of the *pronunciamento* régimes into which so many Latin American nationalisms have degenerated, but differ from them in nature. The Latin American military coups have mostly been to preserve a grossly inequitable social order. The African military intervention has more often been in reaction against the monopoly of power, jobs and privileges by a political élite and tribal or party groupings. In Negro Africa, as in the Moslem world, it must be confessed that soldiers have proved better guardians of the interests of the common man than politicians. Yet military rule is a *faute de mieux*. One is bound to speculate what can come after it. In a situation as fluid as it is in every state in Africa, unfortunately, speculation is the only recourse.

6. MIXED COMMUNITIES

Tribalism is only the extreme form of a more general problem. Africa and Asia are even more prolific in communities of mixed nationality, or no nationality at all, than is Europe. Where there are communities containing two or more distinct, unassimilable, communally conscious and inextricably mixed peoples, the ideal of the nation state can have no relevance. It is only when one analyses the actual composition of what at first seem to be embryo nation states that one realises how mixed many of them are, and that what hope exists of their fusion into united nations, comes only where the political ideal of nationality predominates, as it does in the Americas. Some such states may be considered as examples.

More than half the population of Morocco, and 30 per cent of that of Algiers, is Berber, distinct in language, culture, and locality from the Arabs.[34] Although converted to Islam, the Berbers have not accepted Moslem law.[35] Racially, they are European and not Semitic, and they respond easily to Gallicisation.[36] The fear of losing the Berbers to French civilisation was one of the deepest sources of anti-French feeling among the Arab intelligentsia of North Africa.[37] The Berbers lived in tribal conditions which have been compared to those of the Highland clans of Scotland before 1745,[38] but now their isolation is being rapidly broken down. Experience suggested that if the Arab movement against French rule in North Africa approached anywhere near success it would have as its inevitable concomitant a Berber movement against the Arabs. So

[34] Monroe, pp. 117, 129–30.   [35] *id.* p. 118.
[36] *Survey of International Affairs*, 1937, I. 526.
[37] *id.* p. 527.   [38] *id.* p. 526.

far this has not happened and a common allegiance to Islam may preserve the integrity of the states of the Moghrib.

Egypt only has small and innocuous minorities, but Syria has Syrian Moslem and Christian Lebanese, as well as Alawite and Druse. Israel still has an Arab population. In Iraq the proportion of minority population amounted to some 27 per cent out of a total population of under three millions, according to the census of 1920,[39] though they are divided into a large number of small groups, among whom only the Kurds present a serious national problem.

Of the mixture of peoples in India I have already spoken. Ceylon has a communal problem which has brought about the failure of one constitution. In the Burmese parliament, as well as Burmese, there were Karens, Chinese, and Indians. Malaya has so many Chinese and Indian immigrants that the Malays had sunk, some twenty-five years ago, to a minority of 44.7 per cent in their own country.[40] Throughout the East Indies, Chinese, and in some areas Indian penetration, created a new national problem, for the appearance of which, as well as of the quarter of a million Eurasians of the Dutch East Indies, Western influence is really responsible. Western enterprise started the great economic development in south-east Asia and the East Indies which called for a much larger supply of labour than the local population was able or willing to supply. Western government also provided the conditions of law and order without which the immigrant Chinese and Indians would have been rapidly and efficiently liquidated by the native peoples. In Lower Burma a million Indian immigrants, compared with a Burmese population of about ten millions[41] flocked into the agricultural labour market, into government offices and the railway service.[42] Burmese nationalism was primarily directed against this Indian threat,[43] though

[39] *Survey of International Affairs*, 1934, pp. 115–6.
[40] Emerson, Mills, and Thompson, p. 78.
[41] *id*, pp. 70–1. [42] *id.* p. 163.
[43] *id.* p. 165. *Cf.* J. L. Christian, *Modern Burma*, 1942, pp. 239, 258.

there is also fear of Chinese infiltration from the north-east.[44] It found expression in anti-Indian riots, and led to the tragic flight of the Indian community when British military control of Burma was lost. If the same fate did not also overtake immigrants elsewhere in the Japanese conquests it was doubtless because Japanese imperialism needed their labour as much as Western imperialism did. The point to be remembered is that their presence creates a multi-national community, and that as national—or communal— feelings become stronger in the East, the difficulties will increase.

This is not the place for a full consideration of the problems involved in the countries of multiple nationality. For many of their minority communities the theory of national self-determination had disastrous results The influence of Western ideas on the treatment of minorities in the East may be illustrated by developments in the Islamic world, in which dividing lines had formerly been communal, based primarily on religion, that is, and not national or territorial. The system of cultural autonomy, which prevailed in the ancient Iranian and Arab empires, was developed under the Ottomans by the creation of *millets*, with spiritual autonomy, and a considerable degree of self-government in the administrative and judicial fields, including control of properties, education, churches, marriage laws, and civil rights. By the beginning of the twentieth century there were as many as fourteen Christian *millets* in the Ottoman Empire.[45] The Young Turks of the Committee of Union and Progress changed all this: they adopted a policy of centralisation and westernisation, including a plan for breaking down the *millet* system and making the Empire nationally more homogeneous. During the first World War, when Ottomanism and pan-Islam proved to be weapons that broke in their hands, the Turks fell back upon nationalism;[46] but even before 1914 they had gone so

[44] Emerson, Mills, and Thompson, p. 167.
[45] Sir Harry Luke, *The Making of Modern Turkey*, 1936, pp. 98–9.
[46] *id.* pp. 131, 155, 157.

far with the policy of turkification as to provoke strong re-
actions from their non-Turkish subjects. The revolt of the
Arab provinces against the Young Turk policy, and the
subsequent break-up of the Ottoman Empire, once again
showed the consequences of such a policy for a multi-
national state.

With the rise of nationalist movements a much more
ruthless attitude towards minorities became general in the
Near East. The Anatolian Greeks were driven from Asia
Minor, the Kurds were subjected to forcible turkification,[47]
anti-Semitism became strong in North Africa,[48] Iraqui
troops massacred Chaldaeans and Assyrians. Nationalism
was the more intense in the Islamic countries because it was
'not a native disease but an exotic infection whose ravages
were the greater in so much as the patients had not been
inoculated against the germ.'[49] The process of nationalising
the state was carried farthest in Kemalist Turkey, where
the principle of national sovereignty was enshrined in the
first article of the Constitutional Law of 1921, which declared, 'Sovereignty resides in the Nation without limitations and without conditions.'[50] The subsequent abolition
of the minority rights guaranteed in the Treaty of Lausanne
(Articles 37–45) to Jewish, Armenian, and Greek Orthodox
communities was merely a natural corollary of this principle.
They were replaced by the individual safeguards of the
Swiss civil code—'a mere shadow' of the rights that had
existed under the *millet* system[51]—but the Western powers
could hardly protest against the adoption of a policy based
on their own theoretical principles and actual practice.

In Turkey, and in a few other countries of the East,
minorities were so weak as to make the creation of nation-
states by such ruthless methods a practical proposition. But
where minorities were larger, and Western commitments
greater, the minority problem has seriously complicated the
achievement of self-determination. Minorities in subject

---

[47] *Survey of International Affairs*, 1928, p. 337.   [48] Monroe, pp. 131–2.
[49] *Survey of International Affairs*, 1934, p. 114.
[50] *Survey of International Affairs*, 1925, I. 50.   [51] *id.* p. 71.

countries naturally looked for protection to the imperial power, and the temptation to make use of a minority against a restive majority was obviously great, though experience suggested that such a policy normally led to disaster, both for the sovereign power and the subject peoples. The classic example of this is the Protestant minority in Ireland. The schism in Ireland was completed by British use of the Ulster Orangemen as a barrier against the national liberties demanded by the Irish nationalists. In Syria the French, by attempting to make use of the Catholic Maronites of the Lebanon, exacerbated without solving the problem of Syrian government. It is not to be concluded from these examples that the duty of an imperial power is to grant its subject nations self-determination regardless of the interests of any minorities, as the British Government did in Iraq: responsibility is an attribute of power. A colonial people that claims the right of self-determination for itself should not disregard the rights of smaller peoples. On the other hand, if a minority is weak it should not be encouraged by outside support to demand political rights which its size and situation do not afford any reasonable hope of its being able to possess peaceably.

The truth is that where there are largely intermingled communities the total philosophy of the nation state is inapplicable. In these countries the principle of national self-determination represents an evasion, not a solution of the problem. Where, as in Egypt or Iran, there are only small national minorities, they can be assimilated, or tolerated, without any danger to the survival of a nation state. Where, as in Burma, the immigrant population is recent and has no deep roots, the desirability of allowing it to re-establish itself is clearly open to question. But such comparatively simple situations are the exception. In many countries peoples of different national cultures live side by side, but are so alien from one another in their language, race and religion that the formation of a single national cultural community is not to be conceived.

But if cultural nationalism is impossible, what of the

political idea of the nation? The conception of the homogeneous nation state is irrelevant in such conditions, but might not the differing peoples in countries such as Syria, India, Malaya, form a political nation, as Welsh, Scots, and English have in Great Britain? The Latin American states are conspicuous examples of the possibility of creating nation states on a political basis out of the most disparate human material. In some countries this may be possible, but in many of the countries we are discussing political union is a comparatively new thing, imposed by Western imperialism. In many of these newly created political entities there is no denying that the conception of political unity such as is necessary to support political nationality does not exist. 'To maintain that Palestinian citizenship has any real meaning,' reported the Peel Commission on Palestine in 1936, 'is a mischievous pretence. Neither Arab nor Jew has any sense of service to a single State.'[52] Chinese in the Netherlands East Indies were first the enemies and then the victims of local nationalism,[53] whilst the nationalist movements in the various islands lack cohesion, and there is general resentment at Java's predominance.[54] In Ceylon, communal hostilities increased with the progress towards self-government and involved the breakdown of the constitution. It would be premature to conclude that institutions of self-government cannot operate successfully in any of the multi-national countries of the East, but there is enough evidence already to prove the difficulty involved in the attempt to shape them in the mould of the nation state as the West has conceived it. Nevertheless nation states they are determined to be and the strength of nationalism is such that no cage can be strong enough to confine it or rival power equal to challenging its dominance. At best it may be tamed by concessions; at worst the solutions will be found, as they have already been, in massacre or flight.

---

[52] *Survey of International Affairs, 1936*, p. 742.
[53] *id.* p. 194.   [54] *id.* p. 184.

III. Regionalism and Federalism

One last word remains to be said. If nationalism persists in
the East, it has been said, while Western control is eliminated, the result will be a balkanisation of the East.[55] The
recognition of the rights of the smaller national communities, it may be added, will surely intensify this process.
The reverse should in fact happen, because while the
traditional theory of national self-determination looks forward to the establishment of independent and sovereign
nation states, unfettered by external influence or internal
divisions, the smaller communities are often too small to
aspire to such complete independence. They can only find
political security and economic well-being in a federal
relationship with other regions or with some larger state.
If federalism has a future in the Western world, where the
tradition of the sovereign state has been so strong, it is not
less likely to find appropriate conditions for its development
in the East.

---

[55] *Nationalism*, pp. 335–6.

PART IV

Conclusions

XIV. Self-determination as a Regional Problem

I. The Value of Nationality

THE TIME has come to draw the threads in this discussion of self-determination together. Clearly, the idea of the self-determination of the peoples of the world into homogeneous nation states is unworkable: over too great a part of the world's surface the nations cannot be territorially separated in this way. The failure of self-determination in practice reflects an inadequacy in theory. In the face of its record we are compelled to question the possibility of clinging to the principle of self-determination and the belief in the nation state that goes with it. Yet nationalism is a sentiment that the contemporary world cannot ignore in its political arrangements. Nor is it desirable that nationality should be ignored. Civilisation owes much of what is best in it to the mutual influence of its different nations, with their varying traditions and outlooks, upon one another. The elements making for uniformity in the modern world are so many and so strong that we cannot afford to reject any force that holds out a hope of keeping them in check. Nationality is a spiritual bond and consolation to the individual. It is a fact that the great things in the heritage of the West have often been the work of the little peoples—an Athens or a Florence, Elizabethan England, or the seventeenth-century United Netherlands. Even within a single state diverse national elements have often contributed essential ingredients to its greatness. Would the British achievement have been what it has been if Irish, Scottish,

and Welsh had not been added to English? What the city-
state did for ancient Greece and medieval Italy, the nation
has done for modern Europe. It has been, and remains, a
forcing ground for art and letters, for religious and social
idealism.

Now national communities are not very easily made:
they grow in the course of centuries, as environment and
history develop particular ways of life and habits of mind
that are passed down almost unconsciously from generation
to generation. National tradition may, of course, contain
much that is bad, as well as much that is good. It needs to
be purified and re-interpreted with every changing generation. But it cannot be totally abandoned without a loss of
that sense of belonging to a special place and a distinct
community, which is a psychological necessity for the
individual. It should perhaps be observed in this connexion
that we are not here reverting to the idea of national
determinism. The individual is naturally most likely to feel
conscious of membership of the community in which he is
born and bred, but kinship is less important in determining
his community than environment.

Community spirit of the kind we are describing is naturally primarily local. Since the modern development of
transport, populations have become much more mobile, and
therefore tend to think of themselves as belonging to larger
units. Herein, as well as a cause, is also a partial justification, of the existence of larger states. But there is still a need
for the national community, as a base on which the more
transient local connexions of the modern industrial world
may rest, and in which they may find a more permanent
frame or setting. Empires or federations, implying extensive
sovereignties or confederations of peoples, cannot fill this
gap. They do not rest on the conception of a single patch of
land, with the society living on it, which, since we have left
behind the blood-tie of the primitive tribe, and unless we
propose to revert to a peculiar, communal religion as the
bond of society, is essential to the sense of community.
Empires and civilisations are too large, too shapeless, too

diverse. In the modern world only a community intermediate in size between the small local unit and the empire
can provide that communal setting without which industrial man is truly *déraciné*. The nation is such a community
and can be justified on such grounds. But is it in this capacity identifiable with the state? We may believe that in
some cases it is; nationalism and the theory of self-determination certainly make this assumption. But in many
cases it obviously is not. National consciousness is often
provincial or regional. If we hope to reach any constructive
conclusions it seems to follow that we must analyse the
problem of national self-determination from this point of
view.

II. *The Centralised Nation State*

Behind the theory of self-determination, as I have said, there
lay the assumption that the world could be divided into a
limited number of fairly large, independent nation states.
Until recent times that would have seemed a justifiable
view to take. So long as the state confined its activities
mainly to the political field, and in particular paid no
attention to the language and culture of the masses, and left
to peculiar subdivisions, such as Alsace, their traditional
institutions, the assumption was not directly challenged.
Even in France the centralisation of the *ancien régime*, which
has been exaggerated, affected the powers of the aristocracy
much more than it affected the lives of the people.

A new era began with the French Revolution. The spirit
of the revolutionaries carried the ideal of national unity—
the nation *une et indivisible*—from political life proper into
every sphere of social activity. To give effect to the new
conception of the democratic nation state a rigidly centralised system of government was set up, as a result of
which the nature of the state was drastically altered. In
place of the former provinces, which had a considerable,
though varying, local self-consciousness and life of their own,
France was divided into a large number of *départements*,

to administer which Napoleon created his system of *préfets*.

The departmental and prefectoral system of administration did not remain confined to France. It was spread throughout Europe by the Napoleonic empire, and fitted in too well with the needs and ideas of the time not to be continued or copied by the restored governments after 1815. From the point of view of administrative efficiency it was a great improvement on the methods of the *ancien régime* everywhere. So long as regional or minority feelings were dormant it encountered no very strong opposition, and when these feelings grew stronger in the second half of the nineteenth century, governments came to rely all the more on the rigid administrative structure, which, having generally been drawn up with little reference to regional divisions, was suited for use as an instrument for the repression of regional aspirations.

The peace settlement of 1919, which represented the high-water mark of democratic nationalism, saw the idea of the centralised nation state pushed to its farthest point. The new states that were then set up adopted this model with all the greater enthusiasm because they felt the need to achieve unity—or the appearance of unity—as rapidly as possible.

III. Regionalism

1. FRANCE

The strength of the forces behind the policy of centralisation, and the assiduity with which it was generally applied, should have led, one would have thought, to complete success. On the contrary, the striking fact has been the increasing vigour of regionalist opposition, even in France, the home of centralisation. French regionalist tendencies first became evident in the mainly literary and cultural movement inaugurated in Provence by the poet Mistral. A Breton movement followed this, and took a rather more political form. The literary genius of Maurice Barrès in *Les Déracinés* appealed to the strong provincial sentiments that still survived in many parts of France. The geographer, Vidal de la Blache, gave the new movement a scientific backing by adding the conception of geographical regions to the sentimental memory of the old provinces. The idea of economic regions was also spreading, and made great progress between 1914 and 1918, when the partial breakdown of the central administration and the necessities of the war led to the division of France into economic regions.[1]

On the whole it was the right wing in French politics, especially the monarchists, with their sentimental longing for the ancient provinces, who were the most active in support of the regionalist idea. But the attack on the prefectoral system was also supported, on more democratic grounds, by constitutional lawyers such as Henri Berthélemy and Jèze. 'Like their predecessors,' declared the latter, 'the *préfets* of the twentieth century are the natural enemies of the public liberties.'[2] Similarly, Berthélemy wrote in 1901: 'Centralisation is the cause of our dependence: we are not free because we have not yet succeeded in breaking the bars of the cage in which the Emperor enclosed us.'[3]

It was not until after 1918, however, that the problem of regionalism presented itself in France in an acute form, with the recovery of Alsace. When the flags had been taken down and the rejoicing ceased it was gradually realised that it was not going to be as easy as had been expected to put back the Haut-Rhin and the Bas-Rhin into the positions they had occupied alongside all the other French *départements* fifty years earlier. The incorporation of Alsace in the French state had been one of the conspicuous successes of the *ancien régime*. The Protestant religion there had been protected by exceptional arrangements; the use of the local Germanic dialect was equally free—German was even the official language in Alsace;[4] and in order not to disrupt

[1] *Cf.* R. K. Gooch, *Regionalism in France*, 1931.
[2] G. Jèze, *Du rôle des préfets en France*, 1911, p. 273.
[3] H. Berthélemy, Preface to *Essai sur le gouvernement local en Angleterre*, par. E. Jenks, 1902, p. xiii.
[4] Vidal de la Blache, p. 53.

economic relations between Alsace and the states of south Germany, it was classed as a *province d'étranger effectif* and left outside the French customs frontier.[5] After the annexation to Germany, Alsace-Lorraine was formed into a separate imperial territory, put under a governor and given its own provincial assembly. Unsuccessful in winning the affections of the Alsatians, German rule stimulated the development of what a French writer in 1913 described as 'perhaps the most marked provincial autonomy in the world.'[6] It was inevitable, therefore, that the attempt after 1918 to re-establish the centralised government of the French Republic should have met with bitter opposition and the development of a strong autonomist movement, which was intensified by the resistance of the Alsatians to the anti-clerical legislation of the Third Republic. Politicians from Paris attempted to damn the autonomists by representing them as traitors in the pay of Germany. A German commentator said, more fairly: 'The emigrants from Alsace-Lorraine have always been warning the German public against misjudging as a desire to return to Germany what in reality is merely a struggle of Alsace-Lorraine for cultural liberty and home-rule.'[7]

In no other part of France has regionalism reached as high an intensity as in Alsace, but the strength of provincial sentiment, and the desire to escape from the dominance of Paris, cannot be mistaken by any impartial observer. It is still partly true, as Barrès declared, that French nationality is made up of provincial nationalities.[8] The unity of France, writes a Breton nationalist, is a governmental myth.[9] This is an exaggeration, but it can hardly be denied that the maintenance of the system established by the Revolution and Napoleon has produced internal tension. This does not mean that France is on the point of disintegration: it does mean that the centralisation of the last century

[5] *id.* pp. 56–7. [6] Seignobos, p. 3.
[7] O. E. Lessing (ed.), *Minorities and Boundaries*, 1931, p. 13.
[8] M. Barrès, *Scènes et doctrines du nationalisme*, I. 80.
[9] M. Duhamel, *La Question bretonne dans son cadre européen*, 1929, p. 115.

and a half has not proved entirely satisfactory even in its original home, one of the oldest and most united nation states in the world.

2. SPAIN

The example of France is evidence that even in the most long-established and apparently united of Western nations strong regional sentiments may still persist. Spain teaches the same lesson with much greater force. The Alsace, and far more than the Alsace of Spain, is Catalonia, with a population of some four and a half millions, 20 per cent of the total population of the country. As has been shown above, in the Middle Ages the Catalans had formed a distinct Latin nationality, with a separate language and a sense of separate identity, though divided between the south of what is now France and the north-east of Spain. The French Catalans have been absorbed in the French nation, but Spanish Catalonia preserved many of its privileges and separate institutions up to the eighteenth century. Only after the war of the Spanish Succession, when Philip IV and his French advisers introduced the ideas of the Bourbon unified state, was the attempt to destroy them begun in earnest, and the nineteenth century saw the full suppression of Catalan peculiarities. The criminal law of Catalonia, its mercantile law, its separate courts, its money were abolished, and the Catalan language was excluded from the schools. In 1834 Spain was divided into forty-nine provinces, each under a governor, on the model of the French departmental system.

As the century progressed, however, a revival of the Catalan language and culture manifested itself. Industrial progress distinguished Catalonia, and especially the great city of Barcelona, from the rest of Spain. A demand for the restoration of the regional liberties of the province rapidly followed and a political party aiming at autonomy was formed. In 1932 Catalonia obtained its own local legislature and administration, control of education, and equality for the Spanish and Catalan languages in the schools, rights which were lost when the Fascist rebellion of General Franco, with Italian and German assistance, overthrew the republican régime. But it cannot be believed that the suppression of the Catalans is likely to be permanent, or that they will ever be anything but a perpetual source of dissension and weakness to Spain unless they are given at least the degree of autonomy enshrined in the Catalan Statute.

Regionalism is nowhere else in Spain so clearly marked as in Catalonia. But in spite of centuries of union, patriotism in Spain remains local. 'Separatism,' says Señor de Madariaga, 'is the first impulse of the politically inexperienced Spaniard,'[10] The Spaniard is first a Galician, Asturian, Castilian, Andalusian, Basque, or Catalan.[11] In 1906 a nationalist party was founded at Bilbao by the Basques, and despite the weakness of the cultural, historical and political bases of Basque nationalism,[12] the experience of the Spanish Civil War proved that Basque particularist sentiment was no illusion. In Galicia also there has been a provincial cultural revival. If four hundred years of persistent effort at centralisation have failed to unite the country under the dominance of Madrid, that is surely something like proof that even if this object were worth achieving, it is not likely to be achieved.

3. BELGIUM

That regionalist movements are not confined to the larger states may be shown by the example of a country as small as Belgium. After the revolution of 1830, led by the French-speaking upper-middle classes, it seemed likely that as a separate national community the Flemish would disappear, all the more because the line of cleavage cut across both the old medieval divisions of the country and its later administrative divisions, which had followed the same lines.[13] But

[10] S. de Madariaga, *Spain*, 1942, p. 184. [11] Bowman, p. 151.
[12] De Madariaga, p. 181.
[13] F. Passelecq, *La Question flamande et l'Allemagne*, 1917, pp. 33–4; Van Gennep, p. 186.

the division between the French and Flemish speaking population is no recent or artificial creation: it is embodied in a linguistic frontier that has changed hardly at all for over a thousand years.[14] When regional nationalisms began to appear in Europe it was natural that a Flemish movement should be among them. There were certain limiting factors which held back Flemish regionalism. Economic connexions between the two parts of Belgium were close. The Flemish movement did not originally arise from any desire to join the Dutch, from whom the Flemings were separated by history, religion, and culture, and who on the whole despised them, while there was acute economic rivalry between Antwerp and Rotterdam.[15] The demand was primarily for linguistic equality and cultural autonomy. It progressed rapidly after 1918, aided by economic and educational inequality between the two parts of Belgium. Economically Flanders was backward and poor. All the institutions of higher education automatically used the French language, even the great Catholic University of Louvain, although the Walloon area had strong anti-clerical elements while the Flemings were devoutly Catholic. During the German occupation of the Second World War the Nazis were able to make use of the Flamingant movement. After the war the Dutch began to show rather more interest in their Flemish brethren, though without any serious suggestion of irredentism. What really changed the position was a shift in the balance of power within Belgium. The Catholic Flemish population was growing far more rapidly than the Walloons, and at the same time Flanders was becoming industrialised and ceasing to be merely a backward area in the state. Students were the spear-head of a movement which burst into open violence and seemed to threaten the whole existence of the state, but even in such threatening circumstances the extraordinary tenacity of the political state was manifested. The French-speaking Walloons will have to reconcile themselves to being no longer

[14] S. B. Clough, *A History of the Flemish Movement in Belgium*, 1930, p. 5.
[15] Clough, pp. 266–8, 270.

the dominant partner and having the lion's share of the good jobs. A division of the country by which the Flemish part went to the Netherlands and the Walloon part to France might seem to provide a plausible solution, but one which is politically inconceivable unless both parties to the conflict were to lose all sense of balance. Closer relations with the Netherlands may help to ease the situation of a Flemish nationality within a Belgian state. The danger may indeed soon come from the opposite direction of a Walloon move for union with France. As the interests of the countries of Western Europe become increasingly mixed up with one another, such cross-currents may cease to be dangerous and become bands of union between states instead of bones of contention between them.

4. REGIONALISM ELSEWHERE IN EUROPE

It is not my object in this chapter to make a general survey of the lesser European nations, but their significance can only really be appreciated when it is seen how many distinct regions there are to be taken into account. Among them we should not forget to include those smaller territorial units which have already obtained political recognition. An example of a small regional unit that has achieved independent national status is the Grand Duchy of Luxemburg. Although a separate principality since the fifteenth century, Luxemburg only became a member, though a minute one, of the European state system as a result of the manœuvres of the great powers in 1839, when it protested against the independence that was thrust upon it. In the following hundred years the little duchy became proud of its independent status, and a referendum of 1919 gave a majority of nearly 80 per cent in favour of independence. The American experts at the Peace Conference of 1919 came to the conclusion that 'a really independent Luxemburg is an impossibility, from both economic and military reasons,'[16] and the Luxemburgers, who for three-quarters

[16] Hunter Miller, *Diary*, VI. 47.

of a century had had a custom union with Germany, recognised this to the extent of voting, in a plebiscite of 1919, for an economic union with France. But since France, for the sake of good relations with Belgium, declined the proposed union, a customs, railway and currency union between Luxemburg and Belgium was concluded in 1921. An interesting fact is that such an arrangement has proved quite compatible with political independence. It did not prevent the grand duchy from preserving its separate government, and even, in 1920, being admitted as a member of the League of Nations.

Three other small nations which obtained temporary independence in 1919 were the Baltic States. In the British Isles, the Channel Islands, the Isle of Man, and Northern Ireland are regions possessing local autonomy. In addition to those regions that have had their aspirations recognised, however, there are many more that remain up to the present unsatisfied. One cannot study the question of the disputed areas in Europe without becoming aware that many of those which were claimed by two different states in 1919 were in reality not particularly anxious to belong to either. Their inhabitants were far more conscious of their traditions and interests as separate regional communities than of allegiance to either of the powers which were conflicting over them.

Thus a Macedonian delegation protested to the American Secretariat-General at the Conference of Paris that Macedonia had been refused a plebiscite because it was known that the result would have been a demand for autonomy. If the mixed population of Macedonia had been allowed to dispose of itself by popular vote, it claimed, the result would have been in favour of self-government under the protection of the Allied Powers.[17] Similarly, Stambulisky argued at the Lausanne Conference that Eastern and Western Thrace should have been made into an autonomous region under the control of the League of Nations or the great powers. Only thus, he held, could liberty be ensured for all the

[17] *id.*, XVIII. 67–8.

diverse elements in their population, none of which constituted an important majority.[18]

A delegation from Teschen petitioned for its formation into an independent state.[19] The Commission on Teschen reported that the inhabitants of the province showed no marked national tendencies and were from that point of view 'as if in a state of lethargy,' despite the attempts of Czechs, Germans, and Poles to conquer their allegiance.[20] What seemed lethargy to those who were trying to decide to which of the surrounding nations Teschen could be attached, may merely have been local particularism, such as might have been anticipated in a province that had existed as a single administrative unit since the beginning of the fourteenth century and in which local tradition was strong.[21]

A German writer on Upper Silesia in 1931 declared that national feeling was then very little developed in the province. 'The Upper Silesian feels Upper Silesian in the first place.'[22] This opinion was supported by the evidence of G. Kaeckenbeeck, President of the Upper Silesian Arbitral Tribunal, who commented on the marked reluctance of the Upper Silesians in the territory transferred to Poland to declare themselves for either Poland or Germany until they were forced to do so.[23] 'One fact remains,' says another witness, 'that, whether on this or the other side of the political boundary, the Upper Silesians have been, are, and will be one and the same people.' If asked what they are, the great majority, he adds, will answer, 'I'm a man from here.'[24]

Another small district which manifested a desire for political independence after 1918 was the Tyrol, where the local legislature, hoping, it is true, thereby possibly to save the Southern Tyrol from incorporation in Italy, voted in

[18] T. I. Geshkoff, *Balkan Union: a road to peace in South-eastern Europe*, 1940, p. 63.
[19] Hunter Miller, *Diary*, XV. 109.
[20] Hunter Miller, *Diary*, XVIII. 113.   [21] Temperley, IV. 363.
[22] Lessing, p. 99.   [23] Kaeckenbeeck, p. 130.
[24] W. J. Rose, *The Drama of Upper Silesia*, 1936, pp. 223, 276.

favour of the constitution of the Tyrol as an independent republic.[25] A further motive was the long-standing antagonism between the Tyrol and Vienna.[26] In another Alpine province of Austria, the Vorarlberg, the local diet proclaimed its independence as early as 3rd November, 1918. In April, 1919, a plebiscite obtained a majority of 80 per cent for incorporation in Switzerland.[27] As with the Tyrol, there were doubtless special reasons at the time for these moves, but nevertheless they indicate the strength of local patriotism compared with Austrian national sentiment.

At the opposite extreme of the former Austrian domains, the 'Carpatho-Ruthenes' are described as marked by a 'narrow particularism.'[28] After all the debate in high quarters over the real national affiliations of this people, if a census of the whole population were taken, writes Macartney, 'probably the vast majority of the peasants, above whose heads the whole controversy has really passed, would still describe themselves either by some local appellation such as "Hutzul" or as "Rusins," meaning thereby their own local brand of Carpatho-Ruthenes.'[29] A more recent observer confirms the view that the normal attitude of the Ruthenian peasant is to regard himself as a 'man of the place', with no outside allegiances.[30] In such a very backward area, of course, this sentiment may be due mainly to political immaturity. At any rate, the same writer declares that the experiment of 1939 in autonomy left the peasantry cold.[31] Within the former Habsburg Empire, Croatia, Slovakia, Slovenia—the list is not exhaustive— also constituted regions inhabited by populations more conscious of their local identity than of any broader affiliations.

Even in a single city the sense of local particularism can be stronger than any other allegiance. The American Commissioner appointed by the Peace Conference to report

---

[25] Lessing, p. 23.   [26] Albrecht-Carrié, p. 159.
[27] Wambaugh, *Plebiscites since the World War*, I. 513–4.
[28] E. Wiskemann, *Undeclared War*, 1939, p. 215.   [29] Macartney, p. 240.
[30] M. Winch, *Republic for a Day*, 1939, p. 9.   [31] *id*. p. 265.

on the sentiments of the population of Fiume reported that nationality in the city was poorly defined, in many cases families being divided in allegiance.[32] The salient feature of the situation in Fiume, he declared, was 'the general desire of the people for a more or less autonomous form of government.' This he attributed mainly to economic considerations, though it was a fact that Fiume had always possessed a considerable degree of local independence.[33] In Memel also local sentiment had considerable strength. A Commission of the Conference of Ambassadors declared in 1923 that the majority of the inhabitants favoured the constitution of a free state.[34]

I have confined my illustrations to Europe, but in the previous chapter we saw that similar considerations apply to the Arab world and to Africa and Asia as a whole. A realistic attitude to the whole problem of nations and states, then, would begin, not with a theory, but with the basic and unalterable fact of the situation—the existence of a large number of historically conditioned communities, some of which are independent states, others among which are so small and so patently incapable of political independence that they are not normally termed nations. But even such tiny communities as those of Jersey or Guernsey are nations in all but size and capacity for political independence, although evidently they do not constitute nations as the term has been used by nationalists and as it enters into the theory of self-determination. The difference between the native communities of these isles and those of Alsace, Catalonia, Wales, or Croatia, and again between these and England or France, is one of degree, not of kind. Indeed, it has even been claimed that the larger nations are less fundamental phenomena than regional communities. 'Nations,' it has been said, 'dominate the present. Other forms of areal organisation conceivable in the present are destined to dominate the future, unless the nations in their

[32] Hunter Miller, *Diary*, VI. 464.   [33] *id.* p. 460.
[34] T. V. Kalijarvi, *The Memel Statute: Its Origin, Legal Nature, and Observation to the Present Day*, 1937, p. 79.

day destroy the areal groups of people upon which all such forms are based.'[35] We may add that there seems little likelihood of the latter development coming about. Enough should have been said to show that self-determination, if it is to mean anything, cannot stop, as was believed in 1919, at the nation state. Far too many regions have developed a separate cultural and political consciousness of their own; if they are not nations, they are at least sub-nations, and demand recognition as such. Yet for most of them to aspire to independent statehood would be ridiculous. The consequent problems cannot be evaded, either in theory or in practice.

IV. The Region as the Expression of Self-determination

We have now apparently established two positions which are not on the surface easy to reconcile with one another. On the one hand, the attempt to divide the world into a limited number of unified nation states has only produced increasing internal and international tension; on the other hand, to give all the nations and fragments of nations political independence as sovereign states would involve the maddest balkanisation of the whole world. This conclusion, however, need only follow if it is deemed that the nation state, as it is commonly understood, is a necessary condition of the existence of the rights of the nation. I have tried to show that this is not so.

The European nations of the contemporary world were mostly created, I have said, during the Middle Ages. They were the product of centuries of growth. Now political and social life in the Middle Ages was normally on an intensely local basis. This was the natural result of prevailing economic and political conditions, and it found intellectual expression in a federative pattern of thought, which is well defined by Gierke. 'The properly medieval system of

[35] R. S. Platt, *Conflicting Territorial Claims in the Upper Amazon*, in C. C. Colby (ed.), *Geographical Aspects of International Relations*, 1938, p. 276.

thought,' he writes, 'started from the idea of the whole and of unity, but to every lesser unit, down to and including the individual, it ascribed an inherent life, a purpose of its own, and an intrinsic value within the harmoniously articulated organism of the world-whole filled with the Divine Spirit.'[36] This federalistic conception of the community of mankind was undermined first by ecclesiastical tendencies towards centralisation, and then by the rise of the modern sovereign state. But although the smaller medieval nations were in many cases overlaid by later political developments, they have rarely been stifled, and the twentieth century has seen their rebirth to political life.

This is the basic element in the European situation, for the facts of medieval politics were still, in 1939, the underlying realities in the international life of the German, Baltic, Polish, Danubian, and Balkan lands. The statesmen of this huge area, which is the geographical heart of Europe, still thought and worked in terms dictated by a thousand years of history. Henry the Fowler and Barbarossa, Wenceslas and Sigismund, the Emperor Charles with his Golden Bull, the Serb and Bulgar Empires, the Hussite Wars and the Battle of Mohacs—these were the true political background of Masaryk and Beneš, Pilsudski, Dolfuss, Horthy, and Hitler. The attempt to organise Central Europe, the Europe of the Holy Roman Empire and the Ottoman Empire, into a series of compact nation states, broke on the rock of historical fact. The solution of 1918, well-meant and idealistic, dictated as it may have been by the circumstances of the moment, was none the less ill-conceived and doomed to disaster. Central Europe was not and could not be made into a coherent pattern of nation states; it was a patchwork quilt, a mosaic of medieval fragments.

Even in Western Europe nationalism has in many parts been the parent of regionalism, which here also is a rebirth of medieval particularism. Smaller nationalities, such as the Scots, the Welsh, the Bretons, the Catalans, and so forth,

[36] O. von Gierke, *The Development of Political Theory*, trans. B. Freyd, 1939, p. 257.

which had been brought into membership of the larger nation states, such as Great Britain, France, or Spain, have awoken to a sense of their separate identity. Marchlands, like Alsace, which had been incorporated in modern states, have reasserted their individuality.

To maintain the principle of the centralised nation state is to sacrifice all such lesser entities. The attempt at a national delimitation of states in Central and Eastern Europe involved a process of exchange, expulsion, or massacre of minority populations and even so has only been partially complete.

The emergence into political self-consciousness of the smaller communities was a development which did not enter into the calculations of the theorists of self-determination. Its consequence has been to produce a dilemma from which, on the basis of this theory, there is no escape. Either, in the name of the nation state, the aspirations of these lesser units must be rejected—and then what of the principle of self-determination on which the nation state has been supposed to be founded?—or the right of these tiny communities to political independence must be recognised, which is to reduce the principle of self-determination to an absurdity. It is to be observed, moreover, as has already been said, that the distinction formerly drawn between Western and Central or Eastern Europe in this respect no longer holds good. Europe west of the Rhine is no more capable of being divided into clear-cut homogeneous nation states than is Europe east of the Rhine. All we can say of both areas is that in them some communities are large enough and are in possession of sufficient traditions of political independence to constitute separate states, whereas others are not.

The first task, therefore, of a realistic international policy would be to attempt to construct a regional map of the world. In drawing this up a number of areas of mixed populations would be found, for which special treatment would be required. It should be explained that this regional map would not be compiled by following language, race, culture, religion, or any other single criterion. Switzerland, sub-divided into its cantons—themselves historic and not linguistic or religious entities—for example, would constitute a single region; Norway and Sweden would form two separate regions. The one criterion of the existence of a distinct region would be the sentiments of its population. A national region might be as large and populous as England, or as small as Luxemburg. If this were the groundwork of our political system, we should surely be justified in claiming that it was built on the conception of real self-determination, as opposed to national determinism.

Given the existence and claims of these lesser communities, how are they to be dealt with? Are we to attempt to break down into their component parts the traditional and historically validated state entities? But Flanders cannot become an independent state, neither can Alsace, the Tyrol, or Macedonia. The division of the Caucasian peoples into a host of petty and warring sovereign states was not really a desirable consummation, as it was certainly not a lasting one. On the other hand, can we propose the restoration of Habsburgs, Romanovs, Hohenzollerns, and even of the house of Abdul Hamid, or of successors who would be no better, at the head of great imperial conglomerations in which the national interests and spiritual self-respect of a host of weaker regions and nationalities are sacrificed to the glory of one ruling nation? Even if it were possible to put the clock back to 1914, we should hardly wish to do so.

The Versailles solution was evidently not satisfactory. Above all there was the problem of the nations that were not given political recognition in 1919. The Ukrainians of Poland, the 'Ruthenes' of Czechoslovakia, the Slovaks, the Croats, and many other minorities, constituted permanent centres of internal disturbance and of temptation to foreign intervention. They provided a potential 'Fifth Column' in many of the so-called nation states. It was assumed that the existence of close linguistic or other ties provided a sound basis for uniting in a single nation state communities which had historically been divided. But compulsory union did not bring the Czechs and Slovaks closer together. On the contrary, the Slovak consciousness of separate nationality markedly increased between 1919 and 1939. The very closeness of Serbs and Croats to one another seemed to intensify their mutual hostility.

Where there is a genuine desire for union, of course, it is to be welcomed: it is quite as legitimate an expression of self-determination as the desire for separation. Where unity is not desired, the alternative is evidently to accept a regional basis for political life wherever local sentiment appears to demand it. This might involve a re-drawing of the map of Europe, so as to look much more like the medieval map than that to which we are accustomed. One's immediate reaction to such a suggestion is that it would mean a balkanisation of Europe more extreme than anything proposed at Versailles. It offers, moreover, a sinister resemblance to the way in which the Germans, by playing on local particularist sentiments, undermined existing states, and divided south-eastern Europe into a collection of petty ethnic units, all dependent on, and therefore subservient to, the German Reich. As C. A. Macartney observes, 'To split up Eastern Europe into a series of self-regarding national states, with frontiers drawn as nearly as possible to the ethnic line, would merely perpetuate the atomisation introduced by Germany.'[37] But this, while a possible result of self-determination pushed as far as possible towards its logical conclusion, is not a necessary one. It only follows if we accept the principle of the sovereign nation state. Substituting the idea of local autonomy, a new and entirely different vista of possibilities is opened up. The recognition of the right of local autonomy restores the alliance between democracy and national feeling, which centralisation has done so much to break. The frustration of democratic institutions in the centralised nation state is well put by Ruggiero, who asserts: 'It is notorious that the democratic administration of communes and provinces, instead of

[37] Macartney, *Problems of the Danube Basin*, 1942, pp. 116, 153.

something genuinely autonomous, became a mere link in the bureaucratic chain.'[38] Genuine self-government and total centralisation are incompatible.

This line of approach to the national problem is not entirely new. There were thinkers who realised the weakness of the nation state idea, and who, neglected in the nineteenth century, may on this point be coming into their own in our day. Proudhon was a tireless critic of the great nation state. Acton I have already quoted. A little later Le Play described 'the pretended principle of nationality' as the flail of the century. We may look back also to another notable figure of the last century as, with many eccentric ideas, at least in this connexion, a prophet of the future. 'Universal peace will be impossible,' wrote the Russian anarchist, Bakunin, 'so long as the present centralised states exist. We must desire their destruction in order that, on the ruins of these forced unions organised from above by right of authority and conquest, there may arise free unions organised from below, by the free federation of communes into provinces, of provinces into the nation, and of nations into the United States of Europe.'[39] The principle of building from below is both more democratic and more realistic than the nation state theory of 1918. Where regions with a separate national consciousness exist, even if they are smaller than the communities we are accustomed to regard as nations, they must be treated as the basic elements in the pattern of European society. This is the first principle of the new self-determination. It is only the beginning, of course, and not the end of international reconstruction. We must next ask within what limits regional autonomy, if it is admitted that it is desirable, is possible.

V. Scope and Nature of Regional Autonomy

Assuming that, wherever there are regional communities with a sentiment of their own separate identity, special

[38] Ruggiero, *History of European Liberalism*, 1927, p. 374.
[39] Quoted in E. H. Carr, *Michael Bakunin*, 1937, p. 331.

autonomous institutions to cater for them should be
established, the next problem is the distribution of powers
between central and regional governments. One suggested
solution is the separation of political from non-political
activities. This was the principle advocated in Karl
Renner's plan for the Habsburg empire. It has been criticised on the ground that the great expansion of state activity
in modern times makes any attempt to distinguish between
political and non-political 'Utopian',[40] and we must agree
that 'politics' no longer has the limited connotation it had
in the recent past.

A similar proposal, though put in a rather different way,
is the dissociation of politics from nationality, which, it has
been said, is 'merely the distinguishing of two things which
are in their nature distinct and ought to remain so.'[41] The
suggestion is that each state should exercise political sovereignty within its territorial limits, while each nation forms
'a cultural community, independent of territorial considerations, which would organise the cultural life of all its
members throughout the world.'[42] The truth behind this
suggestion should not prevent us from seeing the dangers it
involves. If my analysis is valid, nationality in modern
times has a political character, which concessions in the
purely cultural field—even assuming that a line could be
drawn between political and cultural—would not satisfy.
Moreover, I have argued above that nationality normally
involves relationship to a specific territory; regional sentiment does so even more clearly. A purely cultural association would give no scope to this territorial sentiment. Finally, from the point of view of national security and international peace, there would be considerable potential
danger in the organisation of 'cultural' nations on a world-
wide basis, overriding all state frontiers. Is it likely, or even
possible, that such organisations would remain non-
political? In this connexion, one cannot but remember the

[40] *Nationalism*, p. 291.
[41] Macartney, *National States and National Minorities*, p. 463.
[42] *id.* p. 469.

part played by the *Auslandsdeutsche* in the German National Socialist movement.

As a matter of fact, however, the cultural claims of more or less scattered peoples do not present the real problem. The Jewish question, outside Israel, is irrelevant to this discussion. The Irish are scattered throughout the British Commonwealth and the United States: they only presented a specifically national problem in Ireland itself. The enforcement of minority rights is an adequate solution for scattered minorities, in the treatment of which neither self-determination nor regional autonomy is involved. The problem of regional and national self-determination only exists where there is a recognisable area, however small, which the nation, or sub-nation, can consider its own on the basis of occupation; and any attempt to satisfy true national demands must in some sense be political, that is, it must deal with rights of government. It must further be recognised that the ordinary rights of democratic local self-government in towns and counties, communes or *départements*, are not an adequate answer to the demand for regional autonomy. It is an essential element in the claim of nationality that the nation or sub-nation should be treated as a unity. Even names are important in this connexion; the sum of Haut-Rhin and Bas-Rhin does not make Alsace.

Moreover, this regional government must be one which the inhabitants can regard as their own. The degree of democracy achieved may vary with the political level of the local community, but in one way or another the people should be associated with their regional governments. Where representative government in any form is not possible —there are few areas in Europe in which this could be the case—it is all the more important that the administration should be in the hands of local personalities. There may be backward regions, such as Slovakia and Ruthenia formed in Czechoslovakia, where this rule would be difficult to apply. The central government ought in this case to establish institutions for the training of young people from the backward region to fill local posts, and a quota should be fixed for the absorption of a specific number of these each year. The end to be aimed at is not a narrow national segregation, but that the lesser nationalities in any state should have equal opportunities open to them, and be represented in a fair proportion to their population in all the public services, and that in each recognised region with a distinct national or regional sentiment the public services should on the whole be conducted by members of the local nationality.

We have not to decide in detail what powers regional governments ought to possess. Generalisation is difficult on this matter, for local conditions vary widely. It may be said, however, that cultural interests should be under separate control wherever there is a distinct national or regional sentiment. This is particularly important in relation to religion, education and language. The subject of minority languages as a whole is one which presents many difficulties. Van Gennep declares that the problem of an administrative language is insoluble in a heterogeneous state.[43] If this is so the solution is surely to have none. Switzerland gets on very well with three—for some purposes, four—languages; South Africa and Canada with two. The principle to be followed seems so obvious that one wonders why so much fuss has been made on this matter. If in a state two languages are each used by large sections of the population, then for all common purposes the state must be bilingual and all official business be conducted and recorded in both languages. If one nation is in an appreciable minority, then its language should be used, so far as is desired, for all official business within its own region, with resort to translation wherever it may be necessary for members of the majority nation.

Turning to more strictly political questions, one condition is fundamental from the start. There can be no question of regional autonomy of any kind in a rigidly centralised state. A decentralised administration is a *sine qua non* of regionalism. Local government, that is, must follow the British or

[43] Van Gennep, I. 91.

the American model, not the French. To attempt a detailed analysis of the varying powers that might in different circumstances be assigned to a regional government would take too long. It must be remembered that the establishment of regional control of the functions of local government would in itself be a step towards enhancing their importance. The central administration would perforce have to ride a regional administration with a lighter rein than it can small, artificial units of local government; the very size of the regional unit would promote its importance. Regionalism, as Charles Brun points out, is a constructive principle, because it builds up larger and stronger provincial entities.[44]

The increasing complexity of modern government is sometimes adduced as an argument against regional devolution, but in fact its bearing is rather the contrary. It does not necessarily mean that the duties incumbent on a regional government to-day must necessarily be light, or its powers insignificant. The more the burden on the central authorities increases, the greater the need for devolution, in the interests of efficiency, to a coherent unit of a size capable of effective governmental action. Nor in proposing to base regional administrations primarily on the national or regional sentiments of their inhabitants are we necessarily flying in the face of economic and political efficiency. 'The modern regions of orientation and organisation of society— the commercial and circulation regions,' to quote a geographical student of regionalism, 'are in general closely coincident with the historical politico-cultural provinces. The fact is self-evident in the small independent states.' The same writer points out that even in Germany, although the appropriate regional divisions cut across the small interlocked state territories, 'their boundaries often correspond, in fact, with old political boundaries.'[45]

There are, of course, necessary limitations on regional

[44] Ch. Brun, *Le Régionalisme*, 1911, pp. 80–1.
[45] R. E. Dickinson, 'The Meaning of Deutschland', in the *New Commonwealth Quarterly*, October 1942, VIII. 58

autonomy. But in asking what the state is entitled to claim, we must be prepared to answer the question, not in terms of sovereignty, but in terms of utility. The state, that is, can claim whatever powers are necessary to enable it to fulfil its functions adequately, and those functions are defence from external attack, preservation of internal law and order, and the promotion, in so far as it lies within the power of a political organisation, of a good life for its citizens. Under the last heading is included economic prosperity, but it was shown in Great Britain by the Second World War, though forgotten soon after, that economic considerations, which might have seemed to demand centralisation above all, while requiring, it is true, central planning, also favoured regional execution.

If, moreover, we consider the good life of individuals in society from a broader point of view as including the non-economic values, the significance of an active regional spirit and a consciousness not merely of absence of repression, but of scope for positive action, on the part of the smaller nationalities or regional communities in the state, is a vital element in the spiritual well-being of the community. Nor does the free play of the national spirit of the smaller nationalities necessarily hamper the growth of a broader patriotism. That loyalty to the larger state is most safely built on the foundations of national liberty is the lesson that the history of the British Commonwealth of Nations teaches, both in its failures and in its successes, and the lesson is being reinforced by the experience of the Union of Socialist Soviet Republics.

A special virtue of the regional solution for the problem of national self-determination is that it has no necessary affiliations with any particular social or political system. In France it has had the advocacy of such diverse thinkers as Barrès and Proudhon. In Spain, Basque Catholics and Catalan syndicalists can join hands in its support. It is recognised in communist U.S.S.R. and in capitalist U.S.A. 'This kind of autonomy,' declared Charles Maurras in 1898, 'can be founded on the most opposed philosophical and political doctrines.'[46] To the pure theorist such an argument may seem shocking, but to the practical politician, who recognises how unlikely is the establishment of uniform social and political doctrines and institutions throughout the world, it will appear as a conspicuous merit.

Finally, in recognising the rights of the small, and often hitherto neglected, national or regional communities through the medium of local autonomy, we should be following out the lines already indicated by practical experience. Economic and military conditions in the contemporary world are undoubtedly tending in the direction of greater unities; yet the intensity of national sentiment in the smaller communities will prohibit the restoration or survival, not merely of great empires, but even of many of the lesser states, unless it can receive some satisfaction. This is a conflict of loyalties which has already had to be met by the greater imperial combinations of the Western world, and the lesson to be drawn from their experience is unmistakable. The Habsburg, Romanov, and Ottoman empires crumbled. Germany, employing similar methods of conquest and domination, singularly failed to win the allegiance of the small peoples clustered round her, which on geographical and economic grounds seemed naturally fitted to form part of a German sphere of influence. On the other hand, by recognising—in different ways and in varying degrees—the national liberties and rights of self-government of the smaller nations within their imperial boundaries or spheres of influence, the United Kingdom, the United States, and the U.S.S.R. have won a measure of willing support. It is hard to resist the conclusion that this is, at least in part, attributable to their recognition of the linguistic and cultural rights, the economic interests, and the desire for local autonomy of the small nations, which, whether nominally independent or not, fall under the shadow of their economic and military power.

[46] C. Maurras, *L'Idée de la décentralisation*, 1898, quoted in M. Barrès, *Nationalisme*, II. 211.

XV. National Independence and Economic Interdependence

I. Self-determination and Economic Nationalism

THIS DISCUSSION up to the present has not questioned the assumption that while there are nations, or fragments of nations, for which circumstances prohibit more than regional autonomy, self-determination in independent political units is still open to many of the smaller communities, where historic or other circumstances provide the right conditions. But this can only be considered a possibility if it is assumed that political independence for small states is still practicable in the modern world.

Unless this is true the idea of self-determination will require not to be limited and qualified as we have suggested, but to be abandoned altogether. An examination of this assumption, therefore, must be our final task. But before we proceed to consider how far self-determination for small states is a political possibility, we must discuss the economic conditions in which it has to operate, since political independence is usually taken to involve independent control of economic policy. A common criticism of small states is the assertion that self-determination for the smaller communities has as its concomitant the adoption of policies of economic nationalism, which are harmful to those they are supposed to benefit and deleterious to world prosperity. If self-determination for small nations means a suicidal economic nationalism, the less we have of it the better.

There is a tendency in the discussion of this question to divide states into 'bad' states and 'good'—those, that is, that do, and those that do not pursue policies of economic nationalism. This distinction is not borne out by the facts. As the Van Zeeland report said: 'We do not find on one side states devoted to a policy of complete autarky, and, on the other, states faithful to a strict observance of international free-trade.'[1] The verdict of the League of Nations Economic Committee in September, 1937, was that 'Every country seeks, and seeks rightly, to protect its own economy.'[2] Economic nationalism, indeed, is merely the contemporary form of a universal phenomenon. Separate societies have always competed with one another in the economic field since the days when primitive tribes fought for the better hunting-grounds or the more fertile pastures. If economic nationalism was less marked between states in the Middle Ages than it became later, this was only because they had hardly reached self-consciousness as economic units. With the rise of the modern state, economic nationalism, or what has been called Colbertism, developed. It has been particularly associated with the name of Colbert only because his was the most thorough and able application of generally accepted ideas. Its basic principle is embodied in his conception of trade as a form of war. 'The trading companies,' he declared, 'are the armies of the king, and the manufacturers of France his reserves.'[3] States, on this view, can only flourish at the expense of their neighbours. France, Colbert declared in 1669, was prosperous not only in itself, but also 'in the condition of want which it has created in the neighbouring states. Extreme poverty appears everywhere; only Holland still resists.'[4]

Adam Smith equally admitted the basic fact of political rivalry between states, but, unlike Colbert, he held that it was possible to dissociate international trade partially from the struggle for power. Except where considerations of national defence complicated the issue, trade, he believed, was normally advantageous to both parties, instead of being a rivalry in which one side must necessarily lose and the

[1] *Survey of International Affairs, 1937*, I. 73.   [2] *id.*
[3] P. Boissonade, *Colbert, le triomphe de l'étatisme*, 1932, p. 6.
[4] S. B. Clough, *France: a History of National Economics*, 1939, p. 21.

other gain. *The Wealth of Nations* was an attempt to free international economic relations as far as possible from the dominance of considerations of power politics. But in relation to British policy, Adam Smith's free trade might be regarded as a more enlightened form of economic nationalism. It was pre-eminently in the interests of a state that had a valuable start in the process of industrialisation, an extensive commerce and sea power. Other states, lacking these advantages, lagged behind in appreciating its practical benefits, and with the rise of the idea of the nation state during the nineteenth century, economic nationalism at last really began to justify its name. Before the French Revolution, when the nation had been only another word for the state, its economic interests had been conceived mainly in terms of the political interests of the ruler. After the state had been identified with the people, economic nationalism could take on a new and a broader significance. The emotional appeal of nationalism now became the driving force behind economic policies, that had hitherto relied on the interest of the government; and the philosophy of free trade, which had achieved considerable success while it could be presented as a defence of the interests of the people against those of the government, gradually lost the democratic appeal which had been one of the chief sources of its strength.

The triumph of economic nationalism was naturally aided by the growth of the idea of national self-determination. Autarky—self-sufficiency—though etymologically distinct, has a close relationship with autarchy—absolute sovereignty. Small nations that had achieved political independence did not feel secure in the enjoyment of it while remaining in economic dependence. Their concern that political gains should not be annulled by continuing economic dependence is in part the explanation of the economic nationalism manifested after 1918 by the successor states. No peculiar dose of original economic sin need be attributed to them. The same phenomenon has been exhibited by the British dominions and even by colonial

territories in so far as they have been able to gain control of
their own economic policies. The evidence of history entirely
confirms the view that 'economic nationalism is the outcome very largely of ideas which gather about the conception of political independence.'[5]

Economic nationalism is, moreover, not peculiar to
small states. The same political motivation dictates the
economic policies of the greater powers. As a general rule
it may be agreed that 'the economic ambitions of states are
to be expressed in terms of power.'[6] Now power in the last
resort means military strength, the dependence of which on
economic resources is more than ever obvious to-day. When
wars were fought by small mercenary armies, the actual
control of transferable wealth in the form of financial
resources was an important factor in military strength, and
small states like Venice and the Dutch Republic could raise
powerful forces and hold far greater feudal realms, which
lacked the wherewithal to pay their armies, in check. After
war had been nationalised by Frederick the Great and the
French revolutionaries, resources of men and material became more important than finance, and the smaller states
were turned increasingly into pawns in the struggle for
power. Since 1914 the economic resources required for the
efficient waging of war have become far greater. The first
result of this development was an intensification of economic nationalism on the part of both great and small
states. Mussolini declared to the National Council of Corporations in 1937, 'In a world like the present, armed to the
teeth, to lay down the weapon of autarky would mean to-
morrow, in the event of war, putting ourselves at the
mercy of those who possess as much as is necessary to wage
war without limits of either time or materials.'[7] Economic
nationalism reached its logical conclusion in what the
Germans termed *Wehrwirtschaft*.

It might be argued that, pushed to the end, this line of

[5] N. Angell, 'The New Imperialism and the old Nationalism', in *International Affairs,* January 1931, X. 74.
[6] Hawtrey, p. 26.   [7] *Survey of International Affairs, 1937,* I. 66.

development must be fatal to the pre-suppositions of economic nationalism. No single state to-day, with the exception
of the United States and the U.S.S.R. can contain within
its own borders the necessary resources for a world war.
China may in due course be added to these, but the irrefut-
able logic of economic facts seems to condemn other states
to drop out of the race for world power. The greater states
of Europe can no longer maintain their industrial machines,
either in peace or war, except by drawing on supplies
from the whole world. It seems impossible to avoid the
conclusion that autarky, developed in a desperate bid to
guarantee the economic bases of power, has on a broader
view become merely a confession of failure.

Our argument now runs—economic nationalism is an
aspect of the struggle for power, which ultimately means
military power. Only the greatest powers—American and
Russian—possess the economic resources necessary for
modern war. For most states, it seems to follow, economic
nationalism has lost its *raison d'être*. It is natural to ask, therefore, whether it can survive, whatever be the future of
political sovereignty, unless it be in the great world powers.
Can we therefore draw the conclusion that economic
nationalism is not to be feared as a consequence of a policy
of self-determination for small nations, and that if this is
accepted as a desirable political objective we need not be
restrained by fears of undesirable economic consequences?

II. *Economic Nationalism as the Expression of Sectional Interests*

This conclusion would be logical enough: its weakness is
that the motives behind economic nationalism are by no
means so simple as it assumes. It is usually taken for granted
that economic nationalism is in fact what it purports to be,
and that, although it substitutes power for welfare, it
represents the interests, so conceived, of the nation or state
as a whole. Is this assumption justified? Is there in the
economic sphere a common national interest? I do not deny

that there are normally certain fundamental economic interests which are common to the community as a whole, but, at the same time, as long as a community contains groups in differing economic positions, so long they will also have differing economic interests. Even if the whole division of the community into classes were eliminated, other oppositions would remain. In fact, of course, we know that the influence of sectional interests in the community, far from being reduced to the minimum, is in most countries a leading factor in government. It is a mistake, therefore, to say that economic nationalism is not stimulated by economic motives. But what passes as economic nationalism is usually the economic interest of the dominant group or groups in the state; and this is rarely or never the majority of the population. In some circumstances it may be closely related to what in an ideal scheme might be regarded as the general national interest: in others it may be directly opposed to it. It might even be said that the first charge against policies of economic nationalism is that they seldom are, in fact, what they profess to be. The common criticism is that they are national, but not economic. It would be truer to say that in practice their motivation is economic enough, but that it is not national. Economic nationalism is most often merely the reflection of sectional interests, masquerading as the common interest.

We have now reached two conclusions concerning economic nationalism which have an important bearing on the economic consequences of the right of self-determination. In the first place, in so far as it is pursued in the quest for power economic nationalism, under modern conditions, is irrelevant to all but the greatest states. Secondly, what passes as economic nationalism is normally only the operation of the selfish interest of particular classes or groups.

III. *National Economic Planning*

Both as a form of the quest for political power, and as an agency for the satisfaction of the selfish interests of particular sections of the community, it may be argued that economic nationalism for small states is an absurdity. If political independence involves economic independence in these senses it is to be condemned. Must we conclude that small communities have no separate economic interests of their own, and that whatever self-determination they may have in the political sense, its extension into the field of economic policy is either impossible or undesirable? Such a verdict would require qualification. The economic dependence of the smaller nations on their relations with greater states is undeniable, but there are also certain dangers in this dependence. Any country which concentrates its productive resources on one or two basic products is at the mercy of the world market, sometimes at the mercy of a single consuming country. 'The justifiable criticism that economic nationalism is wasteful and only makes things worse,' it has been said, 'must be tempered by a realisation of the not unreasonable desire of certain countries to achieve greater economic security through a diversified economic structure.'[8] A policy of economic nationalism may be supported by the welfare argument as well as by the power argument: the totalitarian states employed the latter, the British dominions the former.[9] Changes in productive structure could do much to remedy the poverty of many of the smaller communities. Countries like Egypt, Cuba, or the Philippines, instead of relying on a single crop, might grow more of their own foodstuffs; the states of Eastern Europe might find an outlet for their surplus agricultural population by industrialisation. If this is economic nationalism it is of a more justifiable kind. It would better be described as economic planning, and whether it is well or ill done, in a sense it is inevitable. The true criticism of the economic policies of many small states in recent times has not been that they promoted the economic interests of their own peoples, but that they failed to do so.

[8] *The problem of International Investment*, Royal Institute of International Affairs, 1937, p. 33.
[9] Hancock, II. 270.

*IV. National Sovereignty and
International Economics*

At this point, however, another difficulty appears. Even if a case can be made out in favour of economic planning, can a small state pursue its own economic ends regardless of the policies adopted by the rest of the world? The truth is that unless a small state is as geographically isolated and undeveloped as, say, Tibet, it cannot be other than dependent on its economic connexions with larger communities. It cannot raise the standard of living of its people without foreign imports; it cannot pay for these unless it has access to the markets provided by the greater states; it cannot improve its agriculture or develop its industry without the aid of foreign capital. Here has been in the past one of the main sources of danger to political independence. Backward small states have had in effect the choice between poverty and independence, or economic development at the price of political subjection. Nor, indeed, has the introduction of foreign capital invariably brought economic advantages. In many small and undeveloped countries any possible surplus was soaked up by the foreign investor, the native bureaucrat and military preparations. A large proportion of the foreign capital directed towards the Balkans between the wars was dissipated in corruption or to meet budget deficits.[10] Much foreign investment, moreover, has been directed by political rather than economic considerations. It is natural, in the light of the experience of Eastern Europe, as well as of some American, African and Asian peoples, that some small nations should have come to fear rather than to welcome foreign aid, and attempt to drag themselves up, if they can, slowly and painfully by their own efforts.

But such results have not been invariable, even in the past. Foreign capital has rarely been a danger to states with stable political systems. The British dominions and the stronger South American states profited greatly from British

[10] S. Pribichevich, *Living Space*, 1940, p. 216.

and American investment, without paying any price in political dependence. It is too often implied that the only possible economic relation of a small state to a great one is that of exploitation. In fact, both by supplying capital and providing markets, the economically stronger partner in such a relationship can, and often has, served the economic interest of a small and poorer nation equally with its own. But during the period before the Second World War, the international investment system of the world broke down, and the great powers proved incapable of restoring it. The tragedy for most of the new small states of Eastern Europe was that they were never brought into the broad stream of the economic life of the world. The lesson of this experience is not that small states cannot be recreated, but that it is no use giving them political independence unless the great powers are prepared to co-operate also in the promotion of their economic activities. The lesson has perhaps been learnt now: the greater states should be aware that in their own interests they cannot ignore the economic conditions of the rest of the world. A depressed area is a potential source of unrest, whether it is inside or outside a particular political boundary. In so far as the great powers desire political stability, they must also desire general economic prosperity. The conflict of economic interest between great powers and small nations is therefore not a fundamental fact of the international situation.

There is another sense, however, in which the fragmentation of the world into small states may be regarded as harmful to economic prosperity. Modern industry can only reach its highest level of efficiency when it is producing for a large market. In a system of closed national economies the industries of the small state cannot have this market. But in such a system neither peace nor prosperity is to be hoped for, anyhow. Even at the height of the economic nationalism states could not become self-contained economic units, and the small states that were most successful economically were those that were able to build up a position for themselves in a wider nexus of economic relations.

This brings us to the fundamental fact of the situation. It must be recognised that the smaller nations, whether they are politically independent or not, are bound to rely economically on their relations with greater units. Such states as Luxemburg, the Central American and Caribbean states, or Eire, for example, cannot stand by themselves economically. A nation such as the Norwegian is confined to dire poverty and starvation unless the trade of the world is open to its ships. Whatever the demands of self-determination, the smaller nations, if they wish to prosper, can only do so by integrating their economic policies into broader economic systems. It must be frankly recognised that the economic viability of most of the smaller nations is inevitably dependent on the policies of their greater neighbours.

The one point we must emphasise is that considerations of political prestige, or the search for an illusory independence, ought not to be allowed to stand in the way of necessary economic connexions. In the economic world self-determination is an irrelevant conception. Economic relations should be settled by considerations of geography, natural resources, and economic development. A state that has political stability and a recognised national independence need not fear the existence of economic ties with greater powers. The establishment of closer economic relations is indeed one step towards taking the sting out of the existence of separate political sovereignties.

Because small states are economically dependent on greater ones it is sometimes declared that they must therefore be deprived of their autonomy. This is an attitude which should be recognised as unnecessarily provocative. The situation can be represented in a much less arbitrary manner. It is not the fiat of the great powers, but sheer force of circumstances that dictates the dependence of the smaller nations. The real choice for the small nations lies between being tossed about helplessly at the mercy of the whim of the great powers and the elemental play of uncontrolled economic forces, or joining in a co-ordinated economic system, in which their voices, if small, will be audible, and their interests taken into consideration. If such a system does not involve political subjection to a greater power—and it may in fact be the only alternative to such subjection—there can be no reason for the smaller nations to oppose it. They have in any case not the power to do so. In the discussion of the economic problems of the world the danger presented by the independence of the small states is a glorified red herring. The attempt to saddle them with responsibility for conditions over which they have no control is at best an error of analysis, at worst an attempt to remove the odium of past economic catastrophes from the governments and ruling classes of the greater powers, on whose shoulders it rightly rests.

The ruling fact of the world economic situation is that its problems cannot be tackled without international collaboration on an extensive scale. In this collaboration the larger communities, with more extensive resources, will naturally have to accept the responsibility for providing the necessary leadership. If the results are satisfactory, the smaller political units will not seriously complain of that. Statesmen of both the greater and smaller nations are beginning to realise these facts and to examine their implications. Lord Avon, for example, speaking of 'the type of relationship which should exist between highly developed, powerful countries and those that have not attained to the same level of economic activity, or have had little experience in self-government,' declared that it must be founded on two principles—'First, the receipt of financial and economic aid must not result in a loss of independence for any country. Secondly, any form of assistance or guidance given to a country unpractised in the art of self-government must be such as to help it to achieve its own development.'[11]

In the conditions of to-day, if we wish to avoid further catastrophe, it is impossible to leave international economic relations to chance and the free play of forces which in fact are not free. International bodies for their co-ordina-

[11] In a speech of 23 July 1942.

tion are a necessity, and it must be recognised that such bodies to be effective must have responsibility and power. 'This means, in practice,' it has been said, 'the transfer to such institutions of some attributes of national sovereignty.'[12] In this sense we are bound to accept the limitation imposed by economic needs on absolute rights of self-government. But this does not mean that political independence is irreconcilable with economic interdependence, or that to achieve economic collaboration the smaller nations must sacrifice their political sovereignty. Such a verdict is misleading because it presents as alternatives two conceptions which are not necessarily incompatible with one another. Sovereignty, as I have said above, is properly a political idea. Its application has varied from time to time. During the seventeenth and most of the eighteenth century, for example, hardly any thinker conceived the possibility that it could affect the sphere of individual property rights. In modern times most Western states have in effect ceased to apply the conception of sovereignty in the field of religion. Similarly, there is no reason in the nature of things why it should continue to dominate international economic relations.

States, moreover, may not prove permanently unwilling to sacrifice that which in fact they do not possess. The experience of the last half-century will have gone for nothing if it has not shown that even the greatest states cannot determine their own economic destiny in independence of the rest of the world, unless they are prepared to sever all their external economic connexions. As for the smaller states, they already have no economic autonomy, and, what is more, know that they do not have it. The truth is, that talk of abolishing national sovereignty in the economic field is unnecessary. It no longer exists. This fact is not necessarily fatal to political independence. The Foreign Minister of Luxemburg pointed out that, although his little state was a part of the economic systems of Germany and Belgium in turn, it managed to reconcile these connexions

[12] Condliffe, *Reconstruction of World Trade*, 1940, p. 388.

with the maintenance of political independence and the development of a separate national sentiment.[13]

Finally, it must be said that there is a danger of our being over-impressed with the scale of modern economic operations, and deducing from the fact that world economic planning is now necessary the irrelevant conclusion that national liberty and self-government for small states is impossible. Modern man is unnecessarily terrified of his economic environment. 'Why,' we may ask with Croce, 'should liberty desert the world, and man descend from being a man to being a slave or a sheep, just because, instead of the few roads and the poor communications of other days, human society has now at its disposal railways and airways, telegraphs and telephones and radio, methods of understanding which facilitate centralisation of government and business? Or because, instead of individual cultivation of land, we are now adopting, or may adopt, agricultural associations or even state agricultural institutions; and instead of free trade, trade which is more or less regulated? Liberty has no objection to make, in principle, to these or similar economic changes, if calculation and economic experience, which are alone competent in these matters, approve of them, in the given conditions, as more useful and more productive than others.'[14] Liberty, included in which are national liberties and political self-determination for a number of small states, is, given a willingness to recognise economic facts, entirely reconcilable with economic interdependence and international planning. Economic sovereignty for small states is a thing of the past, but the determining factors for the application of the political right of self-determination are, as one might expect, political; they belong not to the realm of economics but to that of power politics.

---

[13] M. Joseph Bech in *Rebuilding Europe: Talks of Allied Statesmen with V. Heywood*, 1942, p. 40.

[14] B. Croce, *History as the Story of Liberty*, trans. by S. Sprigge, 1941, p. 234.

XVI. The Limitations
on National Self-determination

I. Why have Small States Survived?

A GENERATION that has seen so many of the illusions of its predecessors shattered will not be likely to protest at the suggestion that no solution will endure which ignores the ultimate facts of power-politics. How do these affect the prospects of national self-determination? Local autonomy may solve the problems of some of the smaller communities, but there are a considerable number of small nations which, because of their history as separate political entities, or their experience of national oppression in the past, will not be satisfied with anything short of political independence and the rank of state. Is it conceivable that, for example, the Dutch or the Magyars, the Finns, Poles or Southern Irish, the peoples of Latin America, the Egyptians, and many other nations, would settle down peacefully to local autonomy in a greater state? On the other hand, however the economic problems of the world may be dealt with, as I have said, we cannot avoid the conclusion that the smaller nations or states are dependent for their economic well-being on the policies of the great world powers. I have suggested that this is not necessarily fatal to their existence as separate political units, but I cannot leave the matter here. Economic resources mean military power, and the concentration of the one in the modern world has as its concomitant a concentration of the other. Is any degree or kind of political independence possible for small states in view of the fact that they are practically helpless, given modern conditions of warfare, from a military point of view?

Students of world affairs were becoming conscious of the existence of this problem even during the first World War. At first the inefficient, or backward, small state seemed to present the real difficulty. 'The chief, the overwhelming problem of diplomacy,' wrote Walter Lippmann in 1915, 'seems to be the weak state. These states are weak because they are industrially backward and politically incompetent . . . The government of these states is the supreme problem of diplomacy.'[1] In the same year the author of *Mitteleuropa* was proclaiming that there was no future for small or even moderate-sized powers in the world. 'Our conceptions of size,' he said, 'have entirely changed. Only very big states have any significance on their own account, all the smaller ones must live by utilising the quarrels of the great, or must obtain leave if they wish to do anything unusual. Sovereignty, that is freedom to make decisions of wide historical importance, is now concentrated at a very few places on the globe.'[2]

A quarter of a century later G. D. H. Cole drew the same conclusion from the events of the second World War. 'The independence of small states,' he said, 'and indeed of all states save the largest and richest in developed resources, is impracticable now that a mechanised army and air force belonging to a great state can simply sweep aside all the resistance that they can offer. The utmost "independence" any small state can hope for in the future is a false independence, behind which lies the reality of complete domination by a greater neighbour.'[3] 'In a world in which the appeal to force still lies at the back of international relationships,' he argued, 'the sovereign state which is utterly unable to defend its frontiers is an anomaly.'[4] It is to be observed that if this is true it does not apply only to states as small and weak as Denmark or Austria. In fact on this basis only the

[1] W. Lippmann, *The Stakes of Diplomacy*, 1915, p. 87.
[2] F. Naumann, *Mitteleuropa*, trans. as *Central Europe* by C. M. Meredith, 1916, p. 4.
[3] Cole, p. 13. [4] *id.* p. 69.

great world powers can survive as independent sovereign entities.

Before we endorse this conclusion, we must at least ask how it was that small states managed to survive in the past. Was it because of their military strength? In the Middle Ages economic and military power was confined within comparatively narrow geographical limits, but for several centuries past the military resources of the greater powers, if not as overwhelming as they are to-day, have been sufficient to enable them to overrun the smaller states whenever they so desired. Why have they failed to do so? Why have a considerable number of smaller states survived to the twentieth century? For the early modern period this question is not difficult to answer. In the sixteenth century a state such as the Netherlands or Venice, aided by its wealth, could defend itself successfully against far greater neighbours. Even in the seventeenth and eighteenth centuries the smaller states were still an appreciable factor in European conflicts. But during the Revolutionary and Napoleonic wars many of the smaller political entities were swallowed up in great powers, or amalgamated with other small states, and while the Concert of Europe functioned successfully those that remained could no longer play a serious part in power politics. European affairs, therefore, were regulated by the great powers during the nineteenth century, while the smaller states on the whole adopted an attitude of neutrality and did not interfere in the quarrels of the great.

It has been said that such neutrality is now a thing of the past, because the neutrality of any state is too great a military advantage to one party in a war or disadvantage to its opponents.[5] It may be suggested that military considerations are perhaps not the only ones in this matter. If the neutrality of Belgium was a handicap to Germany, so was that of Eire to Great Britain, but the one neutrality was violated and the other respected. The effectiveness of the concept of neutrality in fact has always depended upon

[5] Carr, *Conditions of Peace*, pp. 54–5.

the policy followed by the greater states. It meant as little to Louis XIV or Napoleon as to Hitler. The recognition of the right of neutrality has varied in modern times, and the independence of small states become possible or impossible, as a result not only of changes in the scope of military power but of alterations in the attitude of the great powers.

It will be said that in some periods most great powers, and in most periods some great powers, have been aggressive. If we ask how it was that, in the face of such aggressiveness, some small states managed to retain their independence, the most obvious answer is that it was preserved because of the rivalries of their greater neighbours. The great powers allowed small ones to survive, it was generally held before 1914, in the interests of the balance of power. But this leads to a further question how the balance of power was maintained. Now the idea of a balance implies a balancer, and for nearly three centuries this role was exercised by Great Britain. Thus, in the eighteenth century, according to Vattel, when Austria and France were the two principal powers of Europe, the balance was held by England, 'whose wealth and powerful navy have given her a very great influence, without, however, causing any state to fear for its liberty, since that power appears to be cured of the spirit of conquest.'[6] During the space of four hundred years every attempt at European hegemony has brought the dominant power on the Continent into conflict with Britain. Philip of Spain, Louis XIV, Napoleon, Wilhelm II, Hitler—each in turn had to meet British opposition. The failure of successive plans for European empire, and the survival of the smaller states, may therefore be attributed in a material degree to British intervention. It is not suggested, of course, that the British state is singled out from all others by the altruistic character of its policy; but, as Sir Eyre Crowe explained in a famous memorandum, 'England, more than any other non-insular power, has a direct and positive interest in the maintenance of the independence of

[6] Vattel, *Le Droit des Gens*, Liv. III, ch. III, § 48.

nations, and therefore must be the natural enemy of any country threatening the independence of others and the natural protector of the weaker communities.'[7]

The importance of British influence in the preservation of the independence of the smaller states is shown by the consequences that followed when isolationist sentiment temporarily dominated British policy. There was such a period between the Peace of Paris in 1763 and the outbreak of the Revolutionary War. During these years Poland was partitioned and the stage was set for the last French bid for European empire. Again, in the second half of the nineteenth century Britain disinterested herself in European affairs and the great power of the Second German Reich was founded. Finally, in the years before 1939 the policy of the Baldwin and Chamberlain governments led to the belief that whatever happened in Europe Great Britain would take no action, and in the sequel the small states of Europe were toppled over like ninepins. The close association between British interests and the independence of the smaller states is further shown by the fact that the conclusion of each of these three periods found Britain fighting for her life against a great Continental empire. These examples suggest that British intervention has normally been necessary both to the independence of the smaller nations and to the preservation of a Continental balance.

The principle of balance, however, has not acted invariably as a safeguard of the independence of small states. It has been a two-edged sword. To maintain existing proportions of power, the great powers have often annexed territory from smaller states, or partitioned them. British liberal opinion has tended to seize on this aspect of the balance of power for criticism, and clearly history justifies its suspicions. The event which more than any other undermined faith in the balance of power was the partition of Poland. The tendency of the Congress of Vienna was to use the balance as an excuse for abolishing small states. It was

[7] Memorandum of 1 January 1907, in Gooch and Temperley, *British Documents on the Origins of the War*, 1928, III. 403.

denounced, not altogether fairly, by Sir James Mackintosh, in the House of Commons. 'To destroy independent nations,' he declared, 'in order to strengthen the balance of power, is a most extravagant sacrifice of the end to the means.' As the true defence of the smaller nations, he looked, not to the idea of a balance, but to a different force. 'The balancing system is itself,' he said, 'only a secondary guard of national independence. The paramount principle . . . is national spirit.'[8]

This introduces us to a favourite liberal explanation of the survival of small independent states. The strength of national spirit became evident during the last century; it provided the motive force behind many movements for national self-determination. But the more we study these movements, the less the will of the populations concerned seems to have been the ultimate determining factor. The fate of the small nations during the nineteenth century, as since, lay in the hands of the greater powers. Would the Latin-American states have gained and kept their independence without the protection of the barrier interposed by the British navy? Belgium and Luxemburg were the creation of the great powers. The most effective reason why the Balkan states gained their independence, while Poland and Finland failed to do so, was to be found in the policy of the Russian Empire.

But even the policies of great empires are influenced by the climate of opinion, and there has for long been a prejudice in favour of the rights of small independent states. With the sources of this prejudice we need not concern ourselves, but its existence is a fact which the student of international affairs cannot ignore. The various factors I have mentioned all undoubtedly have their importance, but it was not the strength of national feeling in the smaller states, or even the effects of the balance of power, so much as the general recognition that the destruction of an independent

[8] Sir James Mackintosh, speech on the annexation of Genoa, 27 April 1815, quoted in D. P. Heatley, *Diplomacy and the Study of International Relations*, 1919, p. 28.

sovereignty was an exceptional, and normally an unjustifiable, act which ultimately protected many of the small states of Europe, some no larger than a single city, from absorption by the greater powers. Even in the eighteenth century, when the power of the larger states was increasing rapidly, contemporary opinion, influenced by the classical city-state ideal, held up the smaller states for admiration and believed in their independence. During the nineteenth century the growth of the nationalist ideal did much to undermine this view, but in 1919, as we have seen, it still exercised considerable influence.

In this respect a change, comparable in significance to the military and economic developments that have already been mentioned, may be held to have taken place. At least it is necessary to ask whether the influences that formerly upheld the independence of the smaller political communities still survive. Apart from the sentiments of the populations concerned, the three effective forces that we have found at work in the past are the rivalries of greater powers, British interests in Europe, and a general recognition of the rights of independent sovereignty. All these can be summed up in terms of the policies of the great powers. The conclusion to which we seem to be forced by an examination of the military and economic factors is that the survival of small states depends to-day, as in the past, on the policy the dominant great powers adopt.

II. *The Attitude of the Great Powers towards Small States*

If I am stressing the policy of the great states as the essential condition of independence for the lesser ones, it is not meant to imply that the spirit of national independence has ceased to operate, or that it is not still an important factor in shaping the attitude of the world powers themselves. But its scope is necessarily limited by the conception which the great powers have of their own interests. The question which we have to answer, therefore, is whether the independence of a limited number of smaller states is compatible with the essential interests of the great powers. Powers, great or small, are not philanthropists, and where the neutrality of a small state is a serious military disadvantage to a greater power in time of war, the survival of its independence is at least doubtful. Even in time of peace the great powers cannot be expected to abandon what they regard as their essential strategic interests: they certainly will not do so, whether they are expected to or not.

A realistic analysis of the prospects of national independence must therefore take into consideration the possibility of reconciling it with the strategic interests of the dominant powers. This is a problem which I have already touched upon in discussing the development of American, Russian and British imperialism, and I have argued that there are in many cases no insuperable contradictions between the possession of military safeguards and the right of national independence. It has always been possible for one government to maintain armed forces or to hold strategic points within the territory of another by treaty without any implication of inequality,[9] as the Dutch, for example, held the barrier fortresses.

Strategic interests could in the past be safeguarded by the possession of comparatively small points—harbours and fortifications or airfields. But this does not end the concern of the great powers in the affairs of the smaller states. It cannot be to their interest to set up a number of small and unstable states which will be centres of international unrest. Arguments are sometimes used which imply that the existence of small states is a menace to the peace of the great powers because of the quarrels which inevitably arise between them. Thus, one writer says of the small states of Eastern Europe, 'From the time of their inception these ten states have been the cause of endless disputes and risks of war.'[10] This point of view has little basis in fact. Naturally,

[9] *Cf. Survey of International Affairs, 1936*, pp. 694–5 *n.*
[10] O. Dutch, *Economic Peace Aims*, 1941, p. 24.

a small state may become an occasion of war when it is the object of a struggle for power between greater states, as Spain entered into the origins of the Franco-Prussian War; but the real causes of all important modern wars are to be found in the conflicting aims of the great powers, or the aggressiveness of one of them. It cannot be denied that there were frequent disagreements between the smaller states from 1919 to 1939, but it is remarkable that only on two occasions, if we exclude the Greco-Turkish war as being properly a section of the World War left unfinished, did their quarrels approach the point of actual hostilities. One threatened war, that between Greece and Bulgaria, was stifled by the intervention of the great powers, acting through the League of Nations. The other, that between Bolivia and Paraguay, was exceptional in many respects. The experience of the last twenty years suggests that the smaller states are less prone to resort to war than is sometimes supposed, and that if the great powers desire to do so, they can easily see that the peace is kept.

In the third place, it may be said that the great powers cannot disinterest themselves entirely even from the internal affairs of neighbouring small states. This is a dangerous doctrine; it brings back historical memories of the Holy Alliance and at its best justly entails the condemnation that Castlereagh passed on the Tsar's proposal for guaranteeing existing governments. The scheme, he said, 'must be understood as morally implying the previous establishment of such a system of general government as may secure and enforce upon all kings and nations an internal system of peace and justice. Till the mode of constructing such a system shall be devised the consequence is inadmissible, as nothing would be more immoral or more prejudicial to the character of government generally than the idea that their force was collectively to be prostituted to the support of established power without any consideration of the extent to which it was abused.'[11]

[11] C. K. Webster, *The Foreign Policy of Castlereagh, 1815–1822*, 1925, p. 151.

At the same time this argument does not permit us to write off the whole question. Can a bandit state, for example, be allowed to survive as a centre of disorder in the world? Is it safe for a great power to suffer the creation of a hostile régime in a state in close proximity to its own borders? The government of the Soviet Union, which has some experience of such a situation, evidently believes that it is not. What should be done, asks an American writer, if a totalitarian régime were established on the American Continent?[12] As he acknowledges, this question is 'not easy to answer.' It is difficult to lay down any principle of action that would not open the door to promiscuous intervention. We may agree, however, with the view that such a situation is less likely to arise in small states that enjoy material prosperity.[13] A policy aimed at promoting their economic well-being is likely to produce better results than a mere use of force or threats of force. Prosperous communities do not thrive on disorder. Such a condition as is a menace to international peace or domestic security is often a sign of economic distress, to be dealt with by prevention rather than by prohibition, and in the economic rather than the political field.

To sum up, we may say that the rights and responsibilities of the great powers extend to the maintenance of their strategic interests, the prevention of war, the safeguarding of their domestic security, and the promotion of economic progress. None of these policies is necessarily harmful to the independence or legitimate rights of the small states.

III. The Application of National Self-determination

It still remains for us to ask, in general terms, within what limits the nationalism of independent small states can operate in contemporary conditions. National feeling is now so strong an element in the political consciousness of the world that no settlement which does violence on an exten-

[12] Perkins, p. 385. [13] *loc. cit.*

sive scale to this feeling is likely to be accepted except under irresistible pressure, or to survive any longer than it is backed by overwhelming force. The Great Powers could doubtless supply such force, but are not likely to co-operate peacefully in such a policy. There certainly has to be force behind any settlement, but the course of wise statesmanship is to minimise rather than maximise the need for it. The Great Powers, moreover, are committed to a territorial settlement based on a general recognition of the right of nationality, including in many cases the establishment of political independence. Their acceptance of the general principle has been reinforced by specific engagements. Even a state of such doubtful validity as Albania had its right to independence recognised by Great Britain, the United States, and the U.S.S.R. The second World War gave rise—and the fact is significant—to much less talk about rights of self-determination than the first, but the same problems of national independence were posed at its conclusion.

For many nations, as I have said, political independence must be taken for granted. No one would challenge the principle in relation, for example, to the Dutch or the Swiss, the Turks or the Mexicans. Although in other cases independent statehood may be out of the question, all nations, or sub-nations, should exercise self-determination, within the limits of what is practicable, in the form of regional autonomy. The first problem, therefore, is the identification of communities, either national or regional, with a separate political consciousness of their own. Wherever the existence of a separate national community is in serious dispute the most logical method of solving the question is by popular vote. This method the Great Powers have conspicuously avoided. The plebiscite is admittedly a difficult instrument of international policy, and experience has demonstrated that unless its application is surrounded with ample precautions, it is better not used at all. There is sufficient evidence to show that the plebiscite *can* be, though it rarely has been, employed satisfactorily, but the whole problem of plebiscitory technique has been dealt with so thoroughly by Wambaugh that it is not necessary to enter on a detailed discussion here.[14]

1. THE PROBLEM OF FRONTIERS

Plebiscites may be of use in determining whether a real national spirit sufficiently strong to justify the recognition of regional rights of self-government exists. In such cases the public would be asked, not 'Do you wish to belong to Austria, or Italy, or Yugo-Slavia?' but 'Do you wish for Tyrolese or Slovenian autonomy?' The use of plebiscites in the delimitation of frontiers is more open to criticism, though if self-determination means anything it cannot be entirely excluded.

Over the problem of frontiers the Paris Conference spent far more time than on any other subject. In its deliberations four contradictory principles struggled for dominance— historic rights, natural frontiers, strategic frontiers, and national self-determination. The first I have dismissed as in most cases dangerous and worthless. Practically every disputed frontier in Europe embodies two or more irreconcilable historic rights.

The idea of natural frontiers is more difficult to dispute: it has played a large part in national policy in the past and is still a very influential conception. Against the implied conception of the state as a geographic unity marked out by natural frontiers modern geographers have vigorously protested. The state, they rightly say, is a work of man, which may respect or may override the geographical features that look so imposing on a map. Rivers, it is now generally recognised, are bad frontiers; they are a link and not a barrier between the populations on either side. River valleys indeed have normally been the nuclei of national development. River frontiers are rare in history and have seldom survived over long periods.

Mountains superficially seem more adequate as frontiers. They appear to be destined by nature to act as barriers. We

[14] S. Wambaugh *A Monograph on Plebiscites*, 1920.

find in fact, however, that most of the mountain chains of Europe are inhabited by a similar population on both sides.[15] The Pyrenees divide the Basque nation in two at their western end, and the Catalan nation at the east. The Alps have become the setting of a united nation's life. The Bohemian mountains have Germans on both slopes, the Carpathians have Roumanians, except where a Ukrainian population from the northern slopes has flowed over and down the south side. Even so apparently obvious a frontier as the Brenner does not constitute a major trade divide, is not a national division, for it has German Tyrolese on both sides, and up to 1919 was not even a county boundary.[16]

However attractive the idea of natural frontiers may be, we must accept the verdict of modern geography, which is decisively against them. 'All political boundaries,' writes one geographer, 'are man-made, that is, artificial; obviously, they are not phenomena of nature. Consequently man, not nature, determines their location; we must eliminate, therefore, any distinction between "natural" and "artificial" political boundaries.'[17] We are bound to conclude that physical features provide us with extraordinarily little aid in the determination of the divisions between nations.

The argument may be used that geographical barriers, even if they do not divide nations, are the natural frontiers between states for economic reasons. But no state can now aspire to be an economic unit, or avoid close economic connexions with its neighbours. If there was once an intimate connexion between geographical barriers and economic divisions, the development of world economy has brought it to an end. Economic regions certainly exist, but they have now little relation to any other divisions, and generally bestride the frontier of several states and include elements of various nations. We must recognise, as has been

[15] Van Gennep, p. 164.
[16] R. Hartshorne, *A Survey of the Boundary Problems of Europe*, in Colby, *Geographic Aspects of International Relations*, pp. 187–8.
[17] *id.* p. 164.

recognised in the administration of the Soviet Union, that practically no correlation is possible between national divisions and economic regions.

The strategic argument remains. Military considerations played a prominent part in the determination of frontiers at Paris. Endless discussions went on, for example, over the strategic rectification of the Belgian frontier,[18] as though against a re-armed Germany the petty changes contemplated could be of the slightest importance. There was much concern over the strategic weakness of the Polish 'Corridor', and because at various points territory claimed by Poland had been allocated to Germany it was objected that strategic considerations had simply been swept aside.[19] The history of the invasion of 1939 is our justification for believing that the strategic frontier of Poland was a matter of little or no significance. Similarly, whereas a historian of the Treaty of Versailles declares that subsequent events showed that the strategic boundaries were necessary to Czechoslovakia,[20] my view would be that they showed that, strategic frontiers or no strategic frontiers, Czechoslovakia could not effectively defend her independence against Germany without the military aid of the other great powers. The belief has been expressed that strategic frontiers should be adopted for the defence of a weak country against a strong one.[21] My reading of history would be precisely the contrary. The great empires will certainly take strategic safeguards in the interests of their own peace and security, but no strategic frontier can defend a weak country against a strong one. We might even say that frontiers determined solely by military reasons are invariably bad ones and unstable, unless they are drawn in the interests of very strong powers against very weak ones. The basic defect in the whole idea of strategic frontiers was summed up very clearly by Karl Marx: 'If limits are to be fixed by military interests,' he wrote, 'there will be no end to claims, because

[18] Hunter Miller, *Diary*, Vol. X. [19] Temperley, II. 210, VI. 241.
[20] P. Birdsall, *Versailles Twenty Years After*, 1941, p. 8.
[21] Macartney, *Hungary and her Successors*, p. 491.

every military line is necessarily faulty, and may be improved by annexing some more outlying territory; and, moreover, they can never be fixed finally and fairly, because they always must be imposed by the conqueror upon the conquered, and consequently carry within them the seed of fresh wars.'[22]

Historical, geographical, economic, and strategic considerations will none of them adequately determine frontiers for us. The conclusions we should draw from this brief examination of the problem of frontiers is that none of the arguments put forward to justify the neglect of national divisions, where they are sufficiently clear cut, can be supported in present-day conditions. Frontiers therefore can and should follow national lines where they can be determined.

But the qualification is a big one. The conception of a frontier as an impenetrable line dividing one kind of people from another kind is an artificial modern idea, which bears little relation to the actual facts. The power of medieval states faded as it left the centre and was almost nonexistent before the effective area of power of another state had been reached. In this condition border lands developed a life and character of their own, which has survived in many cases to the present day. It has truly been said that between most states there should be not boundary lines but zones. 'Above all,' writes Haushofer, 'where we wished to make a clean division we have found not lines but belts, zones with a special life of their own.'[23] Under modern conditions frontier lines cannot be replaced by zones, but they need not necessarily have the all-inclusive importance formerly attributed to them. 'The tradition,' writes E. H. Carr, 'which makes the drawing of frontiers the primary and most spectacular part of peace-making has outlived

[22] K. Marx, *Address to the General Council of the International Working-men's Association*, 9 September 1870.
[23] K. Haushofer, *Grenzen: in ihrer geographischen und politischen Bedeutung*, 2nd ed., 1939, p. 26; *cf.* C. B. Fawcett, *Frontiers, a Study in Political Geography*, 1918, pp. 17–24.

its validity . . . The urgent need now is to alter not the location, but the meaning, of frontiers,'[24] This is another way of saying that the limitation or rather the division of sovereignty is the task immediately before us.

2. MULTI-NATIONAL AREAS

The greatest practical problem involved in the principle of national self-determination is presented by borderlands or other areas in which nationalities are inextricably inter-mingled. Where the tangle can be sorted out by an exchange or transfer of populations, this solution is to be preferred to leaving bitterly hostile populations side by side in the same state, but there are regions in which no conceivable transfer of population on a practicable scale could disentangle the nationalities. In a region such as Transylvania, where there is no nation, or rather where there are too many, national self-determination is meaningless. The difficulty presented by territories of mixed nationality outside Europe has been discussed in an earlier chapter. A settlement left to the local nationalities, whether it is disguised as self-determination or not, is likely to be a bloody and probably an unstable one. The only chance of a more or less peaceful settlement in some areas would seem to be by the establishment of an international authority with its own armed forces.

Up to 1918, it is only fair to recognise, there had been a considerable record of failure behind the idea of inter-national government. After 1918 there were a few experi-ments in international government which tell a different tale and on which a very different verdict has to be passed. They were all in what might be called difficult areas— Thrace, Memel, the Saar, and Upper Silesia, and their success is therefore the more remarkable.[25] It suggests that

[24] Carr, *Conditions of Peace*, p. 241.

[25] For Thrace see D. Mitrany, *Effect of the War in South-Eastern Europe*, 1936, pp. 254-63. Appendix IIв, An Experiment in International Government: the Inter-Allied Régime in Thrace.

For Memel, J. Meuvret, *Le Territoire de Memel et la politique européenne*, 1936, p. 36, and Morrow, p. 429.

For the Saar, *Survey of International Affairs, 1934*, pp. 625-6, and Y. M.

even the most intractable national conflicts may not be incapable of a peaceful solution in so far as, and for so long as, the great powers are united on the solution and prepared to uphold it.

3. THE FUTURE OF SMALL NATIONS

The determination, wherever it is possible, of national regions is, however, only the first step towards an international settlement. National self-determination on a territorial basis will provide us with many nations, large and small. The traditions of some of these prescribe their recognition as independent states. For the others, wherever there is a separable national community, self-determination in the form of a degree of regional autonomy varying with circumstances is desirable, wherever it is wanted. But the affiliation of a national region to some larger political grouping is in the nature of things not equally at the free disposal of its inhabitants. Indeed, in many cases it is unsuitable for decision by popular opinion. The affiliations of many small nations are settled beyond challenge by geographical, economic, historical, or other circumstances. Catalonia, for example, cannot be other than part of Spain, Wales of Great Britain, or the Ukraine of Russia. Even where political associations are less obvious, the maintenance of international stability is a vital consideration.

Of the economic dependence of small nations I have already spoken. Their military weakness is even more conspicuous. They may be willing to rely on a system of collective security, but it must be emphasised that the effectiveness of such a system depends entirely on the great world powers. The combination of any number of weak states does not make one strong one. Some observers of the trend of international events might draw the conclusion that small nations that are concerned for their defence in the

---

Goblet, *Le Crépuscule des Traités*, trans. as *The Twilight of Treaties*, 1936, pp. 22–36.

For Upper Silesia, Kaeckenbeeck, pp. 537-8.

near future may be most disposed to seek it in collaboration with some non-aggressive great power or powers whose direct interests overlap with their own. Thus all the other American states are from an economic and strategic point of view more or less dependent on the United States. Australia and New Zealand looked in the past to Britain and now increasingly to America. Such relationships between great powers and small nations, on a basis of national independence and strategic and economic interdependence, may conceivably be extended in the future.

A settled future for Eastern Europe could be most easily envisaged if a similar relationship prevailed between Soviet Russia and the small states in its neighbourhood. Non-aggression, economic assistance from the stronger power, its possession where necessary of strategic bases, the abstention of the smaller states from hostile attitudes, and in general terms the pursuance by both sides of what has been termed a 'Good Neighbour' policy, are the conditions of success for such a system.

Thus, although starting from a recognition of the rights of nationality, we are forced to accept many limitations on its operation in practice. Independent sovereign states are finding that their independence and their sovereignty are not unrelated to their power, which for many of the smaller states is a very minute fraction of world power. Of what use, it may be said, is self-determination if it does not mean a right for a nation to determine its own destiny. But this is precisely what no nation, in the conditions of the modern world, can possibly have, even the greatest. The greater states will naturally exercise the greater control in an economic and strategic sense. This is not a moral but a political fact, a testimony not to their higher ethical standards, but to their power.

But this is not the last word. Power is a result before it can be a cause. The geo-politicians, from Ratzel and Mackinder to Haushofer and Spykman, have defined it in terms of economic resources and space, but resources have to be used by men, and men are moved by ideas. Some geopoliticians have written of the need for annexing this country or that, as though the view of the populations concerned were no factor in the strategic issue. The fate of the German attempt at world empire is a commentary on the penalty of concentrating on material, to the disregard of human, elements. The successful great powers will be those that, among other things, make allowances for the strength in the contemporary world of national feeling, and the future of the world largely turns upon the form in which their inevitable control is exercised. It can undoubtedly take the old form of an aggressive imperialist policy of annexations, but if it does this it will prove self-destructive. Great powers cannot pursue such a policy without coming into conflict. A belt of small states, with two or more greater states struggling for dominance over them, represents the situation from which general war is most likely to result. The influence of a single great power, such as that exercised by the United States in Central America, is far less dangerous from this point of view. If it has aroused the resentment of the smaller nations in the past, this result is attributable to aggressive tendencies on the part of the great powers and the fears of small states: it is not inherent in the situation. The great powers will certainly meet with violent opposition if they seem to ride rough-shod over the rights of other nations. They can only succeed permanently by gaining the co-operation of the smaller nations: however we have to limit the abstract principle of self-determination, this fact remains. But it is a mistake to suppose that there is any necessary opposition between the interests of great and smaller states. If the great powers desire to take strategic precautions and to direct economic policy in the interests of general peace and prosperity, the smaller nations will have no quarrel with these ends. They are more likely to have a grievance against the great powers for not accepting their responsibilities than for accepting them.

IV. National Equality

The final point in this argument is that unless they feel that their equality is respected the smaller independent states will not collaborate willingly with the greater powers. But what do we mean by equality? The principle of equality is not affected by differences of power, and it precedes the idea of self-determination. It is a basic principle of international law, and goes back to the time when a state was personified in the person of its ruler or sovereign body. 'A dwarf,' declared Vattel, 'is as much a man as a giant is; a small republic is no less a sovereign state than the most powerful kingdom.'[26] During the eighteenth and nineteenth centuries, when the chief threat to the liberties of the peoples was to be found in the aggressions of great autocratic empires, it was natural that liberal thought should have regarded the assertion of the equal sovereignty of all states, great or small, as the bulwark of national liberty. This ideal has survived into an age in which, while it still retains its value as a defence against imperialist aggression, it is also in some circumstances a barrier against the consolidation of world peace. The part played by the small states in the League of Nations was dangerous not because their policy was necessarily bad—in many cases it was more enlightened than that of the great powers—but because it involved the separation of power from responsibility and control. The great states, as I have already said, have the power, and must therefore accept the responsibility for military and economic developments. Great Britain and the United States refused to face this fact in the period between the wars, with disastrous consequences for themselves and for the whole world. Power has become more concentrated since then, and its responsibilities have not diminished.

The emotional climate in which the Conference at Paris met ensured that the claims of the small states, though not

[26] Vattel, *Le Droit des Gens*, Préliminaires, § 18; *cf.* Liv. II, ch. III, §§ 35–6.

invariably conceded, should be vociferously asserted and frequently receive recognition. They attached great importance to their rights of independent sovereignty, and on various occasions during the ensuing twenty years they reasserted them. When Briand's scheme for European Union was under discussion he took the precaution of making it clear that the Union was to be based on 'respect for the sovereignty and mutual equality of the states.'[27] Even so, in their replies many of the governments of Europe underlined their unwillingness to sacrifice one atom of their independent sovereignty. The Irish Free State declared that it could not become a member of a combination of states involving 'any derogation from the rights of this country as a sovereign state.'[28] As late as September, 1938, a proposal in the League Assembly for the modification of the unanimity rule was stoutly opposed by Hungary, Poland, and Roumania. 'In no matter, in no dispute in which the interests of a country were at stake,' declared the Roumanian delegate, 'could a solution be imposed upon that country or recommended to it without its consent.'[29] Since then a great deal has been imposed on the Roumanian government without its consent.

Other governments were less rigid in their interpretation of their rights. The ideal of equality, I must emphasise, like most other legal conceptions, is capable of varying interpretations. In the form of the old-fashioned theory of absolute state sovereignty it is a denial of the interdependence of nations and an excuse for perpetuating world anarchy. The Netherlands government, in its reply to the Briand Memorandum, recognised that international co-ordination is impossible unless states are willing to accept limitations on their sovereign rights. It said: 'A conception of sovereignty leaving no place for the voluntary acceptance of certain limitations of the powers of states should, in Her

[27] '*European Federal Union:* Replies of Twenty-one Governments to M. Briand's Memorandum of 17 May 1930', in *International Conciliation* (Carnegie Endowment for International Peace, No. 265), p. 111.
[28] *id.* p. 88. [29] Hambro, pp. 151–2.

Majesty's Government's opinion, be ruled out as incompatible with the essential nature of international relations.'[30] If we cannot make at least this supposition all hope of international co-operation to secure peace and economic prosperity will have to be abandoned. Again, by national equality we cannot mean that all nations are equal in economic or military power, for this would be patently absurd. The conception of equality belongs not to the field of power but to that of rights. If we are saying anything that is worth saying when we talk of national equality, we must mean an equality of rights. We come back then to a fundamental question of political philosophy. If it is agreed that the rights of a nation are to be interpreted not in terms of power or prestige, but in terms of the interests of its citizens, then, when we say that all nations are equal we mean that they all have equal rights to economic, cultural and spiritual wellbeing. It is the precise opposite of the *Herrenvolk* idea.

V. Conclusion

Most of this book has dealt with the problems of the nation state in historical terms. I may be forgiven if in a concluding section I turn to some more general and theoretical considerations. In discussing nationalism I have perforce had to say much about imperialism. It has generally been cast for the role of villain, yet the history of nationalism is full of equally bloody deeds. When we come to the most frightful atrocities, such as were perpetrated by the Germans on the Jews, they seem to appertain to the nature of nationalism rather than empire. At bottom, empire means no more than the extension of power over a large area including a variety of nations. It may represent the dominance of one element, as it usually has, or it may recognise the equality of its national or racial components. Consequently, under the common heading of imperialism diametrically opposed political systems may be included. Certainly imperialism seeks its own interest; as a political

[30] *European Federal Union*, p. 13.

institution it cannot do anything else. Its scope is a function of its power and this is basically military. It is often said that now there are only two actual imperial powers—the U.S.S.R. and the U.S.A., and one potential power—China. Their empires amount essentially to spheres of influence. What a major infringement might bring with it was shown when Russian missiles were discovered on Cuba.

There is a paradox about modern empires, however, which constitutes an automatic limitation. Moderation in its use is a condition of the survival of power. Even after 1918 a wise German policy could have built up a large German sphere of influence in Europe, founded primarily on the industrial strength of Germany. All the states of Europe this side of the U.S.S.R. would have fallen into the German sphere in due course like ripe fruit. Only a wise restraint and the appearance of self-restraint were required. The Nazis were incapable of this. Their failure came from the clash of empires, but was not uninfluenced by the fact that, apart from little groups of collaborationists and the Germans themselves, the force of nationalism was on the other side. Other nations have learnt since then that military conquest and annexation are not as successful as the bases of empire as they formerly were. Political consciousness has become a fact of world-wide significance. Terrorism and guerilla warfare are more than a match for regular armies and air-forces. Even the strongest alien power can only keep a small people in subjection, as the U.S.S.R. does its satellite states in Europe, with the aid of a party inside the state. Albania is the exception which proves the rule. Rather more than a generation ago, General Smuts declared that an independent South Africa would have to seek the guarantee of a great power.[31] Much weaker states have since then seemed able to do without it. The paradox of empire is that to-day an imperial power can only retain its power by not exercising it, and can only preserve the appearance of unity by sacrificing it. Again, in

[31] Walker, *The British Empire*, p. 204.

the past imperial aggression has been justified by alleged economic necessity. The war for German *lebensraum* sounds ironical when a much more prosperous Germany is confined within much narrower limits. Empires have been connected with the conflict of economic interest between rich and poor; but such conflicts have not been identical with those between an imperial power and its dependencies, and a politically conscious nation is no longer good material for economic exploitation.

The great totalitarian dictatorships, monopolising economic, political and military power, may at one time have seemed the forerunners of a new order. In fact they represented the nationalism of the nineteenth century run riot, not the state of the future. It should be noted that nationalism, not nationality or even the nation state as such, presents the danger; for the mark of nationalism is that it adds total state sovereignty to the nation. National, economic and ideological differences are explosive material, but the sovereignty of separate states is the spark which fires them. The abandonment of absolute state sovereignty alone holds out any hope of reconciling the self-determination of the nations with a peaceful world order. It implies something like a loose federal relationship between states. The Permanent Court of International Justice has several times pointed out that restrictions on the exercise of sovereign rights accepted by treaty are a manifestation and not an infringement of sovereignty.[32] This is a lawyer's definition. For our purpose it is more useful to point out that they *do* make a difference to the working of sovereignty. The British Commonwealth is an example of a political system in which autonomy is reconciled with great inequalities of size and power. Again, if the government of many states is examined in its domestic aspects it will be observed that there are vast fields in which the state has in practice abdicated its sovereignty; religion for example. In the face of facts the total sovereignty of the state should be relegated to the realm of myth. What this means in

[32] Oppenheim, *International Law*, I, 238, *n.* 3.

practice is the re-assertion of the pluralism of human interests, instead of subordinating everything to the separate nation state. Federalism is really an inadequate term for a mixing of interests—economic, political, cultural, religious and so on—which must run throughout the social fabric. Territorial contiguity is an important element and this explains the growth, even without an imperial nucleus, of the European Common Market. A statement issued by the Norwegian Government in 1942 showed that the leaders of at least one small nation were looking forward to the possibilities of this kind of relationship. 'The Norwegian Government,' it said, 'does not share the fear expressed by some spokesmen of other small powers that permanent collaboration with greater ones is equivalent to accepting domination. On the contrary, it thinks that such a combination of great and small countries, evidently based upon full recognition of the individuality of each one, is a necessary protection for the weaker ones. Such protection cannot be afforded by the mere combination of a few nations which, even after having been merged into one unit, would not possess sufficient strength for security. The four northern states, for instance, do not possess the necessary material resources for their defence against one or more of the great powers.'[33]

It has not been the purpose of this book to draw up detailed plans for the settlement of the national question in the continually altering situation that prevails in the world. It is not possible in this matter to lay down hard-and-fast rules, but only to indicate the general lines on which a means might be found of reconciling the claims of the nations to the right of self-determination with overriding economic and strategic necessities. We conclude, thus, with the basic fact of the international situation, on which we repeatedly find ourselves driven back. The dependence of small nations on the great powers is more absolute now than ever before. For most of the smaller nations in the modern world, moreover, a negative independence is not enough. The

[33] Statement issued by the Norwegian Government, 20 July, 1942.

economic influence of the world powers is inescapable. This is the setting in which the independence of small states must operate. In economic and military matters the great states have the power: they therefore cannot escape the responsibility. But I have endeavoured to show that the exercise of such responsibilities by the greater states is not incompatible with recognition of the liberties of the smaller nations. Finally, self-determination is a matter of degree. The rights of nationality are not absolute: they vary with the internal and external circumstances of each nation; and the great powers cannot themselves enjoy peace and prosperity unless by positive measures they establish the conditions in which all nations, whether they are independent states or not, can feel free from national oppression and able to share in the general progress of the world.

Index

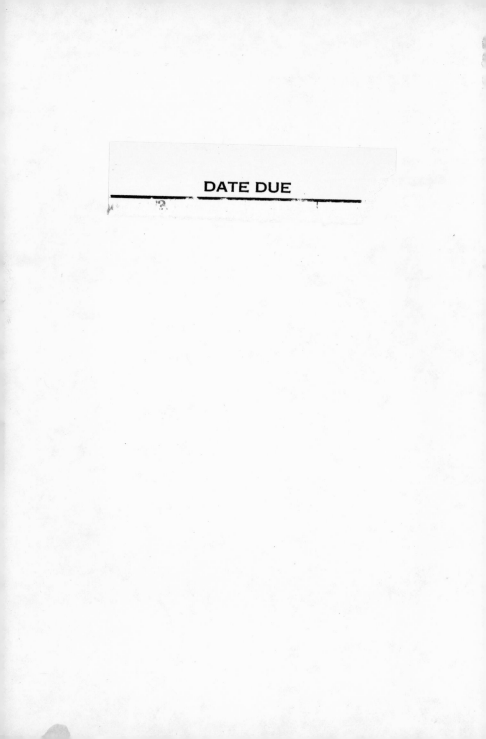

DATE DUE